Women Also Journeyed with Him

Women Also Journeyed with Him

Feminist Perspectives on the Bible

Gérald Caron

Aldina da Silva

Olivette Genest

Marc Girard

Michel Gourgues, O.P.

Élisabeth J. Lacelle

Jean-Jacques Lavoie

André Myre

Jean-François Racine

Foreword by
Jean-Pierre Prévost

Translated by
Madeleine Beaumont

A Michael Glazier Book
THE LITURGICAL PRESS
Collegeville, Minnesota

A Michael Glazier Book published by The Liturgical Press

This book was originally published by MÉDIASPAUL in Montreal, Quebec, Canada, under the title *Des femmes aussi faisaient route avec lui* © 1995 by MÉDIASPAUL. All rights reserved.

1	2	3	4	5	6	7	8	9

Library of Congress Cataloging-in-Publication Data

Des femmes aussi faisaient route avec lui. English.
    Women also journeyed with Him : feminist perspectives on the Bible / Gérald Caron . . . [et al.] ; foreword by Jean-Pierre Prévost.
      p.   cm.
    Papers presented at a meeting.
    Includes bibliographical references.
    ISBN 0-8146-5892-X (alk. paper)
    1. Bible—Feminist criticism—Congresses. I. Caron, Gérald. II. Title.

BS521.4.F4713 2000
220.6'082—dc21

00-026308

Contents

◆ ────────────────────────────── ◆

Foreword

◆──◆

In the wake of the congress marking the fiftieth anniversary of the foundation of their organization members of the Catholic Association of Biblical Studies in Canada (ACÉBAC), meeting for their fifty-first congress in Nicolet, Quebec, from May 29 to June 1, 1994, chose a topic of acute interest in our day: *Feminist Readings and Perspectives in the Interpretation of the Bible*. As is well known, this topic is the object of important and impassioned debates in the different churches. However, it remains an unavoidable question that demands a rigorous and thorough treatment enabling us to resolve certain deadlocks and leading us beyond the sterile confrontations existing within institutions and ideologies. The work of the women and men who are the authors of this collection, *Women Also Journeyed with Him*, is to be placed on the level of the most advanced research allied to a keen concern for theological relevance.

As you are about to begin reading this book, the result of the works presented at the congress mentioned above, I shall not hide from you the reaction of a fair number of European biblical scholars, colleagues, and friends, who upon hearing what the chosen theme was, said, "This is a typical North American preoccupation!" As if such a concern was not also present across the Atlantic! This sort of reaction shows that there is still a long way to go before the seriousness and importance of feminist studies are fully recognized in our ecclesial milieux. Although it is true that sensitivity to feminist questions is especially acute in North America, the following studies will quickly show that it is impossible to treat these questions as purely regional and still less as marginal or peripheral to the theological and exegetical research of today. And this is true on all continents. Feminist concerns arise from all quarters, from diverse sociological, cultural, and religious horizons. The works presented in this collection bear witness to the seriousness of the research in this domain and have the twofold merit of revealing to the

French- and English-speaking public the amplitude and complexity of the current debates and of offering a challenge to exegetical research.

As always at the ACÉBAC, the congress was attended by men and women engaged in biblical research. However, very early on, it became clear that it was essential to place the subject of "Feminist Readings and Perspectives in the Interpretation of the Bible" within a wider context and to use a more inclusive approach to problems, that is to say, within the context of feminist studies in general and more particularly that of theological feminist studies. Élisabeth Lacelle, a theologian deeply engaged in the "men-women" dialogue in the church, has had on more than one occasion the good fortune of being a pioneer as a woman working professionally in theological research. She was entrusted with the task of presenting the purpose of the congress within the specific context of feminist readings and perspectives in theology. Her text admirably fulfills this mandate; it contains an instructive synthesis and a most valuable classification of feminist theological studies of the last quarter century in their phases of *deconstruction, reconstruction,* and *construction.* Besides presenting this vast overall view, Lacelle confronts the crux of feminist theologies and gives us important observations on the alternative Christological readings proposed as counterparts to traditional Christology.

The contribution of Olivette Genest, a well-known specialist on the subject of the semiotic analysis of biblical texts as well as on that of New Testament feminist studies, unveils prejudices and justifies feminist readings and perspectives in exegesis. On the basis of the Biblical Commission's recent document *The Interpretation of the Bible in the Church,* she mentions the progress that has been realized: feminist approaches have finally gained acceptance. At the same time, she deplores the persistence of some prejudices concerning feminist readings of the Bible that are still at work in the Roman text. In the second part of her study, Genest defines what is really at stake in feminist readings of the Bible, that is in fact, the necessity of reconsidering the notions of ideology and power in the interpretation of the Bible, as well as of redefining the task of feminist exegesis and theology. Lastly, she offers a careful assessment of the contributions made by feminist theories to biblical interpretation.

After delving into these considerations, epistemological in character, it is fitting to come back to the text itself, to the Old and New Testaments.

Aldina da Silva has chosen to center her research on woman and love and to look into women's condition in the Mesopotamian and biblical literatures. To achieve her purpose, she concentrates on what the *juridical* texts of the Old Testament and the ancient Near East, principally Mesopotamia, say about women and prescribe for them on the subject of the *three steps of marriage*. For these steps—betrothal, settling into the husband's house, and giving birth—the juridical texts, whether biblical or Mesopotamian, consider the woman to be under the tutelage of her father or husband and see her as a sexual object. Such a conclusion is not surprising: it is not imaginary, as the study of the vocabulary done by da Silva shows. It must be taken into account for a just appraisal of the historical and contingent image of woman which certain biblical texts project.

But there are not only juridical texts: in the collection of biblical poetical passages, the Song of Songs stands out as a wholly innovative work on the subject of the relations between men and women. Jean-Jacques Lavoie, an expert in Wisdom literature, reminds readers of the deeply *gynocentric* character of the Song, which contrasts with the traditional patriarchal pattern found in the majority of biblical writings. For all this, must we go as far as postulating a female author of the Song? This is Lavoie's position, following Solomon D. Goitein and a few recent authors. Such a position will not fail to provoke lively discussions; whatever the outcome of this debate, we must agree with the author of this present contribution that the Song remains a singular voice among the biblical books because of its physical description of woman as well as of her role within the lovers' relationship.

There are four studies concerning the New Testament. The first one, by André Myre, presents female American exegetes and surveys the section in *The Women's Bible Commentary* which supplies a commentary of all the New Testament writings. This is a novel project which deserves a long review in order to show the concrete work of women exegetes and thus to make accessible to the French- and English-speaking public the results of feminist research in the United States regarding the interpretation of the New Testament. According to Myre, this research is "an important cultural and ecclesial revealer." *The Women's Bible Commentary* lacks neither audacity nor seriousness and demands radical reinterpretations of the New Testament. As Myre advises, it will be each reader's responsibility to verify the validity of the hermeneutics proposed by this commentary.

As for Jean-François Racine, he examines the social milieu from which the Jesus movement was born, inasmuch as we may reconstruct it on the basis of the Q source, the hypothetical document on which a large part of the recent research on the historical Jesus is based. Racine presents and critiques the contribution of three feminist approaches of the social milieu of the Q document (Hal Taussig, Luise Schottroff and Amy-Jill Levine). While recognizing that these three feminist approaches differ in their appraisal of the social development of the Q community, the author concludes that there was "an egalitarian social ethos" within this community, in which the traditional patriarchal model was replaced by a model "in which the contributions of men and women tend to be undifferentiated."

It was necessary also to address the important question of Paul's position on the woman's role within the Christian couple and the liturgical assemblies, with the well-known and disputed texts of Ephesians 5 and 1 Corinthians 14.

Michel Gourgues presents us with a brief but highly stimulating study of 1 Corinthians 14:33-36 and the redoubtable saying, "Women should be silent in the churches." The author straightaway acknowledges the anti-feminist thrust of this passage, but the question remains: To whom is this statement to be attributed? To Paul or to some group made up of Judaizing Corinthians whom he opposes? By refining an argumentation already proposed some fifteen years ago (particularly by Neal M. Flanagan and E. H. Snyder), Gourgues concludes that the text in question is a "Corinthian slogan" quoted by Paul which he, Paul, precisely intends to refute in order to establish a new Christian practice which would not impose silence on women in the Christian assemblies. This is a hypothesis worth exploring and in favor of which Gourgues presents a series of new arguments that will remedy the ill-considered use of this "slogan" on the silence of women in the assemblies.

In his turn, Marc Girard spent a long time poring over another difficult text of Paul, Ephesians 5:21-33. The passage is first scrutinized with the help of a method masterfully used by Girard, structuralist criticism. The strict and technical application of this method to Ephesians 5:21-23 is a way of defusing the emotionally charged debate and of better discerning the points of emphasis and contrast in the text itself. First of all, the author acknowledges the "cultural limits of the Pauline discourse" which "presupposes and maintains this *non-egalitarian scheme*" and adopts a "somewhat *fundamentalist reading*" of the Yahwistic story of creation by stressing the fact that "man was created before woman." This being said, Girard nevertheless thinks that Ephesians 5:21-23 contains true theological pearls, especially the idea of the *salvation* and *sacramentality* of the couple. Even on the plane of conjugal ethics, the notions of love as subjection, of fear (understood in the sense of respect) and responsibility set forth by Paul, demonstrate an accomplished theological, pastoral, and spiritual sense and are still worth being part of today's liturgical proclamation.

The study of Gérald Caron, "The Authority of the Bible Challenged by Feminist Hermeneutics," finds its natural place at the end of this collection since it allows us to take up again in a more systematic way a question underlying each one of the studies presented up to now. We must say that Caron had been both the sponsor and enthusiastic supporter of the theme selected for the congress. It is true that the question he treats could have been proposed just as well at the beginning of the congress. But in view of the studies already presented, it appears without doubt as one of the most important results of feminist exegetical discussions. The way the author enunciates the question is to be kept in mind: How or up to what point can a tradition—we speak of a biblical tradition—that is androcentric and patriarchal still be normative for believing men and women of today? The feminist responses to this question are, as one could expect, diversified: they are characterized by rejection, fundamentalism, or liberation. The author dwells here on the liberation current, especially on the positions of Elisabeth Schüssler Fiorenza, Rosemary Radford Ruether, Letty M. Russell, and Sandra M. Schneiders. Beyond the differences, we must recognize that their positions, keenly debated among themselves and in a wider circle of exegetes, lead to a redefinition of the very notion of the *authority* granted to the Bible. A new paradigm is being born: *authority of partnership,* thanks to which women's experience in the process of interpreting the Bible will have to be more seriously taken into account from now on.

In concluding this presentation, I would like to congratulate and thank the women and men who authored the present work for the audacity and quality of their studies. Special thanks go to Olivette Genest, who accepted to supervise the work of preparation for the congress; her suggestions for the development of the theme and the selection of the lecturers were most judicious. I also thank all those who accepted to review the submitted articles and by their remarks contributed to making this collection a work of high quality. Finally, many thanks to Jean Duhaime and Odette Mainville, in charge of the new series Sciences Bibliques and to the managers of Médiaspaul, who received this manuscript with much eagerness and insured its publication with a diligence equal to their professionalism.

If it were still necessary to justify the relevance of the research which is presented to you in this work, let it suffice to note that the first complete day of the congress where these studies were presented coincided with the promulgation of the text in which John-Paul II declared that the discussion of women's ordination was closed from Rome's viewpoint. The question was not on the agenda of the congress. Let us only wish that the discussion may continue in a rigorous way and in the common search for a better understanding and a better experience of the relationship between men and women in the church.

Jean-Pierre Prévost
President of the ACÉBAC

Feminist Readings and Perspectives in Theology

◆ ──────────────────────────────── ◆

Élisabeth J. Lacelle

To speak of feminist readings and perspectives in *dogmatic theology* is to assert that the feminist theological research does not have as its sole object/subject the identity and condition of women in the Christian tradition, but the whole of this tradition, theological as well as pastoral. Feminist theologies took this direction in the 70s. Up to that time, research had been centered on women and their relationships with men; but then researchers discovered that they had to widen their field of inquiry and undertake a rereading of the whole of Christian doctrine and institutions.

It is important to speak of feminist theologies and not of *the* feminist theology. What is called "the second wave" in these studies, that of the beginnings of theological deconstruction and construction, saw the emergence of the diverse—even divergent—visions and methods that characterize feminist theologies. However, they all have the common aim of producing a metapatriarchal theology, with all that is thereby implied for Christian doctrine and institutions.

Here I shall consider more particularly the feminist readings and perspectives pertaining to Christology, and through it, to Christian anthropology as well as to language about God. In order to properly understand the importance of these feminist readings and perspectives, we must first place them in (1) the context of feminist studies in the humanities and social sciences in which they are imbedded and (2) the Christian tradition.

1. Feminist Theological Studies

Inasmuch as they are theological studies, feminist theologies have their own methods as well as their own domain, that is, the Christian tradition. But they accompany what has come to be called Women's Studies, which are interdisciplinary. Like the latter, the former adopt a method intent on keeping together theory and practice, knowledge and experience. Their scientific criticism rests on the postulate that Christian tradition, as it has been transmitted for centuries, is systemically patriarchal and androcentric, at least in its doctrinal and institutional formulations.

The Theologies Underlying Women's Studies

To learn of the places where feminist theologies asserted themselves and developed, we must realize how important Women's Studies have become in researchers' circles interested in academic or other goals, such as pastoral concerns. Most Canadian and American universities today offer courses in Women's Studies, some of them leading to a doctoral degree.[1] Several universities have established a department or center of research in that area. Most offer classes and seminars in various disciplines. In 1990, there were over thirty thousand courses in Women's Studies in the curricula of American universities. All meetings of learned societies and most symposia include them when apposite to the topic under discussion. The increase of support from universities and the significant proportion of grants Women's Studies receive foster the development as well as the scientific advancement and diffusion of the research. The most prestigious prize in the field of religion in the United States, the Gravemeyer Prize ($150,000.00), was given in 1993 to Elizabeth A. Johnson for her book entitled *She Who Is: The Mystery of God in the Feminist Theological Discourse.*[2] Feminist studies are becoming partners in the epistemological debates prompted by the criticism of the modern sciences and, in theology, in ecumenical and interreligious research, whether institutional, ecclesial, or academic.

It would be erroneous to think that feminist studies are an exclusively North American phenomenon. It is true that they have emerged and multiplied in this intellectual and religious context since the end of the 60s. European circles, especially the Anglo-Saxon ones, did not delay long in undertaking similar research. Since 1984, the University of Nijmegen, in the Netherlands, has had a department of studies on

1. The University of York in Ontario is the only Canadian university that offers a Ph.D. in Women's Studies; the Department of Religious Sciences at the University of Ottawa is the only one that offers a doctoral program in Women's Studies in Religion.
2. Elizabeth A. Johnson, *She Who Is: The Mystery of God in Feminist Theological Discourse* (New York: Crossroad, 1992).

women and Christianity. The European Society of Women for Theological Research, a network of women theologians in various disciplines, numbers more than one hundred members today and has held a congress of study every other year since 1986. In 1985, the theological faculty of the University of Lyons in collaboration with the group Women and Men in the Church established a research and documentation center on women and Christianity. The Ecumenical Association of Third World Theologians includes feminist studies, which are growing at an impressive rate in Asia, South America, and Africa.

Because they want to hold together experience and knowledge, praxis and theory, feminist theologians seek not only a university centered environment—which is conducive to exchanges between theorists—but also one alongside universities in order to remain in contact with research groups whose orientation is social or pastoral or both. To cite but one example in Quebec, we can mention a research group named L'Autre Parole (The Other Word) whose theological thinking, since 1976, is based on the lived faith of women who are distancing themselves from the Roman ecclesiastical institution. As a group, it regularly issues its bulletin, and the works published individually by its members do have an impact on the ecclesial conscience in Quebec. Another group, Femmes et ministères (Women and Ministry), established in 1982, gathers women employed by church institutions. An extensive survey has resulted in a sociological analysis of the condition of these church workers;[3] a study on the theological implications of this experiential datum was also recently published.[4] A third group, Réseau œcuménique des femmes du Québec (Ecumenical Network of Quebec Women), was established on March 8, 1988, by Christian Quebecer women from different traditions; this group has already made a significant impact.

I limit myself to speaking of theological and pastoral research, both theoretical and practical, of the feminist consciousness. Despite variations on the methodological and theoretical planes, this research has a common point of departure. It is the postulate that in the domain of theological sciences, traditional knowledge—both in content and method—is structurally affected by one dominant factor: the thinkers and institutions that transmitted knowledge were either mainly or exclusively masculine and imbued with the patriarchal tradition. The present research on the part of women also has one goal: the discovery

3. Sarah Bélanger, *Les soutanes roses: Portrait du personnel pastoral féminin au Québec* (Montréal: Bellarmin, 1988).

4. Lise Baroni and others, *Voix de femmes: Voix de passage* (Montréal: Paulines, 1995).

of views and ways of thinking and knowing, of methods, that integrate women's experience of "acculturated" faith in order to liberate them, individually and as a human group, from a patriarchal ecclesial system perceived as oppressive when it hinders the full growth of women as whole human persons (it equally hinders the full growth of men). All feminist theologies aim at bringing about the emergence of new ways of inhabiting oneself and the world, new ways in closer conformity to the new humanity restored in Jesus Christ. This does not mean that all feminist works reach this goal; like any study, they require validation on the theological level as well as on the ecclesial and scientific levels. In any case, these women theologians do not fail to verify one another and to lend themselves to verification by other groups of researchers of both sexes.

Studies that Emerge from a Recent Sociocultural Context

We must take into account the scientific and sociocultural as well as ecclesial contexts from which these theologies arose at the end of the 60s. The "new wave" feminist studies goes back to the 60s and 70s and those called "second wave" to the 80s. What we have here is a *scientific context* which shows that every study of human reality must be multidisciplinary (aiming at becoming interdisciplinary). At the United Nations Educational, Scientific, and Cultural Organization (UNESCO), the Swiss psychologist Jean Piaget was a pioneer of this in the 70s. This scientific context is also a criticism of the modern sciences with their particular kind of rationality and their prejudices concerning human reality, its relationships with society, the cosmos, and a transcendent reality. On the sociocultural level, women are asserting themselves at the same time that people in general are asserting themselves more and more and new networks of solidarity concerned with human rights are becoming more prominent. It is not by chance that the young and women were the main resisters against the definitions and conditions that the established systems imposed on them and on other marginalized groups—it is this consciousness they expressed. Since then, the hitherto marginalized groups who now speak and act for themselves and their own interests are past counting. This sociocultural context coincided with other events: many peoples and vast human strata, up to then under colonial domination, have gained their autonomy; the charter of the United Nations banning all discrimination against women was adopted and ratified as early as 1981 by the majority of members.

On the *ecclesial* plane, Vatican II opened vast horizons and energized the Roman Catholic tradition during those years. Exchanges between Christian traditions multiplied through institutional ecumenical dialogues and also through groups in academic research and social action. Some churches have acknowledged the full baptismal vocation of women by giving them access to the whole of sacramental and ministerial life. Some churches have undertaken a revision of their liturgical texts and rites where they were more patriarchal than evangelical. This was also a time of openness to other religions.

These circumstances and others, such as developments in the medical and biological sciences and the entrance of women into the legal, political, economic, scientific, and religious spheres are sufficient proofs that feminist studies, including theologies, are part of a sociocultural, religious, and scientific paradigmatic shift in Western culture. Women are not alone in this ever shifting space of transition (space of mutants, some say), but they were born there and today they are present in it with their own discourses. Universities have understood this better than many religious institutions: a whole culture is in the making there, challenging all the scientific disciplines and the overall human undertaking.

Feminist theologies arise from this sociocultural context, as much as from the heritage of Christian faith.

The Phases of Development in Feminist Theologies

Like feminist studies in general, feminist theologies have for the last thirty years traveled an itinerary which we can summarize in three principal phases. A first phase began in the late 60s: the work then was mostly the deconstruction of traditional knowledge and visions, where this knowledge and these visions appeared as "unfulfilled," "partial," and often "biased." At the end of the 70s, a phase of reconstruction began, which in the course of the 80s gave rise to a phase of construction. Today, we find the first two phases and sometimes the third one in the largest part of feminist theological work.

DECONSTRUCTING

The phase of *deconstruction* remains the best known. It happens that some of the criticisms leveled by feminist theologies have remained arrested here. The purpose of this phase is to detect and cleanse the mechanisms of discourses and institutions perceived as patriarchal: what they affirm, how they formulate it, what they conceal, and what they negate. This inquiry uses the hermeneutics of suspicion and thus finds itself relativizing the concepts and methods that have become traditional in theology, as in other disciplines. This hermeneutics is not a female invention. In the course of the twentieth century, theological thinking has questioned the assumptions of classical metaphysics in general, along with those of ahistorical dogmatic discourses and biblical syntheses elaborated without textual or historical criticism. This implies a suspicion concerning the value of the knowledge produced by these discourses. What is peculiar to feminist studies is the systematic extension of the suspicion to any knowledge arising from patriarchal institutions and reflecting, exclusively or quasi exclusively, the masculine view of reality, including postmetaphysical and postmodern knowledge when it shows the same characteristics.

In addition to the hermeneutics of suspicion, heuristic categories make it possible to ask pertinent questions, devise methods, and elaborate alternative theories and formulations. For instance, the category of *patriarchal dominance*. Sociopolitical analyses have had recourse to it. With feminist studies, the category takes on a precise theoretical meaning, that of a sociopolitical system ruled by the father's law and following a hierarchical order predominantly male and perceived as oppressive to women, whether individually or as a collectivity, because of its maintaining them in the position of non-subjects or partial subjects under men's control. In 1970, the American Kate Millett systematically demonstrated that the personal experience of women *is* political and that the political that is men's province *is* personal, and therefore that *the private is public and the public private.*[5] This was a theoretical watershed for feminist studies. The denunciation of the violence inflicted on women, then on children, then on other persons belonging to minorities and therefore vulnerable has its roots here. This denunciation criticizes the "all-powerful father," including the "omnipotent heavenly Father," notions whose deadly effects are found in manifestations of violence in society and religions, including Christianity.

The category of *androcentrism* derives from that of patriarchal dominance, but it can persist in political systems supposed to be democratic or somewhat socialist. Long before feminist studies, the sociologist Lester F. Ward (1843–1913) was, it seems, the author of this term in his book *Pure Sociology: A Treatise on the Origin and the Development of Society* (1903). He understood the term androcentric theory as "the viewpoint according to which the male sex is essential and the female sex secondary on the organic plane; that all is centered on the male, and that the female, although necessary for the completion of the plan, is only the means of perpetuating the life of the planet; otherwise the female is an unimportant accessory and a contingent element in the general outcome."[6] The androcentric theory certainly pervades the an-

5. Kate Millett, *Sexual Politics* (Garden City, N.Y.: Doubleday, 1970).
6. Lester Frank Ward, *Pure Sociology: A Treatise on the Origin and Spontaneous Development of Society*, 2nd ed. (New York: Macmillan, 1925) 292.

thropology that marked centuries of philosophy and theology in the Christian tradition as is demonstrated by Gender Studies in theology.[7]

The third category, that of *sexism*, concerns discriminatory attitudes and behaviors which are systemically alienating for one person, or groups of persons, on the basis of sex. This category entered feminist studies in 1972 with the book of Shulamith Firestone, *The Dialectic of Sex*. As early as 1974, the word and its derivatives appeared in semi-official texts of the Christian tradition, in the report of consultation of the World Council of Churches (WCC) gathered in Berlin, whose subject was Women in Society and the Churches.[8]

In the course of recent years, Gender Studies have proliferated; they are also called studies of the relationships between the sexes, especially in the domains of biblical theology, Christian anthropology, and studies of Christian institutional mechanisms. The category of gender enables us to study the social relationships between women and men throughout history and cultures and to demonstrate that the condition of subordination of women to men is neither "an individual phenomenon, nor a natural phenomenon, but rather a fact caused by the dynamics of the social relationships of the sexes."[9] Is sex itself a biological datum or a cultural one? This is a question unthinkable a few years ago but not today. Even if we suppose that sex is a biological datum, up to what point is it based on a male "gender" and a female "gender"? Up to what point are these a social, cultural, or religious construct? Theories vary. Most of them state that gender is a sociocultural construct based on a hierarchized sexual order whose effects permeate language itself.[10] The social relationships and the religious relationships of the

7. See the study of Prudence Allen, *The Concept of Woman: The Aristotelian Revolution 750 B.C.–A.D. 1250* (Montreal: Eden, 1985), for the philosophical dimension. See Kari Elisabeth Börresen, *Subordination and Equivalence: The Nature and the Role of Woman in Augustine and Thomas Aquinas*, trans. Charles A. Talbot, from the revised French original (Kampen, Netherlands: Kok Pharos, 1995), for the theology of Augustine and Thomas Aquinas.

8. Shulamith Firestone, *The Dialectic of Sex: The Case for Feminist Revolution* (New York: William Morrow, 1970). For the use of this term in Christian documents, see World Council of Churches, *Sexism in the 1970s: Discrimination Against Women*, A Report of a World Council of Churches Consultation, West Berlin 1974, ed. Brigalia Bam (Geneva: WCC, 1975).

9. A. Lafortune, "Rapports sociaux des sexes et marginalisation des femmes dans l'Église," *Femmes et pouvoir dans l'Église*, ed. Anita Caron, (Montréal: VLB, 1991) 161.

10. For the relationship between gender and language, see Olivette Genest, "Langage religieux chrétien et différenciation sexuelle: De quelques évidences," *Recherches Féministes: L'autre salut* 3, no. 2, ed. Monique Dumais (1990) 11–30. For an

sexes are studied in the same perspective, and similarly, the myths and the symbolic systems so fundamental in religious traditions.

Although these concepts and their heuristic function in the phase of deconstruction in feminist theologies are subject to verification as these theologies develop, they remain fundamental.

RECONSTRUCTING

The second phase, called *reconstruction,* took shape at the end of the 70s. It seeks to produce methods and theories leading to alternative Christian theological views and alternative praxis, both of the metapatriarchal type. They are still most often centered primarily on the goal of liberating women and then extending this liberation to every human condition needing salvation—class, race, lifestyle, and so on. Some feminist theologies, called theologies of resistance and/or transformation, are at work where some effects of liberation have already been gained but need either preserving or furthering. A hermeneutics of affirmation replaces the hermeneutics of suspicion: affirmation of complete salvation for any human being having faith in the event Jesus Christ. Anne Carr speaks of a hermeneutics "of generosity" because her way of interpreting affirms that women and men are equally and integrally human; others prefer a hermeneutics of equality between women and men. For my part, I propose a hermeneutics based on the affirmation of evangelical reconciliation in the integral soteriological sense of the mutual exchange which expresses the fundamental acknowledgement of the other as a person endowed with grace in Jesus Christ, a theology of reconciliation still unawakened in our theological tradition.[11]

---

overview of the theological approach to the problem see Anne E. Carr, *La femme dans l'Église: Tradition chrétienne et théologie féministe,* Cogitatio fidei 173 (Paris: Cerf, 1993) 85–126. For femimist theories in Gender Studies, see Christine Di Stefano, "Dilemmas and Differences: Feminism, Modernity, and Postmodernism," in *Feminism/Postmodernism,* ed. Linda J. Nicholson (New York: Routledge, 1990) 63–82; J. Wallace Scott, *Gender and the Politics of History* (New York: Columbia University Press, 1988); Linda A. M. Perry, Lynn H. Turner, and Helen M. Sterk, eds., *Constructing and Reconstructing Gender* (New York: State University of New York Press, 1992). For a Christian approach in the Protestant tradition, see Mary Stewart Van Leeuwen, *After Eden: Facing the Challenge of Gender Reconciliation* (Grand Rapids, Mich.: Eerdmans, 1993).

11. See my book *L'incontournable échange: Conversations œcuméniques et pluridisciplinaires,* selected writings (Montréal: Bellarmin, 1994). I refer particularly to the motif of reconciliation *(katallagē)* in Paul's letters, 1 Cor and Rom, and Pseudo Paul's Eph and Col.

As an alternative to a society and a church of the patriarchal type, these theologies propose an egalitarian society and an ecclesiology of "the community of equal disciples." This well-known formula, made famous by Elisabeth Schüssler Fiorenza,[12] describes neither a community where the members are all on the same footing and identical nor one that is anarchic. The ecclesial order is thought anew in terms of harmony, interconnection, and interdependence with the sharing of responsibility rather than in terms of opposition and of hierarchized relationships between powers, relationships exclusively defined by the persons holding power. Some theologies envisage a partnership between men and women, as well as between ecclesial functions, based on the mutual recognition of baptized men and women as being equally endowed with baptismal grace and with the quality of ecclesial subject it confers; as a consequence, all persons, whatever their sex, race, and so on, are equally empowered by the Spirit for the whole spectrum of vocations. It happens that feminist theological alternatives reflect gynocentered, even matriarchal, outlooks on society and church. Such alternatives see themselves as a necessary step because, as a group of baptized persons, women were never able to collectively and publicly formulate their experience and their visions. That step intends to be strategic; it envisions the recognition of the full humanity of women and men, of their relationships between themselves, with the cosmos, and with God within the event of revelation that is reread in this perspective.

By reconstruction, feminist theologies understand reinterpretations and reformulations of the faith tradition which, not salvific when embedded in patriarchal categories, becomes salvific—for men as well as for women—when set within metapatriarchal categories. In 1982, Rosemary Radford Ruether systematically explored the "pathologies" and "redeeming graces" of the Christian tradition.[13]

Feminist women theologians ask questions, scrutinize the material at their disposal. Like archaeologists of the theological tradition, they dig in archives and any vestige hitherto not brought to light by theo-

---

12. Elisabeth Schüssler Fiorenza, *In Memory of Her: A Feminist Theological Reconstruction of Christian Origins* (New York: Crossroad, 1983).

13. Rosemary Radford Ruether, *Disputed Questions: On Being a Christian* (Nashville: Abingdon, 1982). As early as the end of the 70s, the distinction was made between studies referred to as reconstructionist and constructionist; see Carol P. Christ and Judith Plaskow, eds., *Womanspirit Rising: A Feminist Reader in Religion* (San Francisco: Harper and Row, 1979); compare with their assessment ten years later in Plaskow and Christ, eds., *Weaving the Visions: New Patterns in Feminist Spirituality* (San Francisco: Harper and Row, 1989) Introduction and 1–13.

logical tradition. This brings them to the frontier of theological texts and traditions, and thus to a methodological and theoretical frontier. At this point, certain women theologians recoil and fall back on traditional data, even if it means correcting them when possible, some down to their roots, as do reformist theologies.[14] Others dare to dive into another religious, metachristian space, as do theologies called thealogical and philosophico-religious. Finally, others remain at this frontier of the traditional text as resisters, having the eyes of their intelligence fixed on the eschatological horizons of the Christian faith: they strive to imagine missing elements, possible elements, with a consistency based at once on revelation and reason.

BUILDING ANEW

On this last path, what is sought is no longer reconstruction, but *construction,* anew. This is the third phase that feminist theologies are obliged to face in the name of their twofold loyalty to the gospel and to their feminist faith experience. They elaborate texts which they consider able to cross the frontier and to bring the grace of salvation to its eschatological fullness, to a point where Christian theology has not yet formulated it. Although they are not traditional, these attempts at theological formulations, which I call constructionist, are not anti-traditional. They dwell especially on the Christian eschatological texts, on the figures that these texts set forth, and on the dynamic movement that these figures impart to the text. One can think here of the figures of the Servant and Jerusalem-Zion in the Old Testament, of the figures of the Lamb and the new Jerusalem in Revelation. These figures, at the same time individual and collective, have also a sexual identity and are described in categories of gender; at the same time, owing to their eschatological function, they cause the limits of gender to burst open, inasmuch as genders are differences excluding one another and oppos-

---

14. What is called Reformist Theology goes down to the roots of Christian tradition and demands systemic transformations of its institutions. In Quebec, Marie Gratton, Louise Mélançon, Monique Dumais, Olivette Genest, Yvonne Bergeron, Marie-Andrée Roy, and others represent this tendency, some more radically than others. In general, one can associate this trend with the publications of L'Autre Parole (The Other Word), and the Réseau oecuménique des femmes québécoises (Ecumenical Network of Québec Women) and the international bulletin *Femmes et hommes en Église* (Women and Men in the Church). This same trend is represented in America by Rosemary Radford Ruether, Elizabeth Schüssler Fiorenza, Anne E. Carr, and others, and in Europe by Catharina Halkes, Mary Grey, Ursula King, Marie-Jeanne Bérère, and others.

ing one another or complementing one another. Thus they insert into the text the limit of the text and the possibility of its bursting open into an infinite number of meanings.[15]

This is the most decisive challenge feminist theologies have to face, in my opinion, as well as any Christian theology if it is a theology of God's word. This word happens in human history between the speaking reality that God is and the responding reality that the human being is, woman or man, created as word "in the image" of this word and as its echo. To construct stories, to formulate symbolic systems, to think anew rituals at the edge of a tradition from which one departs only in order to maintain it within the dynamic movement of the word that is its origin, all this is to work in faithfulness to the prophetic and apostolic tradition. John's Gospel is a striking illustration of this.

In the same vein, the theologian Radford Ruether speaks of a critical theological function that today can be put into effect where it never was because it was restrained by a patriarchal religious system whose foundations were not to be questioned. Biblical prophecy never ceased to denounce abuses of power, claiming to speak with the authority of divine revelation itself in order to advance the knowledge of the divine plan in behalf of the life of God's people and in dialogue with them. In continuity with this prophetic current, Radford Ruether urges the elaboration of a "new body of midrashim" as a new textual element, or even as a textual basis for theology which thus would continue the prophetic and messianic ministry of Jesus Christ in the Spirit. According to her, such a textual practice can enable us to speak the divine and make it present in places hitherto unknown: "Where the divine has never been allowed to be present in patriarchal religion. . . . Here women not only claim the right to preach, i.e., to interpret traditional texts. They claim the right to write the texts, to generate the symbols and stories out of their own religious experience."[16] It goes without saying that in order to appropriate to oneself this prophetico-messianic paradigm (I add prophetico-apostolic), a feminist theology and its praxis must create a radical reconceptualization of the event of the Saving Word of God in Jesus Christ.

15. Lacelle, *L'incontournable échange*, 47–59; "La riposta delle chiese al BEM sulla questione 'donne e ministeri' e la strade future per il dialoguo ecumenico," in *Donna e ministero: Un dibattito*, ed. Cettina Militello (Roma: Dehoniane, 1990) 418–443.

16. Rosemary Radford Ruether, "Feminism and Religious Faith: Renewal or New Creation?" *Religion and Intellectual Life* 3 (1986) 16–17; for a good analysis of this method and its hermeneutics, see Mary Hembrow Snyder, *The Christology of Rosemary Radford Ruether: A Critical Introduction* (Mystic, Conn.: Twenty-Third Publications, 1988) 14–26.

At this point we are no longer speaking of patching here and there. And this is what makes the conversation between feminist and traditional theologies difficult, especially the theologies that use for their sole reference point the official theology of the magisterium of the Roman Catholic tradition. On the other hand, one is not free to fabricate any sort of garment. The theological formulations want to clothe the Body of Christ that the Church, born of the Word of God, is; this garment is woven of threads that contain the history of this body, such as it was lived by the witnesses of the faith, the most lowly perhaps even more than those who posed as final and absolute interpreters of God's truth. What is to be sought in faith by a robust and transforming theological practice is the robe which the Body of Christ is called to put on for the marriage of the Lamb, "fine linen, bright and pure—for the fine linen is the righteous deeds of the saints" (Rev 19:7).

As an example of such a practice of construction, one may cite the theological presentation of the Korean Presbyterian Chung Hyun Kyung at the Seventh Assembly of the World Council of Churches, gathered at Canberra in February 1991 with the theme "Come, Holy Spirit—Renew the Whole of Creation." Chung delivered her speech during the opening conference, immediately after Patriarch Parthenios of Alexandria, who treated the same subject.[17] It is easy to imagine the clash of these two theological readings. To quote Chung Hyun Kyung:

> For me the image of the Holy Spirit comes from the image of *Kwan In*. She is venerated as the goddess of compassion and wisdom by East Asian women's popular religiosity. She is a *bodhisattva*, enlightened being. She can go into nirvana any time she wants to, but refuses to go into nirvana by herself. Her compassion for all suffering beings makes her stay in this world enabling other living beings to achieve enlightenment. Her compassionate wisdom heals all forms of life and empowers them to swim to the shore of nirvana. She waits and waits until the whole universe, people, trees, birds, mountains, air, water, become enlightened. They can then go to nirvana together where they can live collectively in eternal wisdom and compassion. Perhaps this might also be a feminine image of the Christ who is the firstborn among us, one who goes before and brings others with her.[18]

This is a novel reading of the biblical stories. It is inspired by an ethnic religious experience, that of the Korean people, stamped by a feminist

17. Parthenios, Patriarch of Alexandria and All Africa, "The Holy Spirit," in World Council of Churches, *Signs of the Spirit: Official Report, Seventh Assembly*, ed. Michael Kinnamon (Grand Rapids: Eerdmans, 1991) 28–37.

18. Chung Hyun Kyung, "Come, Holy Spirit—Renew the Whole Creation," in ibid., 37–46, especially 46.

experience of faith in a Minjung theological context. Chung proposes it as a key for interpreting the theology of the Spirit and Christology. One can understand the shock her words caused to the 850 delegates from some 320 churches; it was felt necessary to add to the program a discussion on the relationship between theology and culture. Archbishop Kirill of the Russian church raised the question in a meeting of the assembly: "It is evident that liberal, radical, and contextual theology has the upper hand over the theology of the apostolic tradition. *We must acknowledge the problem and discuss it*" [emphasis added]. For his part, Emilio Castro, Secretary of the Council of Churches, answered that he wished to debate with Chung her theological presentation and challenge her, but not challenge her right to bring this contribution to the assembly. Here we find ourselves at the heart of the problem of exchanges between those feminist theologies situated on the fringes of theological tradition and the traditional theologies, even when the latter offer a degree of openness to the question posed by the awareness of feminine faith.

Feminist deconstruction, reconstruction, construction, these are approaches and phases found in most theological disciplines today. We must therefore speak of feminist theologies and recognize that they do not deal only with the question of women in the church or with the relationships between women and men in the church but that, beyond these topics, they apply to the whole of the doctrinal and pastoral tradition of the church. The reformist theologies hold various positions regarding the traditional corpus; some are more radical than others. The theologies which I call constructionist certainly are not traditional in the narrow sense of the term, but it remains to be demonstrated that they are anti-traditional if we advert to the deep Christian meaning of tradition. These theologies are now part of the Christian theological production.

2. Feminist Readings and Perspectives in Christology

Christology, understood as discourse on the person of Jesus and his work of salvation, is the crucial point (the *crux*) or the decisive test (the *krisis*) of feminist theologies in their biblical as well as dogmatic formulations. The scandal caused in the early 80s by the exhibition of the sculpture of the crucified Christ as a woman, *Christa,* in the Episcopalian cathedral in New York is a perfect illustration of this crucial problem. The artist, Edwina Sandys, wanted to represent Jesus Christ incarnating, in his person at the hour of effecting our salvation, women's sufferings in society at large, and in the church, as an evil that dwells in humanity and the cosmos; at the same time, she wanted to show the redeeming potential of these sufferings when they become mediators of transformation. It is acceptable to represent the crucified Jew that the historical Jesus was in the form of an oppressed African American or South American male, but to represent him in the form of an oppressed woman created a scandal. However, it is the image of the martyr Blandina that in the early days of Christianity the Christians of Gaul had kept and transmitted.

Christology is the unavoidable test of feminist theologies and the place where their diversities, even their divergences, reside.

Post-Christian *Readings*

Some woman theologians have reached the conclusion that the very fact that Jesus Christ, confessed as Son of God, is of the masculine gender *(aner)* and confessed as such as the Savior and only Mediator between God and humankind, Primordial Image of renewed humankind, renders Christianity fundamentally unable to generate a complete equality as human beings between women and men. Such a tradition betrays itself as patriarchal and androcentric, not only in its formulation, but in its very structure. It is useless to expect from it a true liberation; at best, one might envision less deleterious effects for the condition of women, as the theory of the "loving patriarchal system"[19] proposes it. In 1985, the Englishwoman Daphne Hampson, the first president of the Association of European Theologians, was reaching this conclusion and was taking her place in the ranks of the *post-Christian* theologians, a designation which Mary Daly had applied to herself as early as 1975.

In the first edition of *Beyond God the Father* (1973), Mary Daly writes, "The problem is not that the Jesus of the Gospels was male, young, and a Semite. Rather, the problem lies in the exclusive identification of this person with God, in such a manner that Christian conceptions of divinity and of the "image of God" are all objectified in Jesus."[20] She regards this form of the divinization of Jesus Christ as *Christolatry* at the service of a *Mariolatry:* "The idea of a unique male savior may be seen as one more legitimation of male superiority."[21]

19. Ernst Troeltsch referred to this category in *The Social Teaching of the Christian Churches*, 2 vols. (New York: Harper and Row, 1960). Feminist studies made use of this category; see among others, Schüssler Fiorenza, *In Memory of Her*, 351–391.

20. Mary Daly, *Beyond God the Father: Toward a Philosophy of Women's Liberation* (Boston: Beacon Press, 1973) 79. This was reedited in 1984 and 1985 with a new introduction.

21. Ibid., 71.

Post-Christian theologians see the figure of Jesus Christ as structurally patriarchal: since it is equalled to the divine Being, it serves as a
foundation for a similar divinization of men as a group. Man is thereby
invested with a sacral reality and significance, exemplary or arche-
typal, of which woman can be, at best, a reflection. We know well the
difficulty that in spite of exegetical acrobatics, 1 Cor 11:3 poses to a
feminist theology. According to these theologians, any Christology can
generate only mythical, ritual, symbolic, linguistic, theological, institutional, social, and ecclesial interpretations, interpretations which de-
value women by their dualistic, hierarchizing, fragmenting, not to say
adversarial, character, unavoidably androcentric and sexist. This view
affects also the conception of the relationships between human beings
and the cosmos and even of the relationships between humankind and
God.

Their conclusions lead these researchers to reject any effort at reconstruction and construction of the Christian tradition. They choose constructions, but in another religious space. Thus Mary Daly exhorts
women to start on an exodus from the whole of what is called religious
without them/over them: what is named God the Father, sin in relation
to this father, the Savior Image of this God/Father, the fraternal community under the rule of the Father. By naming themselves from within
this process of liberation, women will begin, she says, to leave behind
their patriarchal identity and will form bonds of solidarity, a *sisterhood*
which will not be a *subordinate mini-brotherhood*. They become a collective figure which Mary Daly opposes to that of the Christ of dogmatics
and which she terms *antiChrist* in this sense. Their communal project of
mutual acknowledgement and liberation becomes an *antiChurch* based
on a cosmic alliance she calls *antiWorld* in this sense. She believes that
this phenomenon signals the end of "Christian idolatry."

> It will, I think, become increasingly evident that exclusively masculine
> symbols for the ideal of incarnation or for the ideal of the human search
> of fulfillment will not do. As a uniquely masculine image and language
> for divinity loses credibility so also the idea of a single divine incarna-
> tion in a human being of the male sex may give way in the religious
> consciousness to an increased awareness of the power of Being in all
> persons.[22]

For these theologians, the end of a God incarnated as a male human
being would signify also the end of the belief in a God who becomes incarnated in a singular form and invests it with an ultimate universal
significance. The problem, an ancient one, arises again in the context of

22. Ibid.

interreligious exchanges open to the recognition of the other. Feminist theologians discuss this problem, in different terms based on their feminist consciousness of faith, while remaining within the Christian tradition.[23]

Christological Constructionist Readings

I call constructionist those theological readings which, while belonging to the Christian tradition, are situated at the edge of its text in order to lead it "beyond the text" in the sense I have mentioned above. Perhaps one could style them emancipationist. According to these persons, biblical revelation, in its evangelical nucleus, carries a "subversive" energy such that in the Spirit, the unheard-of purport of its salvific truth can always erupt as a revelation in the history of humanity. Since revelation took shape in a linguistic and symbolic system limited in the way it formulates meaning, to make absolutes of this linguistic and symbolic system would be to fixate and reify, to idolize the historical moment of a word whose very function is to lead historical laws to limits where they burst open. This would be tantamount to denying to this word its reality and efficacy of True Word.

Now, it happens that Christian women become, individually or in communion with others, a place for the experience of *primary* faith, that is, a faith which did not find place either in the biblical text or in subsequent dogmatic tradition. Thus their experience of violence: women of the biblical tradition lived this experience but did not formulate it themselves. It was recorded in Scripture formulated by men within a patriarchal culture. Nowadays, women as a collectivity express this experience which women theologians for their part formulate in a feminist theology. The figure of *Christa* was the catalyst that prompted numerous women to tell their stories because it spoke to them a liberating word, for example: "I would not have to explain to a male God that I had been raped. God knew what it was like to be a woman who has been raped."[24] These reports cover several levels and can reveal other forms of violence. Radford Ruether sees there a revelatory act of God "where the divine has never been allowed to be present in patriarchal religion, in female sexual victimization by men. The divine is present here . . . one with the female victim, one who knows this anguish, who is a part of it, and who also heals and empowers women to

---

23. See an example in Isabel Carter Heyward, *The Redemption of God: A Theology of Mutual Relation* (Washington, D.C.: University Press of America, 1982).

24. Rosemary Radford Ruether, "Feminist Theology in the Academy," *Christianity and Crisis* 45 (1984) 61.

rise from the dead, to be recreated beyond and outside the grasp of this negative power."[25]

Of course, not every one of these stories is to be held as revelatory. Theological discernment must be used, here as elsewhere, with ecclesial responsibility. Moreover, such stories will become a valuable material of theological interpretation for the church inasmuch as believing women will be recognized as a witness group and a subject of the history of revelation in Jesus Christ. Categories of private revelation and public revelation will have to be reviewed.

Christological Reconstructionist Readings

The feminist reconstructionist readings, which I also call reformist, remain the more numerous and are present in all Christian traditions. They aim at transforming Christian tradition by reinterpreting it and reformulating it from within its fundamental data, and this in a more or less radical way. The criticism and the formulations they offer are less traditional.

Here the problem is neither in the Christological promulgations of Chalcedon as such (that Christ is truly divine and truly human) nor in the confession "Jesus is the Christ" nor even in the fact that Jesus Christ is a man. The problem is in the discourses, the symbolic interpretations, and the institutions deriving from these promulgations which have reinforced the patriarchal and androcentric religious system. The effects of such a system are pernicious not only for the identity and the callings of women—and also men—as groups of baptized persons but also for the whole church's identity and calling, *ad intra* and *ad extra* (within and without).

These theologies hold on to the basic Christological declarations. They do not deduce from the fact that Jesus was a man that masculinity reveals the very structure of God's Word. Rather, they make their own the ancient argumentation, well developed by Athanasius: true humanity includes the whole of humanity and any kind of humanity, truly in-dwelt as such by God; this is the foundation of universal salvation. These theologies hold to this while adding the specific contributions of women's faith.[26] Furthermore, let us note that too literal an

25. Radford Ruether, "Feminism and Religious Faith," 16–17.

26. This is the argument advanced by Archbishop Robert Runcie in his exchanges with the Secretariat for Christian Unity concerning the question of the ordination of women; see *The Vatican and Canterbury Exchange of Letters: Women's Ordination and the Progress of Ecumenism,* in *Origins* 16, no. 8 (1986–1987) 153–160. Some Christian feminist anthropologies are elaborated in this perspective, for instance, that proposed by Catharina J. Halkes, "Humanity Re-imaged: New Directions in Feminist

insistence on the male sex of Christ can raise the question of the incarnation of God in a masculinity not produced by male sperm since its vital human nucleus came exclusively from a woman through God's grace. Some theologians see in that event a revelatory word radically critical of the patriarchal system of laws, even the biological law of fertilization by the male. In this view, Jesus would have extended this criticism, constitutive of his very being in his familial, social, and religious behavior, into a radical rereading of human relationships and their sacred character. This criticism should reach to the centuries-old anthropological discourse which identifies the man as *archē* (beginning) in the act of procreation and which justifies the name of Father for God—"Father Almighty"—because God is the *archē* of creation.

Confronted by a Christology which maintains that a baptized woman cannot represent Christ *in persona*, in her very being, (or the church *in persona*) because of the *"order of creation"*—which, according to this view, the order of grace does not correct—feminist theologies deconstruct in a first phase what in the teachings of Augustine and Thomas Aquinas pertains to the anthropology of the time and its accompanying social and religious outlook more than it pertains to properly Christian Christology. The feminist theologies we are speaking of follow these doctors' example, not by repeating their interpretations, but by adopting a Christian anthropological reading encompassing both the salvific event in Jesus Christ and the human reality that was its beneficiary, inasmuch as it can be known today. Is it not logical to wonder whether today Thomas Aquinas would define woman by her biological destiny? And would he still see in woman an unfinished human being because of her sex and, therefore, by nature or by the order of creation, fated to being dominated by man, the first and exemplary subject and her head both individually and collectively, the only being capable of representing Christ, the Head of the Church? Would he still write today, ". . . it is because the male sex is nobler than the female sex that God chose it when he became flesh. However, in order that the female sex might not be despised, it was fitting that Christ should take his body from a woman"? When speaking of the priesthood, he says that a woman cannot be ordained because she is a physically, mentally, and morally deficient human being; that this is in the nature of things and not only a consequence of the fall; that therefore she is incapable, because of her sex, of publicly representing Christ the Priest, Head of

Theological Anthropology," *Liberating Women: New Theological Directions*, ed. Ursula King (Bristol: University of Bristol, 1992) 75–93. See also E. Meyer, ed., *Femmes dans l'Église et dans la société: Les actes du colloque de Bruxelles*, 9–14 June 1987 (Brühl, Germany: Conférences des Organisations Internationales Catholiques, 1988).

the Church. Thus her innate subordinate status in society and in church is, as it were, inherent in the order of creation willed by God.[27] Would Thomas Aquinas still hold to that interpretation of the original order of creation, hierarchized and dualistic, if he had knowledge of the contemporary biblical and anthropological sciences? Would he still do so at a time when human consciousness realizes that such an order with the system it legitimizes has generated and continues to generate inequalities that alienate women and many other human beings? at a time when in the majority of Christian churches this has been understood and when even the Roman Catholic tradition unequivocally affirms it in the Constitution *Gaudium et Spes* of Vatican II? Constructionist Christologies demonstrate that the problem is not in the Thomistic theological system but in the methodological error of the discourses which continue to apply this system when both theological and human sciences have shown its scientific foundations to be obsolete.

Constructionist theologians extend the logic of today's dogmatic Christology to the question of the salvation of women in Jesus Christ. They ask, "Are women truly saved in Jesus Christ if, simply because they are women, only men can instruct them and guide them?"[28] This is another way of raising the question of the universality of salvation already touched upon above and, as a consequence, the question of the church as a community of salvation. Upon what arguments is it possible to establish a theology of baptismal grace that discriminates according to sex in order to determine who will have access to the sacraments of faith? For feminist theologians, the question demands an answer in a new and urgent way: what is at stake is the veracity of God's salvation in Jesus Christ.

These theologies propose different alternatives. However, all of them require that theological interpretations be linked with the historical experience of faith and that all of them stress the theological principle that to absolutize linguistic and symbolic forms runs contrary to biblical revelation itself. The question to ask is rather: What is the word that dwells in the language and symbolic system in which is expressed the revelation from which the whole of Christian tradition derives its legitimization? This tradition continues to proclaim the event of the death and resurrection of Jesus Christ and the pouring out of the Spirit that sprang from them for the sake of human history in all times and all

27. Thomas Aquinas, *Summa Theologica* 3, q. 1-59; see q. 31, art. 4; 1, q. 92, arts. 1-2; 3 Suppl., q. 39, art. 1.

28. This question is asked by many feminist theologians, including the Brasilian Ivone Gebara; see her interview with Elisabeth J. Lacelle, "Des femmes en mouvement de libération au Brésil," *Femmes et hommes en Église* 55 (1993) 7.

places. The salvation that this word affirms creates or wants to create a new human order with its new human laws, the law of saving grace. This new order (the *novum*) entered history with Jesus Christ, and it produces its effects, here and now, in the Spirit, through those who belong to Jesus Christ, as a church. Any human being who welcomes this salvation is henceforth snatched from every order that causes servitude, imprisonment in one's destiny. If things are so, women are fully humanized in Jesus Christ in the order of creation as well as in the order of grace. With man and like man, woman is at once vulnerable and able to be transfigured in her whole person, including her sex. With man and like man, being baptized in Jesus Christ, she inherits the promise of the whole sacramental life. It is not a matter of denying the twofold identity of male and female any more than of enduring it as an unavoidable genetic fact; it is a matter of *thinking* it with faith in the new Humanity that Jesus Christ inaugurated. This theological task requires that any hierarchizing dualism (soul/body, spirit/flesh, reason/ chaos, man/cosmos, man/woman), at the expense of the unity of the human being, be rejected as unfit for establishing cultural and religious systems. We must tend toward living genuinely dialoguing lives which will produce dialogic theologies keeping on a par, although as different beings in mutual relationships, man and woman created in God's image. These theologies will also proclaim the equal humanity of women and men, a cosmic and sacral coexistence in relationship with God.

The Christological alternatives blaze some trails. The figure of Christ Wisdom/Sophia restores an aspect that had been forgotten or obscured. The collective figure of Christ, both Servant and Jerusalem/ Zion, like that of Mary, both Jerusalem/Zion and Servant, are eschatological soteriological figures echoing one another. Already in the Old Testament, these figures form what Pierre Bonnard calls the great poems of reconciliation in Isaiah.[29]

In this phase of reconstruction, we see beginnings—even though very difficult—of conversation between feminist theologies and traditional theology.

Conclusion

Feminist theologies have reached the point of speaking to one another. They exercise a mutual criticism and exchange questions and

29. Pierre E. Bonnard, *Le second Esaïe, son disciple et leurs éditeurs, Esaïe 40–66,* Études bibliques (Paris: Gabalda, 1972); see also Claude Wiener, *Le deuxième Isaïe,* Cahiers Évangile 20 (Paris: Cerf, 1976) 25–26.

responses. This is the case, for instance, in the United States between African American women (Womanist Theology) who distance themselves from the feminism of their white colleagues and the latter who are careful not to universalize their visions. Feminist theologies have also begun to speak to other milieux of research, even though most of these theologies still resist entering into conversation with traditional circles, particularly if these are functionally linked with ecclesiastical authoritarian discourses. They perceive these circles as unable to meet them as equal partners. One must add that some of these feminist theologians do not make partnership an easy thing.

One of the difficulties that plague these studies resides in their epistemological parameters. Carol P. Christ was right when she wrote in 1987, "Feminist scholarship, as most of us who practice it are aware, requires a paradigm shift, a questioning of fundamental and unquestioned assumptions about canon, ideas, value, authority, and method that operate in the academy and the disciplines."[30] I had pointed this out in 1983 in a multidisciplinary research that explored the paths of a poietic science in which the intellectual act becomes a listening to and experience of the other, of the universe, and of God, at the same time it becomes a listening to and an experience of oneself and of one's relationship with the other, the universe, and God.[31] Such a scientific practice places the researcher and the object/subject under study in a relational mode which fosters a knowledge that can be called "interrevelatory." Its intellectual movement is dialogical (others will qualify it as dynamically dialectical or as correlational), going from the known to the unknown and from the unknown to the known while maintaining an intellectual space into which a new meaning or a new vision may break through. Provided they are correctly conducted, such studies are not subjectivist. Neither are they carried by an underlying ideology—that of the researcher or that of the object/subject under study since this is a conversation between the two. The German writer Maria Mies speaks of "conscious partiality" able to maintain a dialogical or justly correlational distance—of interaction/interconnection—between the two interacting parties.[32] Not all feminist studies succeed to the same degree in

30. See Carol P. Christ, "Toward a Paradigm Shift in the Academy and in Religious Studies," in *The Impact of Feminist Research in the Academy*, ed. Christie Farnham (Bloomington, Ind.: Indiana University Press, 1987) 53–76.

31. Élisabeth J. Lacelle, ed., *La femme, son corps et la religion*, Femmes et religions (Montréal: Bellarmin, 1983) 235–246; see also Lacelle, *L'incontournable échange* 243–261.

32. See Maria Mies, "Towards a Methodology for Feminist Research," in *Theories of Women's Studies*, ed. Gloria Bowles and Renate Duelli Klein (London: Routledge and Kegan Paul, 1983) 117–139.

holding to the asceticism and ethical rigor exacted by such a scientific practice, but most of them strive to reach these high standards. Thus, experience becomes a cultural stratum of a discourse that is contextual, therefore fragmentary, something traditional theology finds difficult to accept because it claims that revelation is universal. However, traditional theological discourse also affirms that revelation is an event, that of the word always bursting into history.

Conversations have begun which are worth pursuing. The search for a "postmodern" paradigm led Hans Küng and other serious theologians to sketch its outlines in four dimensions: biblical, historical, political, and ecumenical. Feminist theologies are an integral part of this. Thus, for the biblical dimension, the problem of patriarchal and androcentric language and symbolic thought is part and parcel of the search for ways to formulate the discourse about God, Christology, ethics, and so on.[33]

Conversations also take place, as I mentioned, in the ecumenical dialogues of the WCC and in certain ones involving two parties. These are most interesting and most important; they are worth keeping track of. An attentive look at the texts produced by these dialogues is sufficient to prove how fruitful they are, even though the price of comprehension is high.[34] It is possible that by meeting one another, feminist theologies and institutional ecumenical theologies may verify one another and exchange visions which will produce a theological tradition and Christian institutions rooted in evangelical faith since its origins and at the same time open to the future. The conditions for this to happen are (1) that confrontations lead to evangelical reconciliation rather than mutual rejection and (2) that the problems of ecclesiastical power may not override the search for truth.

The Spirit of Truth seeks to manifest itself at the heart of the church today through the collective voices of women, something that never happened in the past. I do not believe that feminist theologies and praxis can produce by themselves the liberating transformations they are seeking in faith. But neither do I believe that the church, as a faith community, can effect those transformations without the contributions

33. Hans Küng, *Une théologie pour le troisième millénaire: Pour un nouveau départ œcuménique* (Paris: Seuil, 1989) 237–253; [Hans Küng, *Theology for the Third Millennium: An Ecumenical View,* trans. Peter Heinegg (New York: Doubleday, 1988)].

34. See Commission on Faith and Order, *Confessing the One Faith: An Ecumenical Explication of the Apostolic Faith as It Is Confessed in the Nicene-Constantinopolitan Creed of 381,* Faith and Order Paper 153 (Geneva: WCC, 1991). See also Melanie A. May, ed., *Women and Church: The Challenge of Ecumenical Solidarity in an Age of Alienation* (Grand Rapids, Mich.: Eerdmans, 1991) 179–193.

of feminist theologies and praxis. And biblical sciences are indispensable in such a search.

Feminist Theories in the Interpretation of the Bible

◆──◆

Olivette Genest

Among other results, today's feminist theories have given rise to feminist readings of the Bible, individual and communal readings, intra- and extra-ecclesial readings. They have produced a true feminist exegesis, the object of the present study. We shall call these productions *feminist readings*. The term *reading* allows us to cover its whole gamut: from the elementary visual contact—whether a rapid or a concentrated reading, a scrutinizing or meditative one—to the properly exegetical activity. This activity has acquired scientific tools adapted to its object and little by little has gained its own place among other forms of exegesis in order to arrive at a feminist interpretation of its results and at the theorizing that arises from this interpretation and, finally, at the criticism of knowledge in the field of biblical studies.

Although little known to exegetes, these feminist readings do exist. As proof of this, we can adduce a wealth of publications, already surprisingly vast, in Europe and even more in the United States, in English-speaking Canada, and in Quebec, whether French-speaking or English-speaking.[1] Quantitatively abundant, these publications are

---

1. Katherine Doob Sackenfeld, "Feminist Perspectives on Bible and Theology," *Interpretation* 42 (1988) 5–18; Gayle Gerber Koontz and Willard Swartley, eds., *Perspectives on Feminist Hermeneutics*, Occasional Papers 10 (Elkhart, Ind.: Institute of Mennonite Studies, 1987); Annie Jaubert, "Le rôle des femmes dans le peuple de Dieu: Recherche de critères en référence à l'Écriture," in *Écriture et pratique chrétienne*, Lectio Divina 96, (Paris: Cerf, 1978) 53–68; Elizabeth A. Johnson, "Feminist Hermeneutics," *Chicago Studies* 27 (1988) 123–135; Carol A. Newsom and Sharon H. Ringe, eds., *The Women's Bible* (Louisville: Westminster/John Knox Press, 1992); Carolyn Osiek, "The Feminist and the Bible: Hermeneutical Alternatives," in *Feminist Perspectives on Scholarship*, Adela Yarbro Collins, ed. (Atlanta: Scholars Press,

also qualitatively diversified according to the levels at which the biblical text is read, to its addressees, to the feminist theory that directs its approach, to what tools it borrows from many disciplines, to the self-critical level it has attained. All this reflects the pluralism of feminist endeavors in general.

Another witness to the vitality of feminist published work is the place granted it by the document of the Pontifical Biblical Commission, *The Interpretation of the Bible in the Church,* published on November 18, 1993.[2] Not only is it itemized but it is covered in several columns equal in length to those devoted to long recognized and accepted methods. Since it is detailed enough, this presentation will serve us as a point of departure for organizing these feminist methods of research, pinpointing the grey zones, and uncovering the misunderstandings and prejudices that plague the feminist use and study of the Bible.

Whatever the edition of this document, we find the presentation in part I, section E, among the "Contextual Approaches," next to the "Liberationist Approach." The overall term "contextual studies" is in current use. However, it would fit as well the approaches that were mentioned before in the document: the historical, sociological, anthropological, and even psychological inasmuch as one can date the expression of psychological realities and the cultural area which left its imprint on them. The closest link between liberationist readings and feminist readings is that both are practiced by the subject who reads, from his or her personal situation. From this viewpoint, the two approaches are indeed akin to one another. However, it is also from this viewpoint that the most serious questions concerning them arise.

1985); Letty M. Russell, ed., *Feminist Interpretation of the Bible* (Philadelphia: Westminster Press, 1985); Sandra M. Schneiders, "Scripture: Tool of Patriarchy or Resource for Transformation," *Beyond Patching: Faith and Feminism in the Catholic Church* (New York: Paulist Press, 1991); Luise Schottroff and Annette Esser, eds., "Bibelauslegung und Europäischer Kontext," in *Feminist Theology in a European Context,* Yearbook of the European Society of Women in Theological Research 1 (1993), (Kampen, Netherlands: Kok Pharos, 1993); Elisabeth Schüssler Fiorenza, *In Memory of Her: A Feminist Reconstruction of Christian Origins* (New York: Crossroad, 1984); Idem, *Bread Not Stone: The Challenge of Feminist Biblical Interpretation* (Boston: Beacon Press, 1984); Idem, *But She Said: Feminist Practices of Biblical Interpretation* (Boston: Beacon Press, 1992); Elisabeth Schüssler Fiorenza, ed., *Searching the Scriptures: A Feminist Introduction* (New York: Crossroad, 1993); Mary Ann Tolbert, "Defining the Problem: The Bible and Feminist Hermeneutics," *Semeia* 28 (1983); Denise Veillette, "Exister, penser, croire autrement: Thématique religieuse féministe de la revue *Concilium*," *Recherches féministes* 3 (1990) 31–71.

2. Pontifical Biblical Commission, "The Interpretation of the Bible in the Church," *Origins* 23 (1993–1994) 498–524.

The document recognizes the existence of several feminist biblical hermeneutics, from which it selects three principal forms: The *radical* form rejects the Bible because it is patriarchal—in the sense that it is a product of a patriarchal culture—and androcentric. The *neo-orthodox* form accepts the Bible, provided the women that are oppressed in it are placed among the weak, whose cause the Bible champions in many passages anyhow. The *critical* form seeks to recover the equality of men and women and the egalitarian character of the Jesus movement and the Pauline churches. Let us note that in the document's subsequent paragraphs, this diversity will be reduced to one single position, the best known, that of Elisabeth Schüssler Fiorenza, which in any case would have needed a more nuanced and developed treatment to do it justice. Feminist hermeneutics will pursue one single goal, that is, the historical reconstruction of the position of women in the early Church, through the clues, but also the lacunae, the oversights, the inaccuracies in the writings of the New Testament.

Two paragraphs on the positive contributions to exegesis by women follow. However, ironically, a feminist reading would easily detect, just under the text, the androcentric character of their authorship. Thanks to feminist exegesis,

> women have played a more active part in exegetical research. They have succeeded, often better than men, in detecting the presence, the significance and the role of women in the Bible, in Christian origins, and in the church . . . Feminine sensitivity helps to unmask and correct certain commonly accepted interpretations which were tendentious and sought to justify the male domination of women.

What a progress in these concessions, unthinkable a few decades ago! Including the wish, expressed later on in the document, "that the teaching of exegesis be given by men and women."[3]

But many more refinements would have to be added. It is not through feminist movements that women have been led to exegesis. On the contrary, causes entirely different from the absence of active feminism were at work in the fact that they came to exegesis so late and, at first, in such small numbers. It is not "often" that women succeeded better than men in outlining women's role in the Bible or "in bringing back to light aspects that had been forgotten";[4] rather, they succeeded in contributing the total newness of aspects that had never

---

3. Ibid., III, C, 3, "Teaching," 518.
4. Ibid., III, B, 3, "Roles of Various Members of the Church in Interpretation," 516–517.

been considered. It is not "feminine sensitivity," but a real competence, allied to work, rigor, and great courage, which enabled them to gain acceptance for their conclusions. No one ever resorts to the masculine sensitivity of a male exegete to explain the success of his work. May the day come when, for both men and women, the talk will be only of sensitivity to the text and of becoming sensitized to certain of its aspects when one suffers oppression, whether man or woman.

After the official recognition of feminist exegesis, the document continues by underlining the dangers inherent in its nature, as it does for all the other approaches. "Feminist exegesis, to the extent that it proceeds from a preconceived judgment, runs the risk of interpreting the biblical texts in a tendentious and thus debatable manner." One may regret the pejorative connotation of the term "preconceived judgment." Beyond questions of vocabulary, the problem remains: feminism is an ideology. The following sentences again reduce the exegetical practice inspired by feminism to only historical reconstruction; thereby it "does not correspond at all to the work of exegesis properly so called. It entails rejecting the content of the inspired texts in preference for a hypothetical construction, quite different in nature." Here the writer has forgotten that any historical work is a reconstruction, that exegesis rests upon hypothetical constructions, and that according to the very terms of the document, "several feminist biblical hermeneutics have to be distinguished."

Finally, "feminist exegesis often raises questions of power within the church, questions which, as is obvious, are matters of discussion and even of confrontation." Feminist exegesis hears itself reminded that it "can be useful to the church only to the degree that . . . it does not lose sight of the evangelical teaching concerning power as service." As a unique occurrence in the document, a note stipulates that those opposed to this last sentence requested and obtained that the result of the vote on this sentence be published with the text, that is, eleven in favor, four against, and four abstentions.

While it marks a true progress in the acceptance of the feminist approach among exegetical methods, the text of the Biblical Commission supplies us with a microcosm of the current biases against what it praises. As a basis for discussion, we choose the three pairs of terms placed in opposition which the document lists: so-called feminine contribution versus scientific authenticity, ideology versus objectivity, and politics versus exegesis. These three will underlie our study which (1) situates existing feminist readings, (2) describes accurately their true aims, and (3) evaluates the contribution of feminist theories in the interpretation of the Bible.

1. Feminist Readings of the Bible

Their Classification

In spite of their great abundance and riches, the works produced by the feminist reading of the Bible are invisible to the eyes of exegetical research. Absent or quasi-absent from the bibliographical works in current use, from the reference books mentioned in classes, and from cursive or partial commentaries, the best way to know them, if one is not connected to the electronic networks of feminist research, is by the few typologies that have already been attempted.[5]

With a few differences, these typologies group feminist exegetes, and their works, according to how they evaluate the biblical text. The result is as follows:

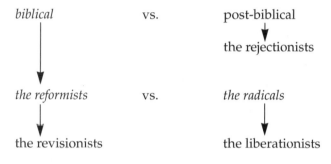

the sublimationists

Those who reject the Bible as being an instrument of the repression of women *call themselves* "post-biblical." They choose to begin afresh either within or without the walls of the Christian tradition. The "biblicals" affirm that it is possible to revise the biblical text or to sublimate its reading to the metaphorical level. Although not completely turning their backs on the Bible, the "radicals" believe any revision to be impossible and attempt to free the Bible from its sexism. They proceed by purifying it from its patriarchal dimension or by rejecting the notion of

5. See among the texts listed in n. 1: Sackenfeld, "Feminist Perspectives"; Koontz and Swartley, *Perspectives*; Johnson, "Feminist Hermeneutics"; Osiek, "The Feminist and the Bible"; Schüssler Fiorenza, *But She Said*; Tolbert, "Defining the Problem."

These typologies concern chiefly North American production. For the European one, see Schottroff and Esser, *Feminist Theology*; Veillette, "Exister, penser, croire autrement."

On the whole, our study reflects the state of North American research.

canon, and, if need be, by amputating the passages they judge irrecon-
cilable with the image of a just God, the defender of the oppressed.

As for the typology of Schüssler Fiorenza, it rests on methodological criteria and on the position of the exegetes within the world of feminisms. It offers ten classes of "Strategies of Interpretation," her own
being at the end of the list.[6]

1. **Revisionist Interpretation**—This cuts through the centuries-old
strata of androcentric interpretation to reclaim the biblical text, believed not to be misogynist; if it were correctly understood, it would
advocate women's liberation. Under this heading, we find works which
distinguish negative texts and positive texts concerning women, male
and female imagery of God.

2. **Text and Translation**—How can we succeed in adequately ren-
dering for our century the androcentric character of biblical texts? Must
we respect it, warn against it, correct it? The translator's preoccupation
with this question bears upon grammatical gender, natural or biological gender, the inclusive language and discourse to be created, the
choice of masculine or feminine variants in the different traditional
manuscripts and materials, the option for a properly feminist version,
the relationship to be maintained with the history of biblical times.

3. **Imaginative Identification**—This takes into account not only the
female characters encountered in the Bible but also those whom it is
legitimate to suppose are present in the narrative framework. Despite
its felicitous findings, this is in danger of veering toward images and
myths of femininity from which, precisely, it intends to free both the
patriarchal text and women.

4. **Women as Authors and Biblical Interpreters**—This exegetical effort aims at recovering texts or portions of texts written by women and
at telling the intellectual history of the interpretation of the Bible by
women. In the first of their objectives, researchers do not expect to necessarily find writings that are liberating for women; as to the second of
their objectives, they already know, through the religious history of
women, that a feminist current persists throughout the centuries.

5. **Historical Interpretation**—Two kinds of works fall under this
heading. The first studies the women in the Bible and their sisters in the
contemporary milieu, women who are Jewish, Roman, and Greek. It

6. See Schüssler Fiorenza, *But She Said*, 20–50.

postulates that the biblical text is the mirror of the reality of women in antiquity. The second requires that a preliminary criticism be applied to this approach. Because the mere compilation of textual and archeological sources fails to detect the character of the ideological construction proper to androcentric texts, these sources must be approached through a hermeneutics of suspicion, they must be submitted to feminist models of analysis and reconstruction, they must be accompanied by sociocritical studies of the daily lives of women and their divisions into social classes. The attention to this preliminary attitude has, in its turn, led to discoveries of unpublished documents.

6. **Sociocultural Reconstruction**—The notion of reconstruction which inspired *In Memory of Her*[7] dominates this sixth class. Here, one finds the illustration, the nuances, and the justification of this notion. With the "New Historicism," history is no longer understood in a positivist sense but as a story deliberately built, as the history of the relationships of and struggles for power. In order to reconstruct the reality of early Christianity, classical exegesis has made use of several models: the geopolitical model, which revealed in the New Testament anti-Semitic, imperialistic, and Eurocentric implications; the theological models, whether Protestant or Catholic, the former seeing a deterioration from Jesus to Catholicism, the latter discerning on the contrary a growth from Jesus to the efflorescence of the Roman papacy; the orthodoxy/ heresy models, the Jesus/apostolic succession models, the charismatic equality/hierarchic institution models.

However, in these sociocultural reconstructions, the androcentric dynamic of the biblical text remains unsuspected and untouched. Therefore, feminist exegesis reexamines these reconstructions in the light of the category of gender and also submits them to the feminist criticism of ideologies. After remarking that history is written from the viewpoint of the winners, it voices its preoccupation with a history written from the viewpoint of those who are marginal and silenced, a history taking into account analyses of women's experiences valued as genuine scientific sources. This feminist reconstruction is not a reckless innovation but rather a test of the preceding sociocultural reconstructions.

7. **Ideological Inscription**—Feminist literary studies, whether formal, structuralist, narratological, or based on the relationship readertext, have succeeded in describing how androcentric texts in general create the politics of gender and the representation of women. These

7. See n. 1.

studies have brought to light a complex ideological construct in these androcentric texts. In order to decode the ideology embedded in the Bible, some exegetes have recourse to a feminist rhetorical criticism. Through the unveiling of the sexual and patriarchal politics underlying the text, these studies seek to break the hold which the androcentric sacred texts have over women, imposing on them identity, prescriptions, and interdicts in the name of religion.

8. **Women as Subjects of Interpretation**—Here the focus shifts from the text to the female reader. The feminist expression of the relationship reader-text shows how patriarchal discourse constructs its reader, male or female, how the categories of gender, race, and class affect his or her way of reading. The purpose of this eighth class of interpretation is to make all readers aware of the textual and sociocultural situation of women and remove them from the auto-alienation generated by the reading of culturally masculine writings presented as normative. Through the light it projects, this way of interpretation seeks to free women's ability to recognize themselves as subjects and, as a consequence, as subjects of interpretation.

9. **The Present Sociopolitical Location of Interpretation**—This strategy of interpretation stresses the connection of the sociopolitical, the global-cultural, the diversified religious locations, and the sociohistorical contexts of biblical readings. For example, the strategy of interpretation of Latin American women proposes a reading different from "other liberation theological approaches" and distances itself from macho culture and religion and takes into account women's daily experience. It is this specifically female ethos which must permeate scientific values and the commitment to the struggles of peoples for justice, self-determination, and freedom.

Here, critical intelligence derives neither from scientific rationalism (even if the approach remains scientific) nor from academic antidogmatism but from the commitment to the fight for the liberation of their own kin.

10. **A Critical Feminist Rhetorical Model**—Schüssler Fiorenza presented in *In Memory of Her*, 1983, her critical feminist interpretation, oriented toward liberating women from the oppression of which they are victims. At that time, she used the framework of historical reconstruction within the hermeneutical paradigm. In 1984, in *Bread Not Stone*, she wanted her method to find its place among biblical studies. Finally, in 1992, with *But She Said*, she intended to set it within the rhetorico-hermeneutical space created by feminist theory.

When she describes it, in this tenth category, she retains her usual vision with its three components, that is, feminist studies, the movements of liberation in church and society, and academic theological studies. In comparison with the other nine categories, she does not bring, she says, a new methodological strategy, but integrates them into "a rhetorical model of a critical feminist interpretive process of transformation." The interaction works on both the nine categories and three components. For instance, feminist religious studies strive to transform biblical interpretation, the academic as well as the ecclesial, thus coupling theoretical concern with a practical goal (p. 41). Regarding academic interpretation:

> A critical construction of feminist biblical interpretation seeks to replace the depoliticizing practice of modern scientific interpretation with a practice of rhetorical inquiry engaged in the formation of a critical historical and religious consciousness (p. 46).

Regarding ecclesial interpretation:

> The shift from a hermeneutical paradigm to a rhetorical one has far-reaching consequences for the theoethical practice of proclamation. By proclamation, I do not mean just preaching but all theoethical inquiry that is concerned with the uses and effects of biblical texts in contemporary society (p. 47).

However, Schüssler Fiorenza brings a new angle, that of rhetoric:

> Indeed, I seek to utilize rhetorical analysis not as one more method of literary or structural analysis, but rather to analyze how biblical texts and interpretations create or sustain oppressive or liberating theoethical values, sociopolitical practices, and worlds of vision (p. 46).

Later on, she adds that "all readers of the Bible must learn how to examine not only the rhetorical aims of biblical texts but also the rhetorical interests emerging in the history of interpretation or in contemporary scholarship" (p. 47). Seen in this way, the definition of her strategy becomes "a religious-ethical rhetoric and feminist pragmatic of biblical interpretation" and "a critical feminist interpretation of liberation" (p. 47).

Because her feminist rhetoric seeks to render audible the voices found both in the text and in its ancient and contemporary contexts, she also has recourse to a creative representation which unites the methods of historico-critical exegesis and the imagination. The historical reconstitution that she practiced in *In Memory of Her* now taps not only the biblical and extra-biblical documents, reread according to the

New History, but also the rhetorical level of the text or texts under analysis.

We must come back to the title, "A Critical Feminist Rhetorical Model," the author gives the tenth category to succeed in comprehending her model. This multidimensional model comprises (1) a textual analysis (a) of the male language of the Bible, perceived as the conventional language; (b) of the expression of the genders in the language and images, an integral part of a framework of common sense where sex is a given; (c) of the references to the other discriminations of the patriarchal system, such as racism, classism, colonialism, nationalism; (d) of the rhetorical level; (e) of the sociosymbolic worlds produced by discourse; and (f) of the way in which the text produces these worlds. It also comprises (2) an imaginary prolongation of what is not said; (3) a historical and social contextual analysis; (4) an explication of the political implications and interests of the text, of its ethical consequences in both its original sociopolitical situation and in the contemporary situation; and (5) a placing of the text in the sociopolitical setting of the scientific biblical research in universities, a research supposed to be rational, neutral, apolitical, value-free, with its notions of language and reality.

The fluctuating borders between these nine classes make it difficult to clearly characterize them. However, all these strategies exist, abundantly represented by their followers. In the domain of exegesis, this profusion forms a distinct field, sometimes uncultivated, sometimes yielding a rich harvest, useful because of the unavoidable questions these studies are beginning to pose to traditional readings.

The specific instruments the early feminists used can be glimpsed between the lines of their presentation. Those who began to work in the human and social sciences soon realized that the female paradigm escaped the basic methods of their respective disciplines. They were obliged to innovate ex nihilo in order to succeed in analyzing it and having it accepted as rightly belonging to the fields of observation of sociology, anthropology, psychology, law, economics, philosophy, and theology. Up to then, women were not a subject of study, except as contained in the family, the structure of marriage, economic production; any report on them was done by the head of the house or the foreman of the workshop. For example, in theology, to place women among the poor and apply to them liberation theology is not sufficient. Again they disappear. Their specific poverty is not taken into account and correcting their material poverty does not rectify their position in the social and religious systems, a position that prevents them from being moderately well-off and prosperous.

Feminists have therefore been obliged to find suitable tools of analysis, some of which are in the process of gaining status methods. We have glimpsed them especially in history and sociocriticism. In their turn, these adaptations belong to distinct feminist theories. We can briefly list them: feminisms of equality, of difference, of oppression/liberation; materialistic, Marxist, constructivist (vs. essentialist) feminisms; feminisms of deconstruction, of language, of criticism of the basic notions of scientific disciplines; and feminisms critical of feminisms themselves. All these paths can lead to particular types of exegesis.

Up to this point, we have looked only at the outlines, the cadastral survey of the body of feminist exegetical work. What universe underlies the various typologies delimited by this survey? What are its characteristics, its problems, its advances, and its fascinating aspects?

Feminist Readings Themselves

FROM THE STANDPOINT OF THE OBJECT OF THE READING

Practically, research can follow one of the three paths of access to the biblical text: *women of* the Bible, the *feminine element in* the Bible, and *women in* the Bible.

In the first path, the exegesis works at discovering the women present in the Bible and results in a gallery of portraits. Publications of this kind are abundant, from leaflet form to book form, from the best to the worst. They make use of the common thematic process, but they innovate by giving biblical status to the theme "woman." As in other disciplines, the recognition of "women of the Bible" by universities as a proper subject for papers and theses is a recent phenomenon. Until recently, it was possible to seriously study, and with profit, the geography, the flora and fauna of the Bible, but the female population of the Bible offered no scientific interest whatsoever.

Along this path, one will find women in their narrative environment. One will find anything, from the poor concubine of the Levite in Judges 19 to the splendid Deborah described in the same book in 4:4-31. Much has been said and remains to be said concerning their presence, their absence,[8] their sudden arrival in the person of exceptional women— exceptional in both meanings of the word: endowed with exceptional gifts and exceptions among their sisters—whose unexpected appearance does not modify in any way the condition of women at that time.

Along the second path, a definition of the feminine element necessarily precedes the analysis. Which definition? and on whose authority?

---

8. There are absences as significant and as motivated as presences, and therefore bearers of meaning. Absence here does not correspnd to the argument *ex silentio,* against which the document of the Pontifical Biblical Commission gives warning to those who work at feminist historical reconstruction.

Woman, "the eternal feminine" and its deep nature, have been defined so often! Here, one will find what one was seeking to find, according to one's preconceived idea and not according to the text. There will also be a more fruitful encounter, that of a discussion on the value of grammatical gender, an inescapable question even if one sees in gender a social construct and not a biological reality.

The third path leads to women in the Bible. Woman and the feminine do not exist, but textually concrete women do; these women are presented in their specific circumstances, and there are also statements on women in general. Here again, the inquiry will turn up a whole gamut of data, from the most negative to the most positive, in a nonlinear trajectory. As an example, let us note the following occurrences, arranged according to the approximate dates of their redaction.

Prov 31:10-31: By reason of its length, this alphabetical acrostic poem in praise of the wise woman cannot be quoted in full. Readers will recognize in it the features of the perfect wife, mother, and homemaker under the patriarchal regime.

Eccl 7:27-28: See, this is what I found, says the Teacher, adding one thing to another to find the sum, which my mind has sought repeatedly, but I have not found. One man among a thousand I found, but a woman among all these I have not found.

Gal 3:28: There is no longer Jew or Greek, there is no longer slave or free, there is no longer male or female; for all of you are one in Christ Jesus.

1 Pet 3:3-4: [You, wives,] do not adorn yourselves outwardly by braiding your hair, and by wearing gold ornaments or fine clothing; rather, let your adornment be the inner self *[anthrōpos]*.

1 Tim 2:11-15: Let a woman learn in silence with full submission. I permit no woman to teach or to have authority over a man; she is to keep silent. For Adam was formed first, then Eve; and Adam was not deceived, but the woman was deceived and became a transgressor. Yet she will be saved through childbearing, provided they [sic] continue in faith and holiness, with modesty.

Negotiating this labyrinth of patriarchal submission and equality, of praises and severe admonitions, the exegete will soon realize that she cannot do without models of feminist analysis. First of all, she needs them to discern, beyond flagrant quotations, the elements pertinent to the object of this study, then to find the means of analysis adapted to her critical approach, means which her classical formation does not supply even though this formation might have been in one or the other of the new methods. She needs these models especially in order to *see* that these women of the Bible are presented in a patriarchal framework, a way of seeing which has only recently become obvious. This framework, with all its nuances studied in feminist sociology, is transmitted by male authors with an androcentric outlook through the medium of androcentric languages and translations.

These women, both in their actual stories and the figures they represent, reach us only through a patriarchal discourse. One cannot overlook this *way of seeing* and the description of this vision if one wants to discuss the normative character of the biblical text concerning "woman's nature" and her place in society and church. In the paragraphs treating of actualization, the document of the Pontifical Biblical Commission enumerates the three steps of the hermeneutical operation that leads to it. The second step is stated as follows: "to identify the aspects of the present situation highlighted or put in question by the biblical text."[9] Now, in the case of "the condition of women," mentioned in the document among the present problems which actualization illuminates, it happens to be the biblical text itself which is questioned by the present situation. In this case, can the text still shed any light on the situation? These remarks do not mean that the deadlock is final. Far from bringing research to an end, they give it a new impetus by supplying the whole picture.

FROM THE STANDPOINT OF THE READER[10]

The fact that the reader of the Bible is a woman, with her personal reactions, whether submissive or rebellious, does not automatically make her reading a feminist reading. The fact that the exegete is a woman, concerned with the theme of women, does not automatically make her exegesis a feminist exegesis, not any more, we may add, than a female exegesis. Differences in perception, viewpoint, mastery and handling of the exegetic technique are not sufficient reasons, in our

9. See Biblical Commission, "Interpretation of the Bible," IV, A. "Actualization," 2. "Methods," 520–521.

10. There are few male readers of feminist reading-exegesis-interpretation. May we be allowed to focus on the female readers-exegetes-hermeneuts, among whom, in any event, a few distinctions are needed?

opinion, to define female exegesis and male exegesis. Exegesis does not proceed from the exegete's biological sex or social gender. What does exist rather are androcentric and feminist exegeses, both practiced by either men or women.

In order to arrive at a feminist exegesis, the reader and the exegete must impress upon their systematic reflection the properly feminist stamp. This exegesis is practiced on the basis of a preferential option for women and with a view to act in favor of the women who, as women, are treated either fairly or unfairly by the biblical texts. The expression "preferential option for the poor" has become familiar to us in the context of the biblical rereadings done by liberation theology. In a parallel manner, the option for women applies to the more specific criticism of the concepts "sexual differentiation," and "sexism" in texts and mores, concepts often submerged and invisible in the manifestations of racism, classism, chauvinism, and ageism.

Feminist exegesis takes its point of departure from an evaluation of the concrete social and ecclesial condition of today's women. Guided by this evaluation, it rereads the Bible, applying to it the hermeneutics of suspicion and scientific feminist criticism. It can choose to work by following any of different feminisms, each at its own degree of development: those which make egalitarian demands, those which lead to Women's Studies and Gender Studies, those which create a corrective *epistēmē* ("knowledge") if the *epistēmē* of the discipline under criticism is no longer sufficient, finally those which criticize feminist theories themselves. As happens in classical exegesis, the diversity of approaches and their handling can give rise to several feminist readings of the same biblical passage. Certain exegetes begin their case for women at the biblical level with an effort to "depatriarchalize" the received text, those variants that have been selected in our critical editions, the translations, and the notes.

Any one of the elements in this rapid characterization can be the object of discussion and lead to various opinions. Whatever the results, what deserves attention first of all are the pivotal questions in this new field of biblical sciences. In its warnings, the document of the Biblical Commission recalls them and we can list them and treat them under three headings, that is, the links of feminist exegesis with ideology, power, and religion; this last link includes the actualization of the Bible.

2. What Is Really at Stake in Feminist Readings of the Bible

Most of the questions raised by feminist exegesis are new. One quickly suspects the possible impact their answers might have, including that of the refusal to raise such questions. However, some of these pivotal questions precede and transcend the most annoying repercussions of any given text reviewed in the light of the techniques of feminist analysis.

Most fundamentally and gravely, what is, de facto, at stake is the value of the readings done from the viewpoint of the reading subject. More than all others, the liberationist approach and the feminist approach share this perspective. The reading subject calibrates her reading according to her existential circumstances. Thus, feminist exegesis is based on women's situation and enters the Bible, intending to put to the text the question of women's condition, to evaluate the answer, and in conclusion, to decide on a plan of action for the benefit of oppressed women. Is this a reading or the pursuit of an ideology? Is this a deeper understanding of the gospel or a passing vagary of North American democracy?

Feminist Exegesis and Ideology

The notion of ideology can be defined in many different ways and it contains a notorious intellectual difficulty. We shall take it in its minimum literal sense; and instead of proceeding from its theoretical meaning towards feminism, we propose to adopt the reverse logical movement, that is, from feminism to its qualification of ideology.

Feminist exegesis is indeed a committed exegesis. It is based on a bias in favor of women and the ideology of feminism gives it theory, method, and modes of operation. Therefore, its specific manner of reading is the product of an ideology. In this case, from its very beginning, this study would compromise the objectivity of its results and deliberately opt for subjectivity. The most polemical fringes of the groups that hold such positions add: the more so if the exegete is a woman. But, if this be true, Christians would be the worst readers of the New Testament.

These considerations overlook a textual fact: the Bible itself is the vehicle of an ideology concerning women, that is, the patriarchal system which permeates Scripture through and through and is perceptible in the vast sequences as well as the little details. An example: the story in the book of Judg 4:17-22 recounts the death of Sisera, killed by the astute Jael. However, it does not tell it as praise of Jael, but as the supreme humiliation of an army general, dying at the hand of a woman. The praise of Jael will be mentioned in the song of Deborah, 5:24-30, but even so, at the end we find an echo of patriarchal ideology: at her window, Sisera's mother repeats to herself that the reason he is late in returning is that he has to gather his part of the booty: "a girl or two for every man."

The analysis of a text must be done over if its ideological variable—although part and parcel of the *object* under study—escapes analysis. Feminists are *objectively* justified when they concentrate their attention on this ideology. With the help of tools developed in other fields, they are in the best position to effectively detect this ideology. The problem is not the existence of the ideological dimension in the Bible but rather the conclusion drawn from it when, without critical work, these texts are applied to today's women. Dealing as it does with consistency between biblical ideology and its application to modern circumstances, feminist ideology is best qualified to examine the conditions for the legitimate passage from the one to the other. An ideological reading becomes the "revealer" of the ideology contained in the biblical text.

In a wider perspective, thanks to recent developments, the debate scientific objectivity/subjectivity is no longer an inflexible dichotomy. Even in the physical sciences, Heisenberg's principle of uncertainty and the postulates of quantum mechanics have come between the two terms of opposition. Renowned practitioners of hermeneutics, such as Hans-Georg Gadamer, have demonstrated the existence and the role of prejudices in the most "uncontaminated" scientific study. In the camp of the feminists, the philosopher Sandra Harding has pointed out in her work in progress that objectivity and subjectivity take on a different meaning according to whether they are considered on the level of epistemology or of the angle of approach. Moreover, at the epistemological level, there is a further distinction to be made between epistemological objectivity and epistemological relativity.[11]

It remains that on the social plane, feminism has acquired an ideological flavor so exaggerated that many women deny being feminists. On the scientific plane, they will take no part in the radical reading attributed to feminism from the outset. Now, radical reading does not mean an exclusive or excluding reading. In other domains, a reading which goes to the root of problems, adopts without concessions the most extremist position in the study of the most exacting problems, would be admired. In contrast, an exclusive reading is practiced by exclusion of other readings and is not necessarily radical. Its ostracism can be used to favor a single aspect of a question; it presents the intel-

11. See Sandra G. Harding, "After the Neutrality Ideal: Science, Politics and 'Strong Objectivity,'" *Social Research* 59 (1992) 567–587. The notes of this article contain references to an abundant feminist multidisciplinary documentation on the subject. See also Mary Daly's discussion on the relationship between subjectivity and objectivity seen from the feminist perspective, in *Beyond God the Father: Toward a Philosophy of Women's Liberation* (Boston: Beacon Press, 1973) 32–34.

lectual danger of undermining objectivity. The avoidance of radicalism is no protection against exclusivism.

Nor does extolling a feminism of the "happy medium" ward off the excesses of subjectivist passion. And what "happy medium" are we dealing with, between what two poles? Between misogyny and the defense of women, that is, between two attitudes, this question calls for an answer. Between two realities, for instance between beaten women and pampered women, is there a happy medium of women more or less beaten or more or less respected? There is no happy medium in questions of justice; there should be no neutrality among the witnesses of injustice. There is no acceptable degree of injustice, and feminism's reason for existence is precisely the eradication of injustice. Neutrality does not guarantee objectivity; one can remain neutral for entirely subjective reasons which prevent one from seeing the objective dimensions of the question under consideration.

In exegesis, is there a happy medium between 1 Tim 2:11-15 and Gal 3:28, between the concubine of Judges 19 and the beloved of the Song? What is the relationship between these two contradictory texts, the reason that would motivate an exclusive choice of the one or the other? These thorny questions are what feminist readings work with.[12]

In the linguistic sciences, recent theories on reading have also revealed the importance of the reading subject in the act of reading. More accurately put, reading raises the question of the subject. On the basis of the act of interpretation that the act of reading already is, the subject is posed as the subject who enunciates, is constituted as subject, is constructed as

---

12. That these questions are thorny is frequently proved by the notes at the bottom of the pages of our Bibles. In general, they show by their very existence a progress over the straight proclamation of a discriminatory passage. 1 Tim 2:11-15 can no longer go without a commentary. In the Traduction Œcuménique de la Bible of 1972, one reads the following commentary on these verses: "In this whole section (vv. 11-15), one must distinguish what pertains to the social context of the time, to rabbinical teaching, and to the immediate concerns of the author of the letter. In any case, it would be an anachronism to project into them the present problems of the cultic ministry of women. When asserting that women are saved through motherhood (v. 15), Paul opposes the heretics who forbade marriage (1 Tim 4:3). When mandating that they receive the teaching in silence, he opposes the excesses of *gossips and busybodies, saying what they should not say* [emphasis added] (1 Tim 5:13). As in Titus 2:3-5, Paul wants to prevent the excesses which the emancipation of women, part and parcel of the freedom of the gospel (Gal 3:28), could have brought about." However, what a malaise this note reflects in its very effort to reestablish the "happy medium"! In its attempt to counteract three excesses, does not the text attributed to Paul betray some other excesses which should be accounted for?

subject.[13] All this means that the subject is not rejected in favor of objectivity. And in feminist exegesis what is practiced is a reading rather than a finicky analysis of the text which often amounts to little more than an autopsy of the meaning.

It can happen that reading creates an anti-subject: the reader is also involved in the reading when he or she objects to the text. Faced with feminist texts, ideology and passion dwell as much in the reader as in feminist discourse. The act of reading could teach the female reader a great deal about herself if she stopped to detect the reasons for her resistances. In these all-important matters, these resistances are not scientifically detached and serene. From this viewpoint, the enunciation of feminist discourse has an advantage because, from the start, it had to make the effort of being and remaining on the scientific plane.

Feminist Exegesis and Power

The second pivotal question raised by feminist exegesis is its attitude toward power. The document of the Biblical Commission saw this clearly: "Feminist exegesis often raises questions of power within the church, questions which, as is obvious, are matters of discussion and even of confrontation." Feminist exegesis cannot not raise them. The ecclesial condition of women, which is at the root of its reading, is not exempt from this omnipresence of power, a component of human reality. In women's case, this power is that of a normative text, that of the magisterium which is its official interpreter, and that of the ecclesial structure which underlies the power of the magisterium. Seen from the viewpoint of the category of gender, these three powers belong to the masculine pole. Their exercise and expressions have consecrated the inferiority of the feminine pole, kept outside their fields of interest.

In ecclesial circles, the word "power" is not well liked because it is linked with too many ambitions, exactions, and injustices. It is true that according to Jesus' teaching, every function conferring authority is service. According to the institutional church's present state of affairs, centuries-old, it would be true that ecclesial service is reserved for the masculine pole of humankind. The exclusion of women from full ecclesial responsibility reveals this embarrassing fact: there is much power in the official exercise of evangelical service. Associated with ordained ministries, the power to exercise certain services, connected to the functions of government, teaching, and sanctification of and in the church, is thereby denied to women.

13. See Louis Panier, "Lecture sémiotique et projet théologique," *RSR* 78 (1990) 199–220, especially 209.

It is not the fact that they are "lay" that makes women incapable of exercising these powers, since laymen do exercise them. In women's case, there is an impediment from birth, their femininity, and this on the authority of certain biblical texts and the theological conclusions the official magisterium draws from them. The absence of consensus concerning the interpretation of these biblical texts gives rise to periodic revivals of their study, independently from the often repeated declarations of the Vatican on the exclusion of women from ordained ministries, the priesthood especially. Although in his letter of May 22, 1994, John Paul II wanted to close the case and put an end to the appeals in favor of women, the exegetical interpretation of the texts remains open. Feminist readings make this their business.

Of necessity, this task obliges them to navigate in the territorial waters of power when their work denounces what the system hides, that is, the present link between ministries and the absolute condition that only males can have access to them. Feminists are useful rather than harmful to the church when—faithful in this to the desires expressed by the document of the Biblical Commission—their exegetico-theological and multidisciplinary studies show that the linkage of power to the male sex has its origins in social practices that exclude women from public offices. But if societies have evolved on this point, the church still lags behind them. And yet, in Jesus Christ it has all it needs to get ahead of them.

Feminist Exegesis and Religious Readings

The third pivotal question raised by feminist exegesis is the extension of its own field. It works not only with the Bible as literary corpus but also with texts which inform the life of the faithful in the church, with all their repercussions on the condition of women. The Scriptures which feminist exegesis scrutinizes are affirmed by a universe of beliefs and believers and are used in the liturgy where believers confess and celebrate their faith. The Scriptures are defined as a canonical, theological, and normative corpus for all Christians. In their total reality, they comprise both the Bible and its "ecological" system throughout the ages, that is, the seventy books of the canon; the orientation due to the choice of variants in the composition of critical editions; the different approved translations; the documents of the magisterium on the theological and pastoral interpretation of the Old and New Testaments; the patristic, spiritual, catechistic, theological, exegetical commentaries; the use of the Bible in the liturgy; the constant interaction of all these components in Christian life.

If and when feminist exegesis and theology analyze this complex organism from the viewpoint of the category of gender, one massive, undeniable conclusion emerges: in the course of twenty centuries, this system was formed and developed around the masculine pole alone. The position assigned to women by the social and ecclesial structures excluded them on principle from the production of Christian discourse in its theoretical, practical, and organizational expressions. Female contributions were perceptible, and this applies to a very small number of women, only in the field of spirituality, or more exactly, devotion. This observation is the reflection of a more global phenomenon: in the history of the West, women's voices were heard only outside official religions, in fringe cultic groups and sects. There, they indeed were heard.

In the particular case of the liturgy, the selection of biblical readings have made only rare peripheral mention of the women of either Testament. With the exception of the Virgin Mary, the way the readings have been apportioned shows us a salvation history lived and realized by men—patriarchs, kings, warriors, prophets, sages, and scribes. For the majority of believers, illiterate or otherwise, denied access to the Bible by decree of the magisterium, the female characters in Holy Scripture never entered Christian memory. Nor did these women, before the intervention of the feminists, gain the status of models for Christians. Here again, we find an echo of the general historical situation, studied by social psychology:

> Individual female contributions . . . will not enter the collective memory as cultural expression of the female gender but will be viewed instead as individual exceptions. Their contents will be re-absorbed into the patriarchal culture without becoming exemplary, i.e. without creating identity prototypes.[14]

The pre-conditions of the reading with which the church surrounds the Book are also part of feminist exegesis. The Bible is presented to believers not only as spiritual food but also as a collection of canonical writings, the word of God and the setting down of God's revelation, whose truth is guaranteed by the notion of Scriptural inspiration. In the literal meaning of the term, the book reaches them through an "ideol-

14. Marisa Zavalloni, "Ego-ecology: The Study of the Interaction between Social and Personal Identities," in *Identity, Personal and Sociocultural: A Symposium*, ed. Anita Jacobson-Widding, Uppsala Studies in Cultural Anthropology 5 (Atlantic Highlands, N.J.: Humanity, 1983) 205–231. On the author's original research in this subject, see also Marisa Zavalloni and Christiane Louis-Guérin, *Identité sociale et construction de la réalité: Images, pensée et action dans la vie quotidienne* (Montréal: Université de Montréal, 1983); Marisa Zavalloni, "'Identity and Hyperidentities': The Representational Foundation of Self and Culture," *Papers on Social Representation* 2 (1993) 218–235.

ogy" to which is added, according to religious affiliation, the "characteristics of the Catholic interpretation" (title of Section III of the document of the Pontifical Biblical Commission).

What happens when feminist exegesis questions this Bible from the viewpoint of the dominated? We have seen that according to the model of hermeneutical operation proposed by the same document, a passage such as 1 Tim 2:11-15 does not question the present situation from which its questioning has sprung but the biblical text itself. However, the idea of discarding this passage because it belongs to an unauthentic Pauline letter does not stand its ground before the notion of canon. And this is the case of all the other passages that have served throughout the ages to establish and "mysticize" women's submission and generate so many theories about their nature, a nature fashioned not quite as much in the image of God as that of men.

In view of all this, feminist exegetes are contesting, in various degrees, the very notions of canon, revelation, and inspiration. This confrontation of their results with the doctrinal statement of the divine authority of the Bible is now in the limelight of feminist biblical interpretation.[15] To carry the debate to this level affects the basic postulates of classical exegesis.

Feminist reading challenges both the faith-filled and theological reading of the Bible and its academic reading. It has gone beyond the ideological passion of the discussion for and against women. It has done more than cause a more active participation of women in exegetical research. According to Thomas S. Kuhn's theory on scientific revolutions,[16] a new paradigm emerges when the basic postulates of a field of knowledge are shaken and when the present state of knowledge does not succeed in answering new questions. All revolutions do not have the amplitude of Kopernik's or Einstein's, but it remains true that the feminist approach is more than the mere instauration of a parallel feminist paradigm and obliges its own discipline to revise its foundations. Few practitioners of academic exegesis have been touched by the dawning light of the new paradigm, but all the same, their own paradigm is no longer able to answer the questions of feminists, of liberationists, and of practical theology.[17]

15. On this precise point, see the reflections of Gérald Caron in his study on "The Authority of the Bible Challenged by Feminist Hermeneutics."

16. "The Structure of Scientific Revolutions," *International Encyclopedia of Unified Science,* 2nd ed., enlarged, vol. 2, no. 2 (Chicago: University of Chicago, 1970).

17. Olivette Genest, "La Critique féministe de la raison théologique," in *Les Bâtisseuses de la Cité,* ed. Evelyne Tardy et al., Les cahiers scientifiques de l'Association canadienne-française pour l'avancement des sciences [ACFAS] 79 (Montréal: ACFAS, 1993) 349–358.

As for feminist exegesis itself, in its lightning course, it often skipped, very rapidly in our opinion, the step of rigorous analysis. As in other disciplines of the human sciences, some proceeded to formulate the theory without a sufficient phase of elaboration. There is still room for works of consolidation, a task the autocriticism of feminisms is engaged in. An exhaustive analysis allied with a correct hermeneutics is not a point of arrival but a point of departure. It leaves untouched the following question: How does one place oneself, as church and as individual, before the Bible? At this point, the answer presupposes a theory of reading, of the dynamic symbiosis reader-text, and a theory of the text. This is still lacking in several feminist endeavors. The results of the revolution in the linguistic sciences have not yet left their mark on them, even though on this point they are more advanced than the works of classical exegesis and theology, and the magisterial interpretation of the church.

3. Contributions of Feminist Theories to the Interpretation of the Bible

Survey of Feminist Activities in Exegesis

With very rare exceptions, women have done feminist exegesis. If one recalls that they were not admitted into schools of theology until the middle 60s and that technical formation lasts for some ten years, the sum of their quantitative and qualitative production deserves attention and admiration. To evaluate this production from the viewpoint of its specific object is to see how much credit its authors deserve.

The early naive reactions have been left behind. As long as this field of study does not acquire a certain "venerability" due to age, one can expect to find traces of these early naive reactions as new exegetes discover this world view. Besides, the early deadlocks have been identified, and either avoided or taken into account in the general way of treating problems. For example, a time of experimentation was necessary to learn the limits of the respective approaches of equality and difference.

Positive results have already been tabulated. Among them, let us mention:

(1) Strategies of interpretation.

(2) Methods of approach borrowed from different feminisms. The absolute necessity of these borrowings appears as soon as one enters this field of analysis. The best formation in exegesis is no preparation for approaching and treating the women's question and the feminist

question. This formation does not supply the suitable tools for discerning, classifying, and especially articulating the pertinent biblical data; this latter escapes its perspectives and methods. A multidisciplinary approach is needed here between exegesis and scientific feminisms and between the feminisms of the various disciplines.

(3) Heuristical categories that illuminate the reading, such as patriarchal system, androcentrism, as well as categories of gender, sexual differentiation, sexism, and "sexage," hermeneutical presuppositions and conclusions.

(4) Appropriate critical markers even more essential than in tried scientific researches. The passion for the defense of a cause is no substitute for the rigorous demands of research; on the contrary, the goal of feminist ideology is better served by rigorous research.

(5) A whole series of operative processes and a metalanguage which are close to the status of method if they have not yet attained it.

Have feminist readings *in exegesis* reached the level of formal theory? Answers vary according to the viewpoint of the evaluation and the nature of the question. In the strict sense of the term, theory appears at the apex of a long process which begins with the verified collection and the construction of data, then passes through the stages of the elaboration of a descriptive language, of its justification by means of a methodological language, of the axiomatic organization of the concepts that have been generated, themselves allowed to settle at the level of undefinable concepts and undemonstrable postulates. The theory thus appears as a hierarchy of metalanguages which have built it and define one another. What remains to be done is to formalize it or transcribe it into formal language. On this score, the effort to make feminist readings of the Bible into theories is only, in our opinion, at the stage of preconceptualization, that is, at the stage of elaboration and explanation of the concepts.

Is it necessary to add that theorization is a dynamic process, always in motion within sciences full of vitality? We ask a question, and not a rhetorical one this time: Must feminist practice arrive at this stage in the biblical field? Feminist exegesis has no ambition to constitute itself as a system which would construct a universe parallel to that of androcentric exegesis. Feminist exegesis is a question, a problem posed to the very foundations of exegesis and theology from within, as is feminism in general in relation to the human and social sciences which are built on the observation of only the male half of humankind.

Answers to the larger question also vary: Is feminism, which is embodied in the multiform reality of feminisms, an epistemology? Of course, yes, when it applies itself—from its chosen point of observation, that is, the unique distance enjoyed by "the other within the system"—to accounting for the ways the different sciences construct knowledge. Is feminism an *epistēmē?* Yes, because feminism has already sufficiently developed to become a field of knowledge in its own right. It has produced a hierarchized organization of propositions specifically adapted to its object, with their combinations defined as possible or incompatible, in the name of certain rules deriving from its identity in the process of constructing itself.

As for feminist exegesis, does it exhibit the qualifications necessary to be called an epistemology and an *epistēmē?* It shares in these qualifications from inside feminism as it were, being its application to the biblical world. Although having their own strong character and being very productive, feminist biblical studies are defined as a province of the feminist universe, as a point of multidisciplinary convergence between feminist literary criticism, feminist historiography, and postmodernist critical theories.

Are we to expect for the future the elaboration of a new theory of biblical interpretation? The whole of the Bible is not explained by its attitude towards women and all that is feminine. Thus, even if it has many a surprise in reserve, the feminist approach is not a theory of interpretation; a way of reading, as illuminating and luminous as it may be, does not render account of the whole contents of such an important collection of writings. The feminist approach is closer to the status of method than most of the new approaches, but neither is a method, without any further cognitive operation, a theory of interpretation. Besides, in no one theory of interpretation can we find the path to an exhaustive reading. But insofar as everything in a text holds together, perhaps the works of feminist exegesis, which demand the revision of so many insufficient and ossified readings, will lead to a significant breakthrough, unsuspected today? Provided they are allied to scientific rigor, such creative approaches have more of a chance to renew, thanks to fruitful questions, the answers we have been satisfied with for too long.

The best prospects still retain something of the character of mere promises. What are the achievements which already guarantee future fruition, although the features of the latter remain always hypothetical?

Contributions to the Domain of Exegesis

Thanks to all the above discussions, we are in a position to succinctly classify and characterize the contributions of feminist readings in the domain of exegesis.

— Concretely, they have brought to this field a great number of works whose authors have had a genuine academic formation and indisputable qualifications. These are badly misjudged when they are labelled improvised borrowings from the biblical material to serve as tools of political strategy, as the first step of legitimate claims to equality.

— They have introduced into exegesis analysis through the category of gender, already well established in several human, social, and economic sciences.

— They have opened a new field of studies, which is a remarkable qualitative advance. Its originality delays its "naturalization" and assimilation. There are reasons for asking what the real causes of the slowness and obstruction on the part of male and female resisters are when publishing firms and learned reviews have already opened their doors to them. That feminist works also proceed by trial and error and occasionally contain rubbish is the fate of any research, especially into unknown territory.

— In this, like other human sciences, they reveal within traditional practice grave deficiencies in the way it constructs the data, treats them, and reads them.

— They have shaken the biblical world by posing the question of women, or the feminine, of the social construct called gender, of the dichotomy of the system man/woman, of its establishment of a dominant/dominated hierarchy, and of the illegitimate projection of this hierarchy onto the plane of essences, natures, and the will of the Creator. This amounts to an iconoclastic unveiling of a large part of the text in contradiction to the presentation of God, Jesus Christ, and the human creature in all its dignity as the image of God.

— They oblige exegetes to face the still more serious question of their relationship with this text, in view of its misogynistic component, a question not fully resolved by recourse to historic distance and sociological explanation. This text is not only a reflection of its time; it speaks, it enunciates. What? And where does this resolution of the problem by historic distance begin and end? Would the answer be valid for theological, Christological, soteriological questions, for the covenant and salvation? Of course, but in what measure? Up to where, if one maintains the affirmations of the text in their integrity?

Liberationist exegesis, less developed than feminist exegesis, is no great help here. It too must find a solution to the difficulties inherent to its approach. It has heard itself reproached with retaining from the Bible only the manifest moments of liberation. How does it reconcile these with the contrary moments of enslavement or with the absence of liberation when the circumstances called for it?

— They submit to judgment the basic notions of their discipline which define the conditions attached to the reading of the book of God's word, normative because canonical. To repeat Kuhn's diagnosis of the history of sciences: when the fundamental postulates of a science are attacked and when the available tools of that science are obviously inadequate to giving a response, one witnesses a mutation of paradigm. Will the explanation given by the paradigm which supplants the old one and imparts a fresh impetus contain a theory of interpretation deriving from feminist work? Movements of creation are unpredictable.

In brief, the interrogation formulated at first by certain exegetes and theologians on the basis of contemporary feminist work and theories has gone beyond itself and surpassed itself. These researchers now pose, unavoidably, a profoundly biblical, profoundly Christian, question since what is at stake is the reestablishment of justice. Their ever growing impact provokes the revision of habits of interpretation that have become insufficient. Is it possible to render a greater service to the advancement of biblical knowledge?

The Condition of Women in Mesopotamian and Biblical Literature

◆————————————————————————————◆

Aldina da Silva

> If the sick are overwhelmed, if they do nothing but speak to them-
> selves, laugh without cause, or else if the pain weighs them down, if
> they utter, "my poor heart!" and dissolve into sighs, they are suffering
> from lovesickness. It strikes equally man and woman.[1]

From time immemorial human beings have been suffering from
lovesickness. The above text, excerpted from a Mesopotamian medical
treatise of diagnoses going back to the second millennium B.C.E., gives
us a touching description of it. The lovesick are described as speaking
to themselves, laughing without cause, overcome with pain, and sigh-
ing incessantly. And—an interesting fact—man and woman share the
same fate: symptoms, causes, and sickness are identical for both sexes.
If the Mesopotamian texts concede the equality of man and woman
when it comes to the suffering caused by lovesickness, what do they
say about love life? Do men and women enjoy the same privileges? As
for the biblical texts, do they show a different vision in the manner of
living the experience of love? We shall attempt to answer these questions in the present study. Since the status of women in the codes of the
ancient Near East and Israel have been the subject of several studies,[2]

---

1. René Labat, *Traité akkadien de diagnostics et pronostics médicaux* (Paris:
Académie Internationale de l'histoire des sciences, 1951) 178–179, lines 6-9.
2. Among others, see P. Rémy, "La condition de la femme dans les codes du
Proche-Orient ancien et les codes d'Israel," *Sciences ecclésiastiques* 16 (1964) 107–127,
291–320; Raymond Westbrook, *Old-Babylonian Marriage Law,* Archiv für Orient-
forschung Beiheft 23 (Horn, Austria: F. Berger, 1988); Martha T. Roth, *Babylonian
Marriage Agreements 7th–3rd Centuries B.C.,* Alter Orient und Altes Testament 222
(Neukirchen/Vluyn: Neukirchener, 1989); F. Zéman, "Le statut de la femme en

we shall focus more particularly on the literary texts concerning the three steps of marriage: betrothal, entrance of the woman into her husband's house, and childbirth. In the study of these three steps, we shall proceed as follows: after a general exposition of the aspects common to the ancient Semitic world, we shall analyze separately the key terms which help us to describe the event as shown in Mesopotamian and biblical writings. The whole of this procedure will enable us to answer the initial questions and to see more clearly the similarities and dissimilarities in women's love life as it is depicted in the Mesopotamian and biblical vocabularies.[3]

1. The Betrothal

> Take a wife according to your choice;
> may you have a son according to
> your heart's desire!
>
> *Sumerian Proverb*

> Young maiden, it is not your brother
> who will be able to choose a husband for you!
> [Understood: only you yourself]
>
> *Sumerian Proverb*

We must first understand that in ancient Near Eastern thought marriage is recommended to everybody. The woman whom no one has "known" and the man who has never taken a wife are judged most unfortunate. Those who die as virgins can even be transformed into demons. The young girl whom,

> like a [normal] woman, no male has ever impregnated,
> like a [normal] woman, no male has ever deflowered,
> [who], in her husband's lap, has not touched his genitalia,
> in her husband's lap, has not drawn aside his garment[4]

Mésopotamie, d'après les sources juridiques," *Science et Esprit* 43 (1991) 69–86; Carolyn Pressler, *The View of Women Found in the Deuteronomic Family Laws* (Berlin: W. de Gruyter, 1993).

3. In this study, we will mention the Song of Songs only rarely because it is a countercurrent piece of writing. On this subject, see the next chapter.

4. Sylvie Lackenbacher, "Note sur l'Ardat-lilî," *Revue d'assyriologie et d'archéologie orientale* 65 (1971) 140. The young girl who has not had sexual relationships is designated as "the one who has not been known [by a man]" *(sa lā lamdat)*, "the one who has not been opened" *(sa lā petāt)*, "the one who has not been broken open" *(sa*

can become a she-demon, Ardat-lilī. This she-demon and her male counterpart are sexually frustrated. They attack young people in order to prevent them from fulfilling their "destiny."

The Bible reports the story of Jephthah's daughter who, knowing she is doomed to die, "bewails her virginity" (Judg 11:37-40). What makes her fate so dramatic is that she will not know the joys of marriage and motherhood. To die a virgin is a misfortune similar to the shame that is attached to sterility, as we shall see below. Thus, according to ancient Semitic thought, virginity is far from being an ideal. The same is true of men. Biblical Hebrew has no word for bachelor and no word for chastity. One of the curses that can strike a man is precisely to be prevented from enjoying the woman he has chosen: "You shall become engaged to a woman, but another man shall lie with her" (Deut 28:30).

In this context, one understands that marriage is an important business, and despite the tone of the proverbs quoted above, it is before all else a transaction between two families. Neither the young woman nor, in many cases, the young man is consulted. Because of the patriarchal regime which prevails in the whole of the ancient East, the choice of the wife is the responsibility of the young man's father or his representative. In general, this choice is made among the close relatives or within the same tribe.[5] This is what we are going to see now.

The Mesopotamian Texts

In Mesopotamia, the wedding is preceded by a written contract *(riksatum)* without which the young woman cannot become a wife *(assatu,* a word different from the word *sinnistu,* which means simply "woman").[6] This contract is concluded between the two heads of the families or between the young man and the young woman's parents. Indeed, she is never one of the contracting parties but only the object of the contract.

---

lā naqpat). According to the ancient Semitic way of thinking, virginity connotes the absence of sexual relationships rather than a positive state of *virgo intacta* ("unsullied virgin"). In any case, neither Sumerian, Akkadian, nor Hebrew have any term to designate the hymen. On this topic, see Elena Cassin, "Virginité et stratégie du sexe," *Le semblable et le différent* (Paris: La Découverte, 1987) 339.

5. However, Esau himself chose his two wives, who moreover were foreigners, but the text adds, "they made life bitter for Isaac and Rebekah" (Gen 26:34-35). See also Gen 29:15-20; 38:2; Judg 14:1-3.

6. On this subject, see Samuel Greengus, "The Old Babylonian Marriage Contract," *Journal of the American Oriental Society* 89 (1969) 506–507; Hammurabi, King of Babylonia, *The Babylonian Laws,* ed. Godfrey R. Driver and John C. Miles (Oxford: Clarendon Press, 1956) 245.

The vocabulary employed, either in the marriage contracts or in Mesopotamian literature in general, confirms this fact. To express a proposal, the most current formula is "to take as wife" *(assatam ahāzum)*. Obviously, the verb *ahāzum* has always the man as subject. The young woman is given in marriage as wife *(martam ana assūtim nadānu)*.[7] Thus, in Mesopotamia, a man marries a woman, a woman never marries a man; she is the object, never the subject of the act. Even when the laws allow her to marry and choose "her heart's man," it still is the husband who takes her:

> . . . When she [the woman] will have raised her children, she will be given a portion like [that of] an heir and the husband who will please her [*mut libbisa* = "the husband of her heart"] will be able to take her.[8]

The ratification of a marriage contract is accompanied by nuptial gifts. The husband-to-be will pay the woman's parents the *tirhatu* in kind or in money.[9] Of course, when a man pays a large sum for a wife, he increases his prestige and that of his family. However, as a rule the *tirhatu* is not very high and depends on the financial resources of the in-laws. A Sumerian proverb, placed in a woman's mouth, points out that no amount of money can equal the worth of a person like herself: "What can the father-in-law give in exchange for his daughter-in-law?"[10]

To the *tirhatu*, additional presents, called *biblu*, are often added as well as several gifts which the man gives his fiancée, especially clothes, necklaces, and bracelets. On the other hand, when the woman goes to her husband's home at the time of the wedding, she takes along a dowry *(seriktu)*, what is "attached to the cloak of the young woman" *(ana qanni rakāsu):* lands, slaves, furniture, garments, jewels. The dowry is the wife's property, which passes to her children after her death or is returned to her family if she dies childless. However, during the wife's life, the dowry is administered by her husband.[11]

7. Millar Burrows, *The Basis of Israelite Marriage* (New Haven: American Oriental Society, 1938) 24.

8. André Finet, *Le Code d'Hammurapi,* Litteratures anciennes du Proche-Orient 6 (Paris: Cerf, 1973) art. 137.

9. On the thesis of the marriage-purchase, according to which the young woman would be sold by her father, see Rémy, "La condition de la femme," 109, n. 7.

10. A Sumerian proverb, 1.169, in Edmund I. Gordon, *Sumerian Proverbs: Glimpses of Everyday Life in Ancient Mesopotamia* (New York: Greenwood, 1968) 130.

11. On the different gifts on the occasion of a marriage, see Samuel Greengus, "Bridewealth in Sumerian Sources," *Hebrew Union College Annual* 61 (1990) 28–88; A. van Praag, *Droit matrimonial assyro-babylonien* (Amsterdam: Noord-Hollandsche

It is probably at the time of the betrothal and in the course of a meal that the rite of anointing and covering the woman's head with a cloak takes place. Indeed, these two gestures are attested in the texts of the Near East. The first is made by the husband's father or the husband himself. This practice symbolizes the entrance of the woman into a new life.[12] The second is made by the husband (or his representative), who covers his wife's head with his own cloak. According to the ancient Semitic way of thinking, the garment, intimately linked with its wearer, is often regarded as the substitute for the person. Therefore, this ritual symbolizes the husband's right of ownership: from then on, the woman belongs to him.[13]

The Biblical Texts

In contrast to Mesopotamian texts, which have given us several marriage contracts, the Bible does not contain any treatise on marriage. It broaches the matrimonial question at random, in narrative rather than juridical texts. These passages show us that, like everywhere else, the proposal is made to the young woman's parents. Nevertheless, the expression "to ask as a wife" (*s'l 'sh*) rarely appears in biblical writings. Actually, it is found only in the question which Solomon asks his mother concerning the eventual and disputed marriage of Adonijah:

Uitgevers Maatschappj, 1945) 128–180; Martha T. Roth, "Marriage and Matrimonial Prestations in First Millennium B.C. Babylonia," in *Women's Earliest Records: From Ancient Egypt and Western Asia*, ed. Barbara S. Lesko (Atlanta: Scholars Press, 1987) 245–255.

12. On the anointment as nuptial ritual, see Jan J. A. van Dijk, "Neusumerische Gerichtsurkunden in Bagdad," *Zeitschrift für Assyriologie* 55 (1962) 70–77; Samuel Greengus, "Old Babylonian Marriage Ceremonies and Rites," *Journal of Cuneiform Studies* 20 (1966) 55–72; Guillaume Cardascia, *Les lois assyriennes* (Paris: Cerf, 1969) 32, no. 15 and pp. 65, 87, 209–212. This custom is also attested in Ugarit: RS 8.208, 6–7; Jean Nougayrol, *Le Palais royal d'Ugarit*, ed. Claude F.-A. Schaeffer, vol. 3 (Paris: Imprimerie nationale, 1955) 110; see Dennis Pardee, *Bibliotheca Orientalis* 34 (1977) 4, 14; Anson F. Rainey, "Family Relationships in Ugarit," *Orientalia* 34 (1965) 19. The Egyptian texts of El-Amarna supply other examples: EA 11, 7.15; 29, 22f.; 31, 11f.; William L. Moran and others, *Les Lettres d'El-Amarna* (Paris: Cerf, 1987); [William L. Moran, ed. and trans., *The Amarna Letters*, English language ed. (Baltimore: Johns Hopkins University, 1992)]. On the symbolism of anointment in general, see Ernst Kutsch, *Salbung als Rechtsakt im Alten Testament und im Alten Orient*, BZAW 87 (Berlin: A. Töpelmann, 1963).

13. On this topic, see our article "La symbolique des vêtements dans les rites du mariage et du divorce au Proche-Orient ancien et dans la Bible," *Bulletin* [of the Canadian Society for Mesopotamian Studies] 26 (1993) 15–21.

"And why do you ask Abishag the Shunammite for Adonijah?" (1 Kgs 2:22) and in the case of the politics of Rehoboam, who "found many wives for [his sons]" (2 Chr 11:23).[14] The ordinary expression was rather "to take as wife" *(lqh l'sh)* or "to take wife" *(lqh 'sh),* or simply "to take" *(lqh).*[15] In this last instance, the immediate context demonstrates that it is a woman who is taken. The verb *lqh* is therefore the technical term used either at the time of the negotiations between the families concerning the marriage or at the time of the marriage itself.

To indicate the action of the wife's parents or of those having authority over her, the expression is "to give as wife" *(ntn l'sh)* or "to give wife" *(ntn 'sh)* or simply "to give" *(ntn).* In the same way as with the expression in the paragraph above, the context determines that it is the woman who is given away.[16]

Finally, for the woman herself, the locution in use is "to become/to be wife of [somebody]" *(hyh l'sh),* or "to become/to be wife" *(hyh 'sh)* or simply "to become/to be [wife]" *(hyh).*[17] These formulas clearly show

14. In contrast, marriage contracts in the Jewish colony of Elephantine (from the sixth to the fourth centuries B.C.E.) explicitly state: "I came to your house *('nh 'tyt bytk)* and I proposed marriage to you *(ws'lt mnk . . . l'ntw)* and you gave her to me *(lmntn ly)."* R. Yaron, "Aramaic Marriage Contracts from Elephantine," *Journal of Semitic Studies* 3 (1958) 29–30; see Pierre Grelot, *Documents araméens d'Égypte* (Paris: Cerf, 1972) 192, 232–233.

15. In the study of these expressions and those that follow, we drew upon Angelo Tosato, *Il matrimonio israelitico: Una teoria generale* (Rome: Biblical Institute, 1982) 68–82. The expression *lqh l'sh* is attested 18 times: Gen 12:19; 25:20; 28:9; 34:4, 21; Exod 6:20, 23, 25; Deut 21:11; 24:3; 25:5; Judg 3:6; 14:2; 1 Sam 25:39, 40; 2 Sam 12:9; 1 Kgs 4:15; Ezek 44:22. The expression *lqh 'sh* is attested 35 times: Gen 4:19; 6:12; 11:29; 21:21; 24:3, 4, 7, 37, 38, 40; 25:1; 26:34; 27:46; 28:1, 2, 6 (twice); 31:50; 38:6; Lev 21:14; Deut 22:13; 24:1, 5; Judg 14:3; 19:1; 2 Sam 5:13; 1 Kgs 16:31; Ezra 2:61; Neh 7:63; 1 Chr 7:15; 14:3; 2 Chr 11:18; Jer 16:2; 29:6 (twice). The expression *lqh* without the addition of *l'sh* or *'sh* is attested 40 times: Gen 19:14; 24:48, 67; 28:9; 34:9, 16; 38:2; Exod 2:1; 21:10; 34:16; Lev 18:17, 18; 20:17, 21; 21:7 (twice), 13, 14; Num 12:1; Deut 7:3; 20:7; 23:1; 24:4, 5; 25:7, 8; Judg 14:3, 8; Ruth 4:13; 1 Sam 25:43; 2 Sam 12:10; 1 Kgs 7:8; 1 Chr 2:19, 21; 4:18; 2 Chr 11:20; Neh 6:18; 10:31; Ezek 44:22; Hos 1:3.

16. The expression *ntn l'sh* is attested 22 times: Gen 16:3; 29:28; 30:4, 9; 34:8, 12; 38:14; 41:45; Deut 22:16; Josh 15:16, 17; Judg 1:12, 13; 21:7; 1 Sam 18:17, 19, 27; 1 Kgs 2:17, 21; 2 Kgs 14:9; 1 Chr 2:35; 2 Chr 25:18. The expression *ntn 'sh* is attested 4 times: Exod 21:4; Judg 21:18 (twice); 1 Kgs 11:19; and perhaps Gen 13:12. The expression *ntn* without the addition of *l'sh* or *'sh* is attested 30 times: Gen 16:5; 24:41; 29:19 (twice), 26, 27; 30:18; 34:9, 14, 16, 21; 38:26; Exod 2:21; 22:16; Deut 7:3; Judg 3:6; 15:2, 6; 21:14, 22; 1 Sam 17:25; 18:21; 25:44; 2 Sam 12:8, 11; Ezra 9:12; Neh 10:31; 13:15; Jer 29:6; Dan 11:17.

17. The expression *hyh l'sh* is attested 19 times: Gen 20:12; 24:67; Num 36:3, 6 (twice), 8, 11, 12; Deut 21:13; 22:19, 29; 24:4; Ruth 4:13; 1 Sam 25:42, 43; 2 Sam 11:17;

that the man is the subject of the action, whereas the woman is only its object. To take or to give a young girl in marriage is men's business. In other words, the woman plays nothing but a passive role. Sometimes, without further ado, she is offered as a prize (Josh 15:16-17). On the other hand, she is required to be beautiful and, above all, a virgin. The text of Gen 24:16 presents us with the portrait of the ideal wife-to-be: very fair *(hy*m*d)*, a virgin *(btl)*[18] whom no man had known. In this perspective, the virginity of a young girl is a familial possession. The girl who allows herself to be seduced throws her family into disrepute and undermines its integrity because she is no longer able to be the object of an exchange.[19] For in the negotiations of the first phase of marriage, the families involved set the amount of the *mohar* to be paid to the parents of the young woman. Does this mean that she is the object of a transaction, of a sale and a purchase? The word *mohar* occurs only three times in the Bible, and always in very specific situations (Gen 34:12; Exod 22:16; 1 Sam 18:25). In the first two cases, a virgin has been raped. In the third passage, there is a plan for marriage between David and Michal. Saul demands as *mohar* "a hundred foreskins of the Philistines."[20] On the sole basis of these three mentions, it is not possible to subscribe to the theory of the marriage-purchase. As Roland de Vaux says, "The *mohar* appears less as the price paid for the woman than as a compensation paid to the family of the fiancée and, in spite of the external resemblance, the two are morally different: the future husband acquires a right over the woman, but the woman herself is not merchandise."[21] Moreover, the verbs "to sell" *(mkr)* and "to gain" *(qnh)* with the meaning of buying are but rarely used in the context of a matrimonial transaction. It is true that Leah and Rachel complain that their father has sold them (Gen 31:15); the father can even sell his daughter to a man

---

12:10; 1 Kgs 4:11; 2 Kgs 8:18. The expression *hyh *sh* is attested 6 times: Gen 24:51, Deut 21:15; Judg 8:30; 1 Chr 2:26; 4:5; 2 Chr 21:6. The expression *hyh* without the addition of *l*sh* or *sh* is attested 11 times: Lev 21:3; 22:12; Num 30:7; Deut 24:2; 25:5; Judg 14:20; Ruth 1:12 (twice), 13; Jer 3:1; Ezek 44:25.

18. The word *btl* does not necessarily mean a virgin in the strict sense, but a nubile girl, as Gordon J. Wenham shows, "BeTÛLÂH 'A Girl of Marriageable Age,'" *Vetus Testamentum* 22 (1972) 326–329; on Deut 22:13-21, see especially pages 330–331.

19. Hence the laws which bind the seducer to pay the young woman's father the "mohar of the virgins" *(mhr btwlt)* and to take her as his wife (Exod 22:15, 16; see Deut 22:28, 29).

20. However, in the biblical texts, the custom of paying the *mohar* is underlying other situations. Let us cite for example the case of Jacob, who had to serve Laban for fourteen years in order to gain Laban's two daughters.

21. Roland de Vaux, *Les institutions de l'Ancien Testament*, vol.1 (Paris: Cerf, 1961) 49.

who designates her as his wife (*ʿmh*) or that of his son (Exod 21:7-11); Boaz explicitly says that he has acquired Ruth to be his wife (Ruth 4:10; see 4:5), but there again we are in the presence of very particular types of marriages.

The fiancé is obliged to pay a sum of money, or the equivalent, and offer gifts besides (See Gen 24:53). But the parents of the fiancée have no such obligation. They can offer her presents (*siluhim*), give her a slave at the time of the marriage (Gen 24:59; 29:24, 29; see Josh 15:18-19), but contrary to Mesopotamian custom, the biblical texts do not mention the obligation of the father to give his daughter any dowry.

Another interesting aspect attested in both the Near East and Israel is the custom for the husband to cover the fiancée with his own cloak. As we have said above, this gesture is often seen as ratifying the marriage proposal. However—an extraordinary occurrence in the Old Testament—it is a woman, Ruth, who asks the man to marry her, "Spread your cloak (*knf*) over your servant" (Ruth 3:9; see also Ezek 16:8).

Between the betrothal and the wedding ceremony a certain amount of time elapses. Biblical texts give us several hints of this. For instance, Gen 19:14, "Lot went out and said to his sons-in-law [*htn*], who were to marry his daughters. . . ."[22] Another probable indication is the particular term which Hebrew uses to express the action of becoming betrothed: the verb *ʾrs*, employed eleven times in the Bible.[23] The subject of this verb is the man (in Hos 2:19-20, it is God). Once more, the object is the woman to whom he becomes affianced or the young virgin (*btl* or *nʿr btl*)[24] or the young girl (*nʿr*).[25] Because the attestations of this verb are rare, it is very difficult to determine its juridical meaning or even its exact translation. However, we know that the betrothal is a definitive commitment. It is a marriage without cohabitation. As a result, the fiancée is regarded as a married woman. If after the engagement she has sexual relations with another man, both are adulterers and must die (Deut 22:23-27).

22. The noun *hatan* means "son-in-law" as well as "fiancé," "husband" (Psalms 19:6; Isa 62:5; Jer 7:34). The verb *htn* means "to become son-in-law," "to marry" (Gen 34:9; 1 Sam 18:22), hence *hoten*, "father-in-law," "father of the bride" (Exod 18:1). The expression for "wedding," "nuptials" belongs to the same root: *hatunna* (Cant 3:11). Similarly, the noun *klh* means both "daughter-in-law" (Gen 38:11; Ruth 1:7) and "fiancée" (Jer 2:32; 7:14).

23. The verb *ʾrs* is attested 6 times in the piel: Deut 20:7; 28:30; 2 Sam 3:14; Hos 2:19 (twice), 20; and 5 times in the pual: Exod 22:15; Deut 22:23, 25, 27, 28.

24. Exod 22:15; Deut 22:23-28.

25. Deut 22:25, 27.

2. The Entrance of the Woman into Her Husband's House

A house without a head is like
a woman without a husband.

Babylonian Proverb

Neither Mesopotamian nor biblical literature knows any word to designate the institution of marriage.[26] Moreover, we have no complete description of the nuptials. As a result, the ceremonies and rites of marriage in the ancient Near East are very little known. But since the family is patrilocal, the nuptial ceremony par excellence is the entrance of the bride into her husband's house. This entrance is celebrated by a banquet offered by the man's family. The marriage contracts speak little about it, but the "codes of law"[27] and the literary texts[28] mention it now and then. All the relatives and sometimes the whole village take part in this wedding meal. In the thinking of the Near East, by eating the food furnished by her husband's family, by nourishing her life with the same victuals eaten together, the bride definitively becomes part of her new family.[29]

Biblical texts mention three wedding feasts: that offered by Laban on the occasion of his daughter's marriage (Gen 29:22); that arranged by Samson at the house of his future bride (Judg 14:10); and that given by Raguel at the time of Sarah's marriage (Tob 7:14). [There is, however, a fourth wedding feast (8:19-20), the fourteen-day feast given by Raguel after Tobias defeats the demon. Trans.] In these three cases, the meal takes place at the young woman's parents', but the circumstances are particular. In the cases of Laban[30] and Raguel, the future sons-in-law

26. Biblical writings mention a marriage contract only in Tob 7:13, a late book. On occasion, the bond between man and woman is called covenant *(bryt)*. Thus in Mal 2:14, the prophet speaks of "your wife by covenant"; in Prov 2:17, marriage is called literally a "covenant of God." And in the allegory of Ezek 16:8, the Sinai covenant becomes the marriage contract between God and Israel. On marriage as covenant, see Gordon P. Hugenberger, *Marriage as a Covenant: A Study of Biblical Law and Ethics Governing Marriage Developed from the Perspective of Malachi* (New York: Brill, 1994).

27. See for instance the laws of Eshunna, arts. 27 and 28, in Marie-Joseph Seux, *Lois de l'Ancien Orient*, Cahier Évangile supplément 56 (Paris: Cerf, 1993) 26.

28. See for example Jean Bottéro and Samuel Noah Kramer, "Le mariage de Sud," in *Lorsque les dieux faisaient l'homme: Mythologie mésopotamienne* (Paris: Gallimard, 1989) 115–128.

29. Jean Bottéro, "Le plus vieux festin du monde," in *Initiation à l'Orient ancien* (Paris: Seuil, 1992) 116.

30. According to certain authors, Jacob's marriage would belong to the *"errēbu* marriage," a type attested in Babylonian law. In this type of marriage, the fiancé,

are away from their kin. As for Samson's marriage, it belongs to a type of arrangement by which the bride continues to live in her parents' house, where the husband comes to visit her.[31] In this last case, it is interesting to note that Samson's family prepares the feast; as we have remarked before, the wedding banquet is, by custom, the responsibility of the husband. This custom symbolizes the obligations the husband has toward his wife. First of all, he owes her food, then clothing and cohabitation (Exod 21:10-11).

The Mesopotamian Texts

It is through the matrimonial ceremony that the man introduces *(sūrubu)* his bride into his family, where she will remain until death (except in case of repudiation). "To enter a man's house" *(ana bīt awīlim erēbum)* is therefore the technical term for marriage when applied to a woman. The husband *(mutu)* then becomes the "master of his wife" *(bēl assati)*.[32] The Code of Hammurabi is very clear on the meaning of this expression. Let us take article 129 as an example; it shows that the husband has the right of life and death over his wife:

> If a man's wife has been caught in bed with another man, the pair will be tied up and thrown into the water. If the master of the woman *(bēl assati)* forgives his wife, then the king will [also] forgive his servant.

Article 161 is also very suggestive:

> If a man has sent a present to the house of his father-in-law, [if] he has paid the *tirhatum*, then [if] his friend calumniates him, [if] his father-in-law has said to the owner of the wife *[bēl assati]*, "you will not take my daughter," he will restitute a double amount of what has been brought to him; besides, his friend will not be allowed to take his wife.

This article shows clearly that the future husband is called "master" of the wife from the time of the betrothal.

---

after he has paid the *tirhatu,* enters *(errēbu)* the family and becomes the adopted son and the husband of the heiress daughter. For further information, see Driver and Miles, *Babylonian Laws,* 134–142; Walter Kornfeld, "Mariage," in *Dictionnaire de la Bible, Supplément 5* (Paris: Letouzey et Ané, 1957) cols. 915–916.

31. What is meant here could be the *"sadiqa* marriage," known to ancient Arabs. The husband does not pay "the price of the fiancée," but every time he visits his wife, he brings her presents (Judg 15:1). On this topic, see Kornfeld, "Mariage," col. 917.

32. Driver and Miles, *Babylonian Laws,* 246, 322.

Thus, Babylonian laws give us to understand that the husband has complete authority over his wife. Sometimes she is called "mistress of the house" *(bēlit bītim)* since the house is her exclusive domain.[33] However, in matters of love, the literary texts specify that quite often the woman takes the initiative. For instance, making love is sometimes called "the daughter-in-law's task" *(sipir kallūti)*.[34] In contrast, the verb *ahāzu* when referring to sexual relations has the man as a subject and means rather "to possess" the woman.[35] Other ways of speaking are "sleep" *(salālu)* with her; "play" *(sāhu, helū)* with her; "know" *(idūm)* her; "succeed in knowing" *(lamādu)* her, which means succeed in making love to her.[36] It is also the man who "comes near" *(tehū)* and recites incantations so that "she may come and he may make love to her."[37] There are indeed a certain number of exorcisms and prayers to insure the success of lovemaking. A man prays "to succeed in having pleasure" *(suhū*, literally, "in laughing"); "to attract a woman" (literally, "to make her come"); "to seduce" a woman *(dabadū*, literally, "to make her speak"); "to obtain that a woman will desire him" (literally, "cast her eyes on his penis"); or "to obtain that the woman may not raise her eyes" to look at "another man's penis."[38] But both man and woman can be said to lie *(nalū)* "on the breast" *(ina sūn)* of their partners; both can be said to arouse the heart *(nīs libbi*, literally, cause the "rising of the heart"). If, during lovemaking, the man touches the woman's genitalia *(kuzba ilputu*, literally "the sensual delight"), the woman also touches the man's.[39] Other expressions are part of the amorous and erotic vocabulary applied to either man or woman: *ramū* and its derivatives going from "to love" or "to be in love" to "to make love"; *huddū*, "to give delight," "to give pleasure to the other"; *kuzbu*, "pleasure," "sexual attraction"; *dādu*, "sexual pleasure" either received or given.[40] Therefore, in matters of love, we note that the woman is the equal of the man; she is neither an instrument nor an object, but a partner.

33. Jean Bottéro, "La femme dans la Mésopotamie ancienne," in *Histoire mondiale de la femme*, ed. Pierre Grimal, vol. 1 (Paris: Nouvelle Librairie de France, 1965) 188.

34. Jean Bottéro, "La Hiérogamie après l'époque sumérienne," in *Le mariage sacré* (Paris: Berg International, 1983) 203.

35. Van Praag, *Droit international assyro-babylonien*, 87.

36. Wolfram von Soden, *Akkadisches Handworterbuch*, vol. A–L (Wiesbaden: Otto Harrassowitz, 1965) 188, 531.

37. Bottéro, "La femme dans la Mésopotamie ancienne," 174–176.

38. Jean Bottéro, "Le manuel de l'exorciste," in *Mythes et rites de Babylone* (Paris: Librairie Honoré Champion, 1985) 104–105.

39. Lackenbacher, "Note sur l'Ardat-lilî," 124, 129, 136, 140.

40. Bottéro, "La Hiérogamie," 203.

The Biblical Texts

In biblical writings, the man is also considered the "master" of his wife *(bʿl ᵓsh)*[41] and the wife the property of her husband *(bʿlt bʿl)*[42] on a par with his house, his field, his flock. On this point, the text of Gen 20:3 is significant:

> But God came to Abimelech in a dream by night, and said to him, "You are about to die because of the woman whom you have taken, for she is a married woman ["she belongs to her master," *bʿlt bʿl*].

The word *bʿl*, which means master over the woman as subordinate, occurs fifteen times in the Bible.[43] Sometimes it is placed in parallel with the word "man" *(ᶜys)*, as in the following passage:

> When the wife of Uriah heard that her husband *[ᶜys]* was dead, she made lamentation for [her master, *bʿl*] (2 Sam 11:26).[44]

One of the verbs meaning "to marry" also belongs to the same root: *bʿl*, "to become the master," "to take possession of."[45] Indeed, in Israel the woman does not have any identity of her own. She is always someone's wife. The locution "wife of . . ." is attested more than 250 times in the Old Testament. One finds the following formulas: "wife of + the husband's proper name" (some 60 times);[46] "wife of + the common name designating the husband" (some 50 times);[47] and "wife of + the

41. Exod 21:3; Deut 24:2; 2 Sam 11:26.
42. Gen 20:3; Deut 22:22.
43. Gen 30:3; Exod 21:3, 22; Lev 21:4; Deut 22:22; 24:4; 2 Sam 11:26; Esth 1:17-20; Prov 12:4; 31:11, 13, 18; Hos 1:18 (in figurative language); Joel 1:8.
44. The term *ᵓys* in the sense of "husband" occurs especially in the juridical passages in which several questions on marriage are discussed: Num 5:12ff.; 30:8ff.; Deut 22:13ff.; 24:1-4 (see Jer 3:1), 5. The term *ᵓdwn*, "lord," is also used in the sense of "husband": Gen 18:12; Judg 19:26; Amos 4:1; Ps 45:12. This title is more often that given by a slave to his or her master or by a subject to the king.
45. Deut 21:13; 24:1; Prov 30:23; Isa 62:5; Mal 2:11.
46. Gen 4:23; 7:13; 11:13, 29 (twice), 31; 12:17; 16:1, 3; 20:18; 24:15; 36:10 (twice), 12, 13, 14, 17, 18 (twice); 38:12; 46:19; Exod 18:2; Num 26:59; Judg 4:4, 17, 21; 5:24; 11:2; 14:15, 16; Ruth 4:10; 1 Sam 4:19; 14:50; 25:14, 44; 27:3; 30:5 (twice); 2 Sam 2:2; 3:3, 5; 11:3, 26; 12:10, 15; 1 Kgs 9:16; 14:2, 4, 5, 6, 17; 2 Kgs 5:2; 22:14; 1 Chr 2:24, 29; 4:19; 7:16; 2 Chr 22:11; 34:22.
47. For example, "your father's wife" *(ᵓst ᵓbyk):* Lev 18:8, 11; "his father's wife" *(ᵓst ᵓbyw):* Lev 20:11; Deut 23:1; 27:20; "your brother's wife" *(ᵓst ᵓhyk):* Gen 38:8; Lev 18:16; "your son's wife" *(ᵓst ᵓbnk):* Lev 18:15; "your kinsman's wife" *(ᵓst ᵓmytk):* Lev 18:20; "your neighbor's wife" *(ᵓst rᶜk):* Exod 20:17; Deut 5:18.

pronominal suffix designating the husband" (170 times.)[48] On the other hand, the expression "man [husband] of . . ." is attested only once with the proper name of a woman (Ruth 1:3); once with the common name designating a woman (Judg 20:4); and some 50 times with the feminine pronominal suffix "my, your, her man."[49] These data show us that in Israel, women are defined by the men to whom they belong.[50] In order to be really respected and protected, a woman had to belong to a man and bear his name. To bear a man's name is so vitally important that Isaiah describes the misfortunes of Jerusalem through the images of anguished women doomed to celibacy and sterility:

> Seven women shall take hold of one man in that day, saying,
> "We will eat our own bread and wear our own clothes;
> just let us be called by your name;
>   take away our disgrace" (Isa 4:1).

When one knows the value attached to the name in the thinking of the ancient Near East, one understands that "to bear the name of a man" means much more than a mere appellation: the woman carries in herself the mark of her belonging to someone.

The various expressions describing sexual relations between men and women confirm what has just been said. The most often used is probably "to go in to *(bw' 'l)* a woman." After his seven years of service for Rachel, Jacob asks his father-in-law to give him his fiancée in these terms:

> Give me my wife that I may go in to her, for my time is completed (Gen 29:21).[51]

48. Gen 2:24, 25; 3:8, 17, 20, 21; 4:1, 17, 20, 25; 6:18; 7:2 (twice), 7; 8:16, 18; 12:5, 11, 12, 18, 19, 20; 13:1; 17:15, 19; 18:9, 10; 19:15, 16, 26; 20:2, 1, 14, 17, and so on.

49. Gen 3:6, 16; 16:3; 29:32, 34; 30:15, 18, 20; Lev 21:7; Num 5:13, 19, 20 (twice), 27, 29; Deut 25:11; Judg 13:6, 9, 10; Ruth 1:5, 9; 2:1, 11; 1 Sam 1:8, 22, 23; and so on.

50. People also said "daughter of . . .," "sister of . . .," "mother of. . . ." See Inger Ljung, *Silence or Suppression: Attitudes towards Women in the Old Testament* (Uppsala: Academiae Upsaliensis, 1989) 22–26. The Mesopotamian texts describe a similar situation. Jean-Jacques Glassner, "Women, Hospitality and the Honor of the Family," *Women's Earliest Records*, 82–84, gives us several examples.

51. See Gen 6:4; 16:2, 4; 19:31; 29:23, 30; 30:3, 4, 16; 38:2, 8, 9, 16, 18; Deut 21:13; 22:13; 25:5; Judg 16:1; 2 Sam 3:7; 12:24; 16:21, 22; 1 Chr 2:21; 7:23; Ps 51:2; Prov 6:29; Ezek 17:44. In Gen 16:2 and 30, it is women who ask their husbands "to go in to" their servants; both are sterile women. In Gen 30:16, Leah asks Jacob to "come in to" her. This is also a particular case since that night Jacob was to sleep with Rachel.

To designate sexual relationships, one finds the following verbs and locutions: "to go to bed with" *(skb ʿm);*[52] "to cause a flow of semen" *(sktb-zrʿ);*[53] "to cohabit" *(sgl);*[54] "to approach" *(qrb);*[55] "to touch" *(ngʿ);*[56] "to attach oneself to" *(dbq);*[57] and "to advance" *(ngs).*[58] All these expressions have "man" as the subject, that is, the initiative is the husband's. The verb "to know" *(ydʿ)* also serves to describe the sexual relations between a man and a woman,[59] and very rarely, between a woman and a man.[60] We meet also with the expression "the woman in his bosom" *(ʾst hyqw)*[61] to speak of the woman who shares the man's bed, but the reverse expression is also used, "the man in her bosom" *(ʾys hyqh),* as in Deut 28:56.

In the Old Testament, it is the man who loves *(ʾhb)* the woman. Outside the Song of Songs, one single text mentions the love of a woman for a man, Michal's love for David (1 Sam 18:20). This exception only serves to further emphasize the central place of the man in matters of love.

Not only does the man love the woman, kiss her *(hbq),*[62] he desires *(hps)*[63] her, strongly desires her *(ʾwh* pi., quoted but once, in Ps 45:12), and falls in love with her *(hsq).*[64] Sometimes he rapes her, as in the cases of Dinah and Tamar:

> When Shechem . . . saw *[rʾh]* her, he seized *[lqh]* her and lay *[skb]* with her by force *[ʿnh].* And his soul was drawn *[dbq]* to Dinah (Gen 34:2).

52. Gen 19:32, 33, 34, 35; 30:15, 16; 34:2, 7; 35:22; 39:7, 10, 12, 14; Exod 22:15; Num 5:13-19; Lev 15:24; 18:22; 19:20; 20:11, 12, 13, 18, 20; Deut 22:22, 23, 25, 28, 29; 28:30; 2 Sam 2:22; 11:4, 11; 12:11, 24; 13:11, 14. In Gen 39, it is the wife of Potiphar who asks Joseph to lie with her in her husband's absence. Lev 18:22 speaks of homosexual relationships.

53. Lev 15:18; Num 5:13.

54. Deut 28:30; Jer 3:2.

55. Gen 20:4; Lev 18:6, 14, 19; 20:16; Deut 22:14; Isa 8:3; Ezek 18:6.

56. Gen 20:6; Prov 6:29.

57. Gen 2:24; 34:3; 1 Kgs 11:2.

58. Exod 19:15.

59. Gen 4:1, 17, 25; 24:16; 38:26; Judg 19:25; 1 Sam 1:19; 1 Kgs 1:4; Ezek 19:7. Compare the expression *ydʿ mskb zkr,* "to know by sleeping with a male," Num 31:17, 18, 35; Judg 21:11, 12.

60. Gen 19:8; Num 31:17; Judg 11:39; 21:11. This verb is also applied to the relationships between two men: Gen 19:5; Judg 19:22.

61. Deut 13:7; 28:54. See Gen 16:5.

62. Gen 29:13; Prov 4:8.

63. Gen 34:19; Deut 21:14; 25:7, 8; Esth 2:14.

64. Gen 34:8; Deut 21:11.

But he would not listen to her; and being stronger *[hzq]* than she, he forced *[ʿnh]* her and lay *[skb]* with her. Then Ammon was seized with a very great loathing *[snʾ]*; indeed his loathing was even greater than the lust he had felt for her (2 Sam 13:14-15).

The young girls in these two stories have not been engaged to anyone. We are here outside the question of marriage. However, it is again the man's pleasure which is envisioned when the sage advises his son to enjoy the wife of his youth:

Let your fountain be blessed,
  and rejoice *[smh]* in the wife of your youth,
  a lovely deer, a graceful doe.
May her breasts *[dd]* satisfy *[rwh]* you at all times;
  may you be intoxicated *[sgh]* always by her love (Prov 5:18-19).

The first verb, *smh* pi., "to be joyous," "to rejoice," expresses the joy that is manifested in a spontaneous and irresistible manner. It is sometimes so overflowing that the man loses control of himself.[65] The second verb, *rwh*, means "to drink to satiety," "to become drunk," "to be fully satisfied." This verb occurs again in Prov 7:18, also in connection with the root *dd*:[66]

Come, let us take our fill *[rwh]* of love *[ddym]* until morning;
let us delight *[ʿls]* ourselves with love *[ʾhbym]*.

In this passage, the invitation is placed in the mouth of the femme fatale who seduces the young man in the absence of her husband. The third verb *sgh*, "to get drunk," is used here to indicate the effect of passion, whether in legitimate or culpable love. In Prov 20:1, it is applied to the effects of wine drinking. In both cases, the man is beside himself. The use of these three verbs is significant: the man fully enjoys his wife; she is a mere object. What is more, the woman who takes the initiative in lovemaking is the adulterous woman. Nevertheless, a Deuteronomic law exempted the man from all public work for a year after his marriage in order "to bring joy to the wife he has taken." (Deut 24:5, JB).

If a man is newly married, he shall not join the army nor is he to be pestered at home; he shall be left at home free of all obligations for one year to bring joy to *[smh* pi.] the wife he has taken (Deut 24:5, JB).

---

65. E. Ruprecht, *"smh," Diccionario Teologico Manual del Antiguo Testamento* (Madrid: Ediciones Cristandad, 1978) vol. 2, cols. 1042–1043.
66. See Ezek 23:3, 8, 21.

We must not forget that the law is one thing and the reality another. The question would be to know whether this prescription was respected.

3. Childbirth

> Woman is the future of man.
>
> *Sumerian Proverb*

According to the model of the patriarchal family, every woman is created to become the wife of a man and the mother of his children. Only motherhood definitively bonds the woman to her husband and to her in-laws. In the case of sterility, the husband can either send her away[67] or take a second wife who will bear children "to his name."[68] And since the gift of a child is a sign of divine benevolence,[69] the woman "whose breasts have not produced milk . . . who has not been called by the name mother, and who has not given a name [to a child]"[70] is looked down upon; she is incapable of holding her place; she misses her destiny *(sīmtu)*. Now the *sīmtu* entails a whole collection of rights and duties; any infraction against it causes a social imbalance.[71] The inability of a woman to give birth to a child is seen as a lack that upsets the established order of family and community.

The biblical texts reflect the same outlook. Sterility is regarded as a calamity which makes the woman a "nobody" in the eyes of those around her. Rachel's case is eloquent: since she cannot bear a child, she gives her servant as a wife to Jacob, saying, "[G]o in to her, that she may bear upon my knees and that I too may have children through her" (Gen 30:3). A baby is born and Rachel exclaims, "God has judged *[ddny]* me, and has also heard my voice and given me a son" (Gen 30:6). Nevertheless, she again finds her place in the group only after having herself given a son to her husband. Joseph's birth has this meaning: "God has taken away my reproach *[hrph]*" (Gen 30:23). We see that sterility is understood by the woman herself and by those around her as a divine "punishment."[72] Is not the child a gift of God (Gen 33:15)?

67. Code of Hammurabi, art. 138.
68. Bottéro, "La femme dans la Mésopotamie ancienne," 192.
69. See for instance the Sumerian proverb 1.160: "to take a wife is men's business, but to have children depends on god."
70. Lackenbacher, "Note sur l'Ardat-lilî," 140.
71. Concerning this concept, see A. Leo Oppenheim, *La Mésopotamie: Portrait d'une civilisation* (Paris: Gallimard, 1970) 211–215; [A. Leo Oppenheim, *Ancient Mesopotamia: Portrait of a Dead Civilization* (Chicago: University of Chicago Press, 1964).]
72. Gen 20:28; cf. Lev 20:20.

The Mesopotamian Texts

"Is it possible to conceive without going to bed?" asks a Babylonian proverb. Of course, "Going to bed leads to nursing" says another proverb,[73] but once a woman is pregnant, she is beset by many worries. The first one is without doubt the fear of miscarrying (literally, "losing one's fruit"). Often, such a mishap is due to the action of certain he- or she-demons, such as the dreadful Lamastu, who are especially hostile to future mothers. To ward off this danger, women have recourse to prayers and rituals as well as to the wearing of necklaces and belts made of different stones having efficacious properties. The most important one is precisely "the birthing stone," the one which protects women against a miscarriage, called *ittamir.*[74]

The second worry concerns the child's sex. Will it be a girl or a boy? The treatises of diagnoses and prognoses, which are rarely concerned with women, devote several articles to methods of determining the baby's sex. For instance, "If the mother-to-be's forehead is full of nevi, the child she is carrying is a boy—a sign of prosperity."[75] The Mesopotamian key to dreams also states that if "a man dreams that someone gives him a seal bearing his name, he will have a name and progeny."[76] As a matter of fact, one of the Akkadian words for "name" *(sumu)* also means "son." Indeed, the arrival of a male heir brings happiness to the father and the in-laws. Because of this boy, the name will be perpetuated and the family gains recognition in everyone's eyes. Thus, the woman becomes the instrument through which the man's future is insured.

The third worry concerns childbirth itself. It is a time when the woman is most vulnerable and an easy prey for demons. The "work of delivery" is accomplished of course with the help of a midwife *(sabsutu,* "the one who knows the inside of bodies"), who cuts the umbilical cord *(bitiq abunnati).*[77] The delivery is surrounded by a whole magico-religious

73. Wilfred G. Lambert, ed., *Babylonian Wisdom Literature* (Oxford: Clarendon Press, 1960) 241, lines 40-44; see also 247.

74. Francois Thureau-Dangin, "Rituel et amulettes contre Labartu," *Revue d'assyriologie orientale* 18 (1921) 161. On the she-demon Labartu-Lamastu, see Walter Farber, "Lamastu," *Reallexicon der Assyriologie und vorderasiastichen Archäologie,* vol. 6 (New York: W. de Gruyter, 1980–1983) 439–446.

75. Labat, *Traité akkadien,* 201, line 6.

76. A. Leo Oppenheim, *Le rêve: Son interprétation dans le Proche-Orient ancien* (Paris: Horizons de France, 1959) 147; [A. Leo Oppenheim, *The Interpretation of Dreams in the Ancient Near East, with a Translation of an Assyrian Dream-book,* Transactions of the American Philosophical Society, new ser. 46 (Philadelphia: American Philosophical Society, 1956)].

77. Bottéro, "La femme dans la Mésopotamie ancienne," 194–195.

ritual to help the woman give birth *(alādu)* easily and without risks. If complications occur, in case of difficult labor or delivery *(pusqu)*, one can always have recourse to "birthing herbs," "birthing stones," and especially incantations.[78] Or else, one appeals to Samas, the Judge God, in a desperate prayer:

> Samas, eminent judge, father of the black heads,
> This woman, the daughter of her god,
> In the presence of your divinity, may the knot of her womb be untied;
> May this woman happily give birth,
> May she be delivered and live, may the fruit of her womb thrive;
> In the presence of your divinity may she fare well,
> May she happily give birth and sing your praises!
> In the presence of your divinity, may evil spells and bewitchments
>   dissolve;
> As a dream, may they vanish.[79]

In extreme cases, one resorts to an operation called *silip rēmi*, "extraction [of the child from the womb],"[80] but then the risks of death for mother and baby are overwhelming. The predictions derived from the circumstances of birth, as well as the medical and divinatory treatises, describe this procedure and the anomalies which often afflict infants.

Allusions to the difficulties of delivery are present everywhere in Mesopotamian literature. We shall give only two examples. The first one is a Sumerian saying: "A sick person is [relatively] well; it is a woman in labor who is [truly] in a bad state" (1.193). The second is drawn from a poem entitled "The Master and His Servant": "Investing money is as pleasant as loving a woman; but getting it back as painful as giving birth."[81] After delivery, the woman is considered "unclean" for thirty days.[82]

The birth of the first child, particularly if it is a boy, is of the greatest importance for the woman. Hitherto called *kallatu*, "young bride," she becomes *assatu*, "wife," since the child is the true fulfillment of the marriage.

Mesopotamian writings do not give us many details on the mother's role in the child's education. After the birth, she nurses *(sūnuqu*, liter-

---

78. M. Civil, "Medical Commentaries from Nippur," *Journal of Near Eastern Studies* 33 (1974) 331.

79. Marie-Joseph Seux, *Hymnes et prières aux dieux de Babylonie et d'Assyrie* (Paris: Cerf, 1976) 217. For other incantations for a woman in labor, see René Labat, *Les religions du Proche-Orient asiatique* (Paris: Fayard, 1970) 285–286.

80. Bottéro, "La femme dans la Mésopotamie ancienne," 195.

81. Labat, *Les religions du Proche-Orient asiatique,* 345.

82. René Labat, "Geburt," *Reallexicon der Assyriologie,* vol. 3 (1957) 179.

ally "suckles") it during a three-year period. If needed, she can have recourse to a wet nurse *(musēnitqu)*, but this is not within the means of everybody. A text tells the story of a woman who, unable to pay the salary of the wet nurse to whom she had entrusted her son, says to her, "Take the infant; he will be your son."[83] Another passage reports that Zuhuntum, the wife of Anum-kīnum, unable to pay her daughter's wet nurse the price agreed upon, food, oil, and clothing, relinquishes the baby to her.[84]

It is the mother also who is at the baby's side when it is sick, as we are given to understand from the following prayer, part of an incantation to soothe a crying baby: "May the child sleep in peace and may its mother, who has work to do, do it quietly while it is asleep."[85] We can also glimpse the motherly care in a text that describes the day of a schoolboy: early in the morning, when the child wakes up, his mother gives him two "little loaves of bread" before he starts for "the house of tablets" (the school).[86] The mother exercises more authority over the girl than over the boy if we believe that the following proverb reflects the reality: "The mother will make a talkative girl keep quiet, but a talkative boy, impossible" (1.185). Another saying exhorts the son to listen to his mother's words: "Pay attention to your mother's word as to your god's word!"[87] However, the Mesopotamian family is patrilinear, which means children belong neither to the mother nor to the mother's family. Only the paternal lineage counts. Article 117 of the Code of Hammurabi stipulates that the father is the master of his children, whom he may sell as slaves if he gets into debt,[88] and Article 135 states that the children "follow the father," that is, they belong to him and live with him, even if their mother should leave the house.

The Biblical Texts

In Israel, childbirth *(ldh)* is also one of the great moments in a woman's life. From early childhood, a girl is taught the necessity of

83. Paul Koschaker, "Observations juridiques sur 'Ibla-Ablum'," *Revue d'Assyriologie* 11 (1914) 37.

84. Vincent Scheil, "Les nourrices en Babylonie et le #194 du Code," *Revue d'Assyriologie* 11 (1914) 175.

85. Bottéro, "La femme dans la Mésopotamie ancienne," 195.

86. Samuel Noah Kramer, *L'Histoire commence à Sumer* (Paris: Arthaud, 1986) 40; [Samuel Noah Kramer, *History Begins at Sumer: Thirty-nine Firsts in Man's Recorded History*, 3rd rev. ed. (Philadelphia: University of Pennsylvania Press, 1981)].

87. Jan J. A. van Dijk, *La sagesse suméro-accadienne: Recherches litteraires des textes sapientiaux, avec choix de textes* (Leiden: Brill, 1953) 105.

88. See arts. 39 and 48 of the Assyrian Laws.

insuring progeny to the family by becoming a mother. When she enters her husband's house, the blessing of her relatives accompanies her as a good omen, as Laban's wish for his sister Rebekah shows:

> May you, our sister, become
>   thousands of myriads;
> may your offspring gain possession
>   of the gates of their foes (Gen 24:60).

The young bride therefore impatiently waits for the moment when she will know she is pregnant *(hrh)*. The verb *hrh*, "to conceive," "to be pregnant," occurs 43 times in the Old Testament.[89] It is often joined to the verb *yld*, "to give birth," "to bring into the world," "to bear a child,"[90] followed by the name of the newborn. For example, "Now the man knew his wife Eve, and she conceived and bore Cain" (Gen 4:1).[91] The construction with the accusative is also frequent, especially in the expression "she bore a son."[92] The name of the father, of the man to whom the woman gives a son, is introduced by the particle *l*: "Sarah conceived and bore *[l]* Abraham[93] a son" (Gen 21:2). When the verb *yld* has the man as a subject, it means "to generate."[94] Thus the father is seen as "the one who begets" and the mother as "the one who gives birth." The father is the progenitor, the mother the receptacle. The children are the father's seed, that is, his descendants.

As in Mesopotamia, childbirth in Israel is not without peril. The Bible cites two cases of women who died giving birth: Rachel (Gen 35:16-19) and the wife of Phinehas, whose name we do not know (1 Sam 4:19-20). The imagery used by the prophets also grants an im-

---

89. Gen 4:1, 17; 16:4 (twice), 5; 19:36; 21:2; 25:21; 29:32, 33, 34, 35; 30:5, 7, 17, 19, 23; 38:3, 4, 18; 49:26; Exod 2:2; Num 11:12; Judg 13:3; 1 Sam 1:20; 2:21; 2 Sam 11:5; 2 Kgs 4:17; 1 Chr 4:17; 7:23; Job 3:3; 15:35; Ps 7:15; Cant 3:4; Isa 8:3; 26:18; 33:11; 59:13; Hos 1:3, 6, 8; 2:5. All these references have the woman as subject, with the exception of Num 11:12, where it is Moses; in Job 15:35; Ps 7:15; Isa 26:18; 33:11; 59:13, the verb is used metaphorically. The adjective *hrh*, "pregnant," occurs 15 times and always refers to a woman: Gen 16:11; 38:24, 25; Exod 21:22; Judg 13:5, 7; 1 Sam 4:19; 2 Sam 11:5; 2 Kgs 8:12; 15:16; Isa 7:14; 26:17; Jer 20:17; 31:8; Amos 1:13. The noun *hrn*, "pregnancy," "conception," is used only twice in the singular (Ruth 4:13; Hos 9:11) and once in the plural (Gen 3:16).

90. Gen 4:1, 17; 21:2; 29:32, 33, 34, 35; 30:5, 7, 17, 19, 23; 38:3, 4; 1 Sam 1:20; 2:21; 1 Chr 7:23; Isa 8:3; Hos 1:3, 6, 8.

91. See Gen 4:17; 38:3, 4; 1 Sam 1:20; 1 Chr 7:23.

92. See Gen 29:32, 33, 34, 35; 30:23; 1 Sam 2:21; Isa 8:3; Hos 1:6, 8.

93. See Gen 21:2; 30:5, 7, 17, 19; Hos 1:3.

94. The verb *yld* is also used in parallel with the verb *bnh*, "to build," in the sense of to generate: Gen 16:2; 30:3. See Deut 25:9; Ruth 4:11; 2 Sam 7:27; 1 Chr 17:25.

portant place to the pangs of childbirth. The woman in labor writhes in pain (Isa 13:8); she moans in giving birth (Isa 42:14); she gasps for breath and pants (Isa 42:14; Jer 4:31); she places her hands on her loins and her face turns pale (Jer 30:6); her heart falters (Jer 48:41); she trembles in anguish (Jer 49:24).

During labor, the man stays away (Jer 20:15). It is the midwife (*yld* pi, literally "the one who helps in childbirth") who assists her.[95] At birth, the umbilical cord *(krt sr)* is cut; the newborn is washed, rubbed with salt, and wrapped in swaddling clothes (Ezek 16:4). The mother is regarded as "unclean" for forty days if she gives birth to a boy (Lev 12:2-4) and eighty days, if she gives birth to a girl (Lev 12:5).

The mother herself nurses the child for three years.[96] Sometimes, as in Mesopotamia, a wet nurse *(mnqt)* is engaged, especially if financial conditions allow it.[97] Immediately after birth, the child is given a name. In most cases, it is the woman who chooses her son's name,[98] but the father may also name him.[99] Sometimes, even the neighbors are the ones to give a name to the infant (Ruth 4:17). Nevertheless, like women, children bear in their names the mark of their belonging; most often, they are called by their first name followed by the father's name, for instance, "Isaac, Abraham's son" (Gen 25:19). The circumcision to which every male child is submitted on the eighth day after birth[100] is the father's responsibility,[101] but in cases of necessity the mother can perform it.[102]

After all we have just said, it is obvious that the woman's worth is linked with motherhood to such a point that she is sometimes called "womb" *(rhm)* by metonymy (Judg 5:30). Her value increases if she gives birth to a male. Rachel's second childbirth, which cost her her life, is illuminating on this point:

> When [Rachel] was in her hard labor, the midwife said to her, "Do not be afraid; for now you will have another son" (Gen 35:17).

Indeed the birth of a son is of the utmost importance. It insures that the name of a man will not be blotted out of Israel (Deut 25:6). A fecund

95. Gen 35:17; Exod 1:15.

96. Gen 21:7; 1 Sam 1:21-23; 1 Kgs 3:21.

97. Gen 24:59; 35:8; Num 11:12; Ruth 4:16; 2 Sam 4:4; 2 Kgs 1:5; 11:2; 2 Chr 22:11; Isa 49:23.

98. Gen 4:1, 25; 16:11; 29:32-35; 30:5-8, 10, 13, 18, 21, 24; 35:18; 38:3-5; Judg 13:24; 1 Sam 1:20; 4:21; 2 Sam 12:24; 1 Chr 4:9; 7:16; Isa 7:14.

99. Gen 4:26; 5:29; 17:19; 21:3; 41:51-52; Exod 2:22; 18:3-4; 1 Chr 7:23.

100. Gen 17:12; 21:4; Lev 12:3.

101. Gen 17:23; 21:4.

102. Exod 4:25; 2 Macc 6:10.

wife, and therefore the presence of many children, are considered the greatest blessing that God bestows on men. The psalmist sings of this good fortune:

> Your wife will be like a fruitful vine
>   within your house;
> Your children will be like olive shoots
>   around your table (Ps 128:3).
> Sons are indeed a heritage from the LORD,
>   the fruit of the womb a reward.
> like arrows in the hand of a warrior
>   are the sons of one's youth.
> Happy the man who has his quiver full of them (Ps 127:3-5).

As everywhere else in the ancient Near East, family life is centered on the father. His authority is incontestable. He enjoys the right of life and death even over his children. In fact, when the fetus is still in its mother's womb, it already belongs to the father, as shown in the following text:

> When people who are fighting injure a pregnant woman so that there is a miscarriage, and yet no further harm follows, the one responsible shall be fined what the woman's husband demands [b⁾ ḥ⁾sh], paying as much as the judges determine (Exod 21:22).

However, in spite of the supremacy of the father's power, when it comes to the children's duties, no distinction is made between father and mother (Exod 20:12; Deut 5:16).

*   *   *

In this study on woman and love, we have followed the three steps which constitute marriage: the betrothal, the entrance into the husband's house, and childbirth. Whether in Mesopotamian or biblical texts, one common point characterizes women's condition throughout, and that is, dependence. As a young girl, she is under the father's authority and responsibility. At the time of the betrothal, she simply exchanges one authority for another, for she is "given" or "offered" as a wife by her father or his representative then "received" and "taken" by her husband. A series of symbolic gestures accompanies this change of dependence: the payment of the *tirhatu* or the *mohar,* the anointing, and the ritual covering of the bride's head with her husband's cloak. Even though the spouses do not yet cohabit and the bride continues to live at her father's, she already belongs to her husband.

The nuptial ceremony par excellence, that is, the second phase of marriage, is the entrance of the woman into her husband's house. "To enter into a man's family" is therefore the technical term for marriage applied to the woman in Mesopotamian texts. At that moment, the husband becomes the "master of his wife." In the Bible, the succession of terms explaining the matrimonial process is as follows: "to take a wife" + "to go in to" + "to be the master [of the wife]." Thus, on both the juridical and anthropological planes, the man is considered the "proprietor" of the woman and she, his "property."

Our study of the love vocabulary has also shown us that the woman is seen as a sexual object. Even though the Mesopotamian literature—contrary to biblical texts—presents the woman as the man's partner in love relationships, her rights appear to be based only on her ability to bear children. In fact, it is the birth of a child that truly fulfills the marriage. Lacking this birth, the woman can see herself sent back to her father's house or replaced by another woman able to discharge the social function for which she was born. The woman who gives a child to her husband gains the respect of her in-laws and society at large. But this child must be a male. It is he who, by reproducing the father's seed, insures the survival of his father. A girl, not reproducing the father's seed, condemns him to extinction.

This study of the marriage vocabulary in ancient Semitic thought has shown us that a woman has no worth of her own. Her role is always defined by her relationship with the man to whom she belongs. The following Sumerian proverb summarizes in some way what we have just said:

> For a man, the woman is the future,
>   [by giving him a large family]
>
> For a man, the son is the refuge,
>   [by prolonging his name]
>
> For a man, a daughter is salvation,
>   [by bringing him assets at the time of her marriage]
>
> For a man, the daughter-in-law is "Hell"![103]

103. Kramer, *L'histoire commence à Sumer*, 137.

Woman in the Song of Songs

◆————————————————————————————————————◆

Jean-Jacques Lavoie

As its name suggests, the Song of Songs is in the form of a song, the most beautiful of songs. As a consequence, to read the Song is not first to decipher words but to listen carefully to musical textures, such as alliteration, homophony, rhyme, repetition, play on words and rhythms. Better still, to read the Song is to play the Song—the verb "to play" being used here also as a musical term. To regard the reading of the Song of Songs as the execution of a musical score "effectuates, actualizes the semantic potentialities of the text."[1] By the same token, being a musical score, the Song can be given different interpretations. The very history of the ways the Song has been read reminds us eloquently that these interpretations are in some way an integral part of the words of this book.[2] For instance, the fact that for almost twenty centuries the authorized readers of the Bible have been men, formed by a strongly patriarchal environment, has deeply influenced the interpretations given to the Song. A few sentences excerpted from a commentary by G. Geslin, published in 1938, will suffice to illustrate our assertion:

> With love, she [the bride] will have all virtues: she will be attentive, hardworking, devoted, faithful; she will be a good housekeeper, clean, thrifty, discreet, industrious. . . . Let us not be surprised that God

1. Paul Ricœur, *Du texte à l'action,* Essais d'herméneutique 2 (Paris: Seuil, 1986) 153; [Paul Ricœur, *From Text to Action,* trans. Kathleen Blamey and John B. Thompson (Evanston, Ill.: Northwestern University Press, 1991)]. In other words, it is the reading which manifests the completion of the text.

2. Readers will find a good survey of the history of the interpretation of the Song of Songs in Marvin H. Pope, *Song of Songs: A New Translation with Introduction and Commentary* (New York: Doubleday, 1977) 89–229; Anne-Marie Pelletier, *Lecture du Cantique des cantiques: De l'énigme du sens aux figures du lecteur* (Rome: Pontificio Istituto Biblico, 1989).

raised the marriage contract to the dignity of a sacrament, a contract through which the young man receives the indispensable help he needs to fulfill the career God has assigned him, and the young woman realizes her mission as man's helper. It is thus that once married, the young woman will remain in the retreat of her home, eschewing any conversation which could compromise her faithfulness or raise any suspicion in her husband's mind. . . .[3]

As to the different allegorical readings of the Song, which always place God or Christ at the center, one could even say that they were made possible only because an androcentric vision was imposed on the book. The theocentric reading of the Song is in fact essentially androcentric, while the anthropological reading of the Song gives back her rightful place to the woman because the Song is essentially anthropocentric.[4] The purpose of this article is precisely to clearly show the importance of the woman's role in this book. To accomplish this, we shall proceed in three stages. First, we shall examine the place that our book reserves for the woman. Then, we shall emphasize the singular images of woman depicted by this most beautiful of all songs. Lastly, we shall raise the question of the Song's author.

1. The Place of Woman in the Song of Songs

What place does the Song assign to the woman? In order to answer this question, we find it useful to scrutinize the text with the help of a few statistical data. Of course, we do not intend to justify our viewpoint simply by additions and figures, but these will help us to have a better look at data which in fact are often unknown. Exegetes have not failed to notice that in the Song it is the young woman who speaks most often. To be more precise, we must add that out of the 117 verses of the Song, 65½ are sung by a woman,[5] 43½ by a man,[6] 4 by women choirs,[7] 1 by the mother,[8] 2 by the beloved's brothers,[9] without counting

3. G. Geslin, *Le Cantique des Cantiques* (Orne: Abbaye Saint-Wandrille, 1938) 48, 61, 66.

4. According to the anthropological reading of the Song, this text speaks first and essentially of human love. Nowadays, the majority of exegetes favors this reading.

5. 1:2-7, 12-14, 16-17; 2:1, 3-9, 10a, 16-17; 3:1-5, 7-11; 4:15-16; 5:2a, 3-8, 10-16; 6:2-3, 11-12; 7:11-14; 8:1-4, 5b-7, 10-12, 14.

6. 1:8-11, 15; 2:2, 10b-14; 4:1-14; 5:1a, 2b; 6:4-10; 7:1-10; 8:13.

7. 3:6; 5:1b, 9; 6:1; 8:5a.

8. 8:15.

9. 8:8-9.

the title, in 1:1, which fits into no class whatsoever. Besides, if one adds that out of the 45½ verses attributed to men, 5 are quotations placed in the woman's mouth (2:10-14), the woman speaks almost twice as much as the man. It is true that in the case of a few verses, the attribution to one or the other person could be debated at length; nevertheless, the data favoring the woman would remain as impressive.[10] In a word, the phenomenon is unique in the Bible.

These statistics also demonstrate that the woman is the alpha and the omega of the Song since it is she who has the first and last word (1:2; 8:14). Her entrance and her exit give the tone of the whole book: contrary to Israel's patriarchal mores, she begins and ends by freely expressing her desire and her love for her beloved (1:2-3; 8:14), but also by using the imperative form, "Draw me" (1:4) and "Make haste" (8:14). In the beginning as well as in the end, the man is therefore subject to the amorous commands of his beloved. However these amorous imperatives are reciprocal. At times they are the woman's: "Tell me" (1:7); "turn . . . be like" (2:17); "come out [and] look" (3:11); "Awake . . . come . . . Blow upon" (4:16); "Come" (7:11); "Set me as a seal" (8:6). At times they are the man's: "follow" (1:8); "Arise . . . come away" (2:10); "let me hear" (2:14; 8:13); "let me see" (2:14); "Open to me" (5:2); "turn away" (6:5); "Return, return" (6:13). A comparison shows once more that, within this reciprocity, the woman uses more imperatives than the man: a total of 12 for the woman, 9 for the man. Masculine domination, unilateral, aggressive, oppressive, and sometimes tyrannical (see for instance Gen 34; Judg 19; 2 Sam 13), yields to reciprocal commands expressing nothing but recognition of the other, love, and tenderness.

2. Singular Images of Woman

Simone de Beauvoir has said that "the liberation of women begins with the womb."[11] Now, in the Song, the woman is not only the first to take the initiative but she is also considered for herself alone. The Song makes no mention of the woman's fecundity. This fact is remarkable

---

10. For example, J. Andreolla and others, *Cântico dos Cânticos: A mais bela cançao* (Sao Paulo: Ed. Paulinas, 1994) p. 30, distribute the verses as follows: 60 are attributed to the woman against 37 to the man, whereas the rest of the book gives parts to the voices of the choir and the narrator. Unfortunately, this commentary, which denounces machismo several times, gives no additional details.

11. Quoted without reference in A. Michel, *Le féminisme* (Paris: Presses universitaires de France, 1979) 97.

when one knows that in women, Israel valued and respected not femininity but motherhood. Woman had worth only as mother to such a degree that she was sometimes called by metonymy *raham* "womb" (Judg 5:30). The stories recording the sterility of the matriarchs are enough to prove that to have descendants was of the utmost importance. But here, woman is no longer regarded as a womb and her sexuality is no longer reduced to its biological and genital dimension. By prizing sexuality only as difference and relation, the Song frees woman from the patriarchal stranglehold. The accomplished woman is no longer necessarily the wife and mother as in Proverbs 31.

The complete absence of a paternal figure also witnesses to this liberation of woman, for it is well known that the unmarried girl was subject to her father's authority and then later on to that of her husband.[12] Moreover, contrary to Israel's patriarchal customs (see Gen 24:67; Ps 45:11; Matt 1:20), it is the man who enters the mother's house (3:4; 8:2); the mother appears four additional times (1:6; 3:11; 6:9; 8). As to the brothers' authority, literally "my mother's sons" (1:6; 8:8), the words of 8:12 and the whole of the book ironically show that it is simply disregarded.[13] The beloved is determined, for all by herself she challenges orders; courageous, for all by herself she confronts hostility (5:7); passionate, for she is lovesick (2:5; 5:8).

These findings, added to what was said above, clearly suggest a matrilocal or matrilinear system or both, perhaps simply a matriarchal one. In brief, not only does the Song ignore the social structures usually symbolized by the father's presence and the mention of progeny, but it reverses the roles.

This reversal of positions is found again in 7:10, which can be read as an allusion to Gen 3:16:

Cant 7:10	Gen 3:16
I am my beloved's and his **desire** [*suq*] is for me	To the woman he said, "I will greatly increase your pangs in childbearing; in pain you shall bring forth children, yet your **desire** [*suq*] shall be for your husband."

12. See the preceding chapter.

13. On this, see the remarks of Daniel Lys, *Le plus beau chant de la création: Commentaire du cantique des cantiques* (Paris: Cerf, 1968) 297; and Yves Simoens, *Le Cantique des Cantiques comme livre de la plénitude: Une lecture anthropologique et théologique* (Bruxelles: Institut d'études théologiques, 1992) 147–148.

The allusion rests on a single word, but this word *suq* occurs only one other time in the Bible: Gen 4:7, a verse placed within a pericope which is akin to Gen 3:9-21. By electing to use this rare word, this verse in the Song is really redirecting the Genesis text and completely transforming it. The curse of Gen 3:16 is changed into a blessing. Desire is a joy, not a judgment. The love relationship is no longer unilateral but reciprocal. Moreover, it is no longer the woman who yearns for the man, as in the patriarchal text of Gen 3:16, but the man for the woman. Not without reason does Phyllis Trible state that the Song of Songs is an excellent example one can adduce to justify a "depatriarchalising" interpretation of the biblical tradition.[14] This interpretation could apply equally to Western tradition as a whole, which, contrary to the Song, has almost always presented the love relationship in terms of dominant/dominated and active/passive.[15]

The Song disrupts, once more, the imaginative functioning of the patriarchal world when it describes for us the "fairest among women" (6:1) with numerous military images borrowed from the masculine world: "Pharaoh's chariots" (1:9); "tower of David, bucklers, shields of warriors" (4:4); "army" (6:4, 10); "ivory tower, tower of Lebanon, [guard at the] gate" (7:4); "wall, towers" (8:10).[16] This upheaval of traditional images is found also in 7:5 where the beloved himself asserts that the king is held captive in the tresses of his beloved.

Finally, the mutual recognition that the other is unique and irreplaceable (2:1-3; 6:9) can also be understood as a criticism of the polygamy practiced by the dominant class.[17]

3. Who Is the Author of the Song?

Tradition regards Solomon as the author of the Song of Songs: it is explicitly written in 1:1; moreover, the Book of Kings presents Solomon as the sage par excellence who composed five thousand songs and had

14. Phyllis Trible, "Depatriachalising in Biblical Interpretation," *Journal of the American Academy of Religion* 41 (1973) 41–47.

15. On this subject, see Michel Foucault, *Histoire de la sexualité*, vol. 2: *L'usage des plaisirs* (Paris: Gallimard, 1984) 57; [Michel Foucault, *The History of Sexuality*, trans. Robert Hurley, vol. 2: *The Use of Pleasure* (New York: Vintage Books, 1980–)].

16. Concerning the tower as military image, see Carol L. Meyers, "Gender Imagery in the Song of Songs," *Hebrew Annual Review* 10 (1986) 213–215, 221.

17. See Cant 6:8; 8:11; Gen 4:19-22; Deut 21:15-17; Judg 8:30-31; 1 Sam 1:2; 2 Sam 5:13; 1 Kgs 11:3; Qoh 2:8. These texts show that polygamy was regarded as a sign of economic prosperity, power, and prestige.

one thousand wives and concubines (1 Kgs 3:12; 11:3). But the date of composition and the place of origin presupposed by this attribution has led to almost all exegetes saying that Solomon could not possibly have written the Song of Songs. The attribution to Solomon in 1:1 is not only fictitious but is perhaps simply a late addition whose purpose was to include the Song among the Wisdom books. Out of the seven mentions of Solomon (1:5; 3:7, 9, 11; 8:11-12), only the title makes him the author of the book. Therefore, it is possible that the original anonymity of this book served, among other things, to hide the work of a woman.

This hypothesis, seeing the Song as the work of a woman, is not new. Already in 1957, Solomon D. Goitein had proposed it.[18] A few years later, Arthur S. Herbert, independently of Goitein, repeated the same idea, but without taking it seriously since in the rest of his commentary he spoke of the author in the masculine.[19] In the 80s, more and more exegetes believed in the possibility of a woman being the author of the Song, whether in whole[20] or in part.[21] Renita J. Weems summarizes well the argumentation of the majority of exegetes when she writes that in this book the emotions and experiences of the beloved and the women of Jerusalem are at the center and this is why the author is probably a woman. There is no evidence, she adds, to support the idea that the Song was not written by a woman.[22]

In any event, this case would not be unique either in Israel or in the Near East. Many Orientalists acknowledge the fact that from the Sumerian to the Neo-Babylonian periods, Near Eastern poetry and prose were often written by women.[23] In Israel, as in the ancient Near

18. Solomon D. Goitein, "Nasim Keyosrot Suge Sifrut Bammiqra'," in *'iyyunim Bammiqra'* (Tel Aviv: Yavneh, 1957) 301–303. The text has been translated and published in English by M. Carasik, "Women as Creator of Biblical Genres," *Prooftexts* 8 (1988) 1–33.

19. Arthur S. Herbert, "The Song of Songs," in *Peake's Commentary on the Bible*, ed. Matthew Black and Harold Henry Rowley (London: Nelson and Sons, 1963) 468–474.

20. See for example André Lacocque, *Subversives: Un pentateuque de femmes* (Paris: Cerf, 1992) 139–140. For Athalya Brenner, *The Song of Songs* (Sheffield: JSOT Press, 1989) 65, 82–83, the editor/compiler could very well be a woman. According to her, passages like 1:2-6; 3:1-4; 5:1-7, 10-16 are so feminine that a man would have had difficulty imitating the tone and texture of these passages.

21. Thus, for instance, Roland E. Murphy, *The Song of Songs*, ed. S. Dean McBride, Jr., (Minneapolis: Fortress Press, 1990) 70; and Alphonse Maillot, "La femme dans l'Ancien Testament," *Foi et Vie* 89 (1990) 44.

22. Renita J. Weems, "Song of Songs," in *The Women's Bible Commentary*, ed. Carol A. Newsom and Sharon H. Ringe (Louisville: Westminster/John Knox Press, 1992) 157.

23. On this subject, see the excellent summary of the research by J. Harris, "The Female 'Sage' in Mesopotamian Literature (with an Appendix on Egypt)," in *The

East, there were women who composed, among other texts, songs and prayers. For instance, P. D. Miller mentions the following texts: Gen 21:16-17; 25:22; 29:35; 30:24; Exod 15:21; Judg 5:1-31; Ruth 1:8-9; 4:14; 1 Sam 1:10, 12-15; 2:1-10; 1 Kgs 10:9; Ps 131.[24] Of course, we should perhaps add the Song of Songs to this list, which is not exhaustive. At least, we are led to think so by the important place the woman occupies in the Song of Songs and by the singular images used to describe her.

Final Remarks

At the end of this brief inquiry, we may state that this ancient text, which many would willingly relegate to museums, offers us an image of woman much more accurate, balanced, and interesting than the rest of the Bible. In this respect, the Song of Songs is not just a singular and exceptional witness within the patriarchal universe of the Bible. As a canonical book, it is also a critique of Scripture. Better still, it unceasingly invites us to autocriticism, and this is why one can only agree with Barbel von Wartenberg-Potter when she writes:

> The feminist movement, intent on the discovery of and emphasis on the traditions favorable to women, would be ill-advised to ignore the biblical tradition: I do not believe that it is less worthy of this research than any other. Patriarchal deformation is omnipresent. Otherwise, we would have to empty our museums, close the concert halls, and burn down the libraries, because they carry a patriarchal culture.[25]

In the end, all that is left to us is to hope that the Song will more and more find place in the liturgy, social imagination, and the anthropological understanding of the relationships between man and woman.

Sage in Israel and the Ancient Near East, ed. John G. Gammie and Leo G. Perdue (Winona Lake, Ind.: Eisenbrauns, 1990) 3–17.

24. Patrick D. Miller, "Things Too Wonderful: Prayers of Women in the Old Testament," in *Biblische und gesellschaftlicher Wandel: Für Norbert Lohfink,* G. Braulick, ed. (Freiburg: Herder, 1993) 237–251.

25. Quoted without reference in A. Geense-Ravenstein, "Qu'est-ce que la théologie féministe?" *Bulletin du Centre Protestant des Études* 42 (1990) 9.

The New Testament in the
Women's Bible Commentary

◆————————————————————————◆

André Myre

Introduction

In order to delineate some ways of looking at the feminist readings of the New Testament, I am using the appropriate sections of a book, published in the United States, entitled *The Women's Bible Commentary*[1] *(WBC)*. The use of a single book—and moreover one quite synthetic in nature—suffers from the disadvantage inherent in any recourse to a limited source of information. However, the number of collaborators (some fifteen for the New Testament), the diversity of their education (Catholic, Jewish, Protestant), and the variety of schools they attended can compensate, up to a point, for this drawback.[2] Therefore, this article will reflect only some readings of the New Testament done by feminists from the United States. But we must recognize that for various reasons, rare are the countries at this time where many women are engaged in a sweeping movement of feminist interpretation of theology and the Bible.

The author of this article is a man. Which should not surprise anyone, for the authors of the *WBC* did not write exclusively for women.

The purpose of this chapter is to present to those who understand French or English or both these feminist New Testament readings, of

1. Carol A. Newsom and Sharon H. Ringe, eds., *The Women's Bible Commentary* (Louisville: Westminster/John Knox, 1992).
2. See the list at the beginning of the four sections of this study. Without wishing to detract from the collaborators' quality and ignore the constraints that bear upon any sort of collective work, we cannot help but be surprised at the absence of personalities as well known as Elisabeth Schüssler Fiorenza and Adela Yarbro Collins.

which they could easily be unaware. We decided to describe these readings at some length so that male and female readers might delve into them and discern their orientations. With the exception of the last pages, readers will find almost no reservations or criticisms in this chapter. The author is not inclined to endorse the whole content of the *WBC*, but he thinks that a systematic criticism—difficult anyhow for this sort of book—would have diverted the readers' attention from his primary objective which is to *make known* this kind of feminist reading of the New Testament. As will be seen from the introduction by Carol A. Newsom and Sharon H. Ringe, the publication of the *WBC* is an important event, and it deserves to be known.

In their introduction (pages xiii to xix), Newsom and Ringe state that although women have been reading the Bible for generations, they have hardly begun to read it consciously *as* women. The Bible has helped in an important way to define women's place in society. But it can be read with profit only if men and women undertake the necessary task. This intuition was already expressed by Frances Willard in 1889:

> We need women commentators to bring out the women's side of the book; we need a stereoscopic view of truth in general, which can only be had when woman's eye and man's eye together shall discern the perspective of the Bible's full-orbed revelation.[3]

However, "so long as women were excluded from both religious offices and educational opportunities, it was difficult for them to enter into the interpretation of the Bible in an authoritative way" (*WBC*, xiii).

Between 1895 and 1898, Elizabeth Cady Stanton with a small group of collaborators produced *The Woman's Bible*,[4] a commentary on the passages of the Bible in which women are mentioned; the misogyny and masculine bias of the biblical text did not escape them. The enterprise remained at a standstill for close to three quarters of a century. However, in the last thirty years or so, much work has been done. Some researchers have sought to find, behind the text, the lived experience of women in biblical times; others have concentrated on passages concerning women. The *WBC* seeks to harvest the fruit of women's biblical research in order to disseminate it widely. The title is a tribute to the work of Stanton. However, the substitution of the plural *women* for the

---

3. Frances E. Willard, *Woman in the Pulpit* (Washington: Zenger Publishing Co., 1978 [© 1889]) 21.

4. Elizabeth Cady Stanton, *The Woman's Bible*, 2 vols. (New York: Arno Press, 1972 [© 1895–1898]).

singular *woman* is meant to show that there is not one single woman's perspective on the Bible, but many different ways of reading it (pp. xiv–xv).

The contributors to the *WBC* come from different traditions and have more or less harmonious relationships with traditional religions. Several join their feminist reading of the Bible to their commitment to social justice. Moreover, they are aware of their North American roots and realize that women from other cultures would feel differently about many things. Finally, for the New Testament as for the rest of the Bible, their commentaries bear upon the portions of the text that explicitly speak of women or are especially relevant to them (pp. xvi–xviii).

After this introduction and just before entering the commentary proper, Ringe treats of hermeneutics in "When Women Interpret the Bible" (pp. 1–9). All through this commentary, women's viewpoints seek to counteract the text itself, in which women are depicted solely from men's viewpoints, absent "as persons working out their own religious journeys." Recent history demonstrates that feminist approaches are many. Some women have a positive approach to the Bible; others see in it an ineradicable misogyny. Still others, African American, Latin American, stress the importance of traditions on Exodus, the prophets, and Jesus himself. In contrast, some deny the very possibility that texts so deeply imbued with patriarchal values could have anything whatsoever to reveal about God or a community in dialogue with God. They go so far as to refuse to read the Bible. The commentary which is the subject of this article is the work of women from the United States who belong to the academic world and their viewpoints must not be generalized.

Ringe's article ends with some remarks on gender and language. The author reminds readers that whereas in Hebrew, Greek, and certain modern languages the nouns have a *grammatical* gender, masculine or feminine, which directs the use of the appropriate pronouns, such is not the case in English, in which most nouns are neuter. The gender of the pronouns attributed to God in English cannot be chosen on a grammatical basis but only on a theological one. As a consequence, many refuse to attribute a gender to God and are content to repeat the word God without using any pronouns. The case of Christ is more complex. For many interpreters, "the idea that women are ultimately dependent on a male for their relationship to God is unacceptable." However, for the author, "theologically, the accent is on the humanity, not the maleness, of the Christ" (p. 8). For women, the work of biblical interpretation is particularly multidimensional and complex.

The *WBC* follows the canonical order for the books of the New Testament. In order to present the characteristics of the commentaries, I shall group the texts differently, trying not to scatter what concerns like books. Ordinarily, I shall omit data such as date, author, authenticity, place of origin, sources, and so on. Most of the time, the writers have adopted in their choices one or the other of the typical conclusions of exegetical researches done in recent decades.

1. The Synoptics and Acts

Matthew	Amy-Jill Levine	pp. 252–262
Mark	Mary Ann Tolbert	pp. 263–274
Luke	Jane Schaberg	pp. 275–292
Acts	Gail R. O'Day	pp. 305–312

One of the characteristics of Matthew's Gospel, according to Levine, is that it "decries various structures that cause social oppression" (p. 252). For instance, it "defines the family unit in terms of mothers and children rather than, as might be expected, fathers" (12:50).[5] And several women assume positive roles without being defined by their relationship to husband, father, or son. They contribute to the life of the Church as do others who are "removed from positions of power" (p. 253). From the very beginning of the Gospel, for instance in the genealogy, Matthew names women who are not part of the traditional domestic arrangements: unmarried, separated, widow, prostitute. Levine goes as far as stating:

> The combination of the originally feminine Spirit and Jesus' lack of a human father . . . indicates the restructuring of the human family: outside of patriarchal models it is not ruled by or even defined by a male head of the house (p. 254).

In chapter 2, Matthew sides with those who are outside the political system, against the political and religious elite of Jerusalem. Afterwards, he defines the role of the father by the model of service exemplified by Joseph rather than by a model of domination. In the following chapter, Matthew stands against those who place their trust in their privileged status with regard to salvation. In the Sermon on the Mount, Jesus addresses the descendants of the slaves of old, who accept to let go of their power. In the texts on adultery and divorce, Matthew's

---

5. The only "father" of whom the Gospel speaks in the context of a new social experiment is the Father in heaven (p. 257).

Gospel prohibits regarding women as sexual objects, and it does not hold them responsible for men's sexual adventures. In chapter 8, Matthew groups together three miracles: the healing of the leper, the centurion's servant, and Peter's mother-in-law. The first one restores full participation in the cult of the Temple; the second announces the entrance of pagans into the Church; and the third "indirectly reveals the Gospel's interest in moving toward a more equal structure" (p. 256).

Not all women are seen in a positive way in Matthew's Gospel, as shown by Herodias and her daughter or the mother of James and John, who wants powerful positions for her sons. For Matthew, anyone, man or woman, who decides to enter secular politics, does so at the expense of his or her social and spiritual salvation. Similarly, in the episode of the ten bridesmaids, it is obvious that even though women are responsible for their own salvation, they lack solidarity among themselves. Besides, the evangelist's male perspective is visible here and there, for instance, in the story of the multiplication of the loaves, where women and children are mentioned as an adjunct to men (p. 258). Here as elsewhere, Matthew reveals that in his church the traditional roles have not been eliminated (p. 261).

But, on balance, Matthew depicts women in a positive manner. They are present all through Jesus' life from his conception and birth to his death and resurrection.

Tolbert's commentary is remarkable chiefly for its introduction. The author begins by presenting the favorable characteristics of women in Mark's Gospel, with a few exceptions: Herodias and her daughter (6:17-29) and possibly the mother of Jesus (mentioned only in 3:31-35, "The True Kindred of Jesus"). It is therefore legitimate to suppose that in the Christian community reflected by this Gospel, there were "strong women leaders and role models" (p. 263). Therefore, it is not impossible that the Gospel's author was a woman (p. 264).

Then, Tolbert sets the Gospel within the Greco-Roman world: flight from the country to the cities, social ills, separation of male and female roles. Given this background, the challenge which the author of Mark's Gospel addresses to the social status quo is surprising (pp. 263–265).

The literary genre is that of the "ancient novel" (p. 265), in which the characters are illustrations of ethical concepts and principles. In this genre, the parables of chapters 4 and 12 are particularly important. All readers recognize themselves in this seed destined for the good soil in order to bear fruit at the risk of their life, security, possessions, reputation. In this Gospel, women especially respond positively (pp. 265–267). The rest of the commentary is devoted to illustrating this.

The most startling commentary is that of Schaberg. It begins with a "Warning" couched in the following terms:

> The Gospel of Luke is an extremely dangerous text, perhaps the most dangerous in the Bible. . . . Even as this Gospel highlights women as included among the followers of Jesus . . . it deftly portrays them as models of subordinate service, excluded from the power center in the movement and from significant responsibilities. Claiming the authority of Jesus, this portrayal is an attempt to legitimate male dominance in the Christianity of the author's time. It was successful. . . . The Gospel attempts . . . [to control] women who practice or aspire to practice a prophetic ministry in the church. One of the strategies of this Gospel is to provide female readers with female characters as role models: prayerful, quiet, grateful women, supportive of male leadership, forgoing the prophetic ministry. The education that the study of Luke offers today involves a conscious critique of this strategy. It is not at all the education Luke had in mind! (p. 275).

This warning is followed by a summary of the Gospel and a source theory. Schaberg insists chiefly on source L, containing material proper to Luke, which speaks a lot about women and comprises traditions according to which women play an important role, even at the level of leadership (pp. 275–277). Then comes a presentation of the characteristics of the Gospel and a few remarks on the questions of date and authorship.

The first part of Schaberg's commentary contains a general analysis of the role of women in Luke. It is true that Luke defends, reassures, and praises women. But he does this in the service of his strategy. If one compares him to the other evangelists, in his Gospel no woman challenges Jesus[6] or initiates a mission to the pagans or has a message to transmit to male disciples. In his Gospel, women are silent (pp. 278–280). Both the Gospel and Acts prove to be strongly androcentric when one makes the breakdown of the passages where men and women are named or treated in an anonymous way or studied from the viewpoint of who speaks and who is spoken to. In Acts only men make decisions in church matters. In the Gospel, women are never called disciples or apostles.[7] Women listen, reflect in silence, never proclaim Jesus as Messiah or Son of God. Present at Pentecost, they receive no mandate. Men receive the task of serving, but the only persons who really do the serving are women and they are never called leaders. Even the parables describe a man's world and circumstances; the parable of the Good Samaritan is a good example of this (pp. 280–282).

6. In Mark's Gospel, for instance, the Syrophoenician woman is the only person who bests Jesus in a debate (p. 269).

7. In Luke's Gospel, the addition of the word "wife" in the list of what the disciple must leave behind (18:29) shows that for the author the disciple is a man (p. 281).

The commentary then turns to five passages. In the infancy narratives, women are fully present, but in their traditional role of mothers, and anyway, the focus of interest is on their sons. It is true that Mary pronounces her admirable Magnificat, a peerless song of liberation sung by the prophet of the poor. But she pronounces it "without an explicit commission to preach," and soon afterwards she is described as a model listener. Her response "is what Luke considers a woman's perfect response to the word of God: obedient trust and self-sacrifice" (p. 285).

The story of Jesus' anointing has been transposed by Luke to the beginning of the Gospel, chapter 7. In Luke, the woman is a sinner, which has for centuries blemished the reputation of Mary Magdalene because her healing is mentioned immediately afterward. Separated from the announcement of Jesus' death, the woman's gesture is no longer that of a prophet whose memory will last forever.

> Given the emphatic nature of Mark 14:9, Luke's editing displays real arrogance. Politically, prophetically, what she has done will *not* be told in memory of her (p. 286).

Immediately after the story of the anointing, in the passage of the women who accompany Jesus, these are "cast in a nonreciprocated role of service or support of the males of the movement" (p. 287). All these women have been cured and show thankfulness, which is never said of the Twelve.

> Luke's depiction of a female-supported, male-led organization has been mirrored down the centuries in many Christian organizations (p. 288).

Luke thus describes [the women as supporting] "a nonegalitarian system that subordinates and exploits them" (p. 288).

In the story of Martha and Mary, the role of service, a technical term applied to eucharistic service, to proclamation, and ecclesial leadership, is devalued in comparison to simple listening to the word. Thus, Luke has the church of his time in mind and contributes to the disappearance of the *diakonia* (ministry) of women (pp. 288–289). Finally, in Luke's last chapters, women fade away almost completely. They vanish into the crowds, their role decreases in comparison with that of men, and their testimony is erased. The faith of the men depends neither on women's testimony nor on the empty tomb. Women's testimony is not essential to Christian faith.

Luke's work has relegated women to the margins of the Christian community and its leadership. According to Schaberg, the "enthusiasm [of women] for Luke-Acts, the most massive work in the New Testament, is enthusiasm for a formidable opponent, not for an ally" (p. 291).

In Acts, according to O'Day,[8] the role of women is restricted because Luke seeks to gain the favor of the imperial authorities—men all. In the episode of the upper room, the male disciples who are present are all named, whereas among the women only Mary, the mother of Jesus, is named; moreover, in the rest of the book, women are very rarely named. The apostolic function is reserved for men. In 16:13, the author briefly mentions a gathering by a river on a sabbath day of a group made up exclusively of women. However, this passage is most evocative:

> This Sabbath gathering suggests that as early as the first century, women believers sought ways to hear their own voices and stories in worship, freed from the dictates of the male-dominated church (p. 308).

At the level of ministries, Luke does not make much room for women. For example, the widows are ministered to by men, but they themselves are not ministering to other widows, as in 1 Timothy 5. In chapter 21, Luke mentions that Philip had four daughters who have the gift of prophecy, but contrary to his relating what men say, he refrains from naming them and reporting the contents of their utterances. Women are marginalized in the Church's early years. In chapter 9, Luke speaks of Tabitha, an important woman in Joppa, the only one to be named disciple in Acts, v. 36, where the feminine word *mathētria* ("female disciple") is used, its only occurrence in the whole of the New Testament. She gave alms and did good works, but for Luke this is not a "service" as is the case for men (6:1-4). In chapter 12, people do not believe Rhoda's words concerning Peter's presence at the door. In Philippi, Lydia plays an important part, but Luke does not attribute to her any leadership role; Paul silences a servant who had a spirit of divination but does not worry about her conversion; for Luke she is unimportant. In Acts 18, it is obvious that Priscilla and Aquila were missionaries and teachers, but Luke never gives them such titles.

From reading Acts, one sees clearly that women played an important role in the Church in its early beginnings. It depended on the largess of women, especially widows. And it is noteworthy that in Acts all the women who are named were wealthy with the exception of Mary and Rhoda. The anonymous ones were poor. But Luke does not really do justice to women, wealthy or poor, to avoid anything "embarrassing or threatening to men in the Roman Empire" (p. 312).

8. One is hard put to understand this change—unexplained in any case—of commentator for Acts.

2. The Pauline Literature

The letters deemed indisputable (Johnson, p. 338) are treated by Gaventa, Bassler, Osiek, and Perkins; the others, by Johnson, Dewey and D'Angelo.

In commenting on Romans, Gaventa wants to help women read the letter by making them see that they too participate in the human condition of rebellion against God (p. 316). They should not be put off by terms like circumcision and uncircumcision (which signify belonging or not belonging to the Jewish people) and man (which means human being). Gaventa insists especially on the list of chapter 16, which comprises many women. All of these women are involved in ministries, a fact that must be taken into account in every evaluation of women's roles in early Christianity.

In her commentary on the letters to the Corinthians, Bassler thinks that women must have played a major role since they asked Paul questions on sexuality (note the use of the word "sister" in 1 Cor 7:15). In his answers, Paul insists on the mutuality of sexual relations, which is exceptional for a man of his time. On the other hand, he seems to have taken a dim view of marriage, probably because, believing the end was near, he could see little reason for marrying. It is also remarkable that Paul invites women to remain unmarried; it is a striking innovation opening the way to the social independence of women. Perhaps the mention of the woman first in the discussion on divorce is an indication that the pressure in favor of it came principally from women who were seeking "freedom on a social level commensurate with their freedom in Christ" (pp. 322–324).

It is unfortunate that Paul is not always consistent in the way he looks at women, for instance, in the famous passage, 11:1-16, where his argumentation is "inarticulate, incomprehensible, and inconsistent" (p. 327). We must note however that he recognizes the right of women to pray and prophesy in church. But what shall we do with the famous "silence" of chapter 14? It is probably a marginal gloss introduced into the text at a late date.[9]

For Osiek, the salutation of Galatians shows that women were marginal and did not need to have a letter addressed to them. In his text, Paul speaks a great deal about filiation, sons, and heirs. We must remember that at the time, daughters did not have the same right of inheritance as the firstborn son. But according to Paul, women have the juridical status of sons before God and are heirs of eternal life.

The renowned text of Galatians 3:28, "There is no longer . . . male and female . . ." receives five different interpretations, but Osiek does not choose among them. Speaking of God the Father in 4:4-7, she declares that to call God "Mother" arouses as many reactions, positive or negative, as the appellation of "Father" did before. When commenting on the text in which Paul speaks of his birth pangs, she says, "Perhaps a man willing to use such an image is not as alienated from women's experience as Paul is often made out to be" (p. 336). Finally, when Paul in his final advice offers a series of values which customarily are considered feminine ideals (patience, kindness, meekness, and so on) perhaps he may be doing "something quite radical: he is holding up traditionally feminine values as ideals for everyone, male and female (p. 337).

In her introduction to Philippians, Perkins regrets that Paul often uses images which speak only of male experience in a letter addressed to a church in whose foundation women played an important role. For instance, the exhortation to suffer like Christ has frequently served to justify women's oppression by their husbands or masters (p. 344). Elsewhere in contrast, the church in Thessalonica seems to have been too poor for wealthy women to have any influence in it. And in a sarcastic comment Perkins says:

> It may be the sudden death of male members of the community that has led to the questions about the dead. Women were too constantly victims of early death in childbirth for their fate to cause much comment (p. 350).

Finally, because in his letter to Philemon Paul speaks of Onesimus as his child and his heart and asks Philemon to treat him as a brother, Perkins remarks:

9. On this point, see the study of Michel Gourgues in the present book.

This example demonstrates the need for new patterns of naming as the basis for changing deeply ingrained patterns of domination. Women struggle with this problem today as racist and sexist stereotypes make it difficult to see "the other" as a "beloved sister or brother" (p. 363).

In commenting on Ephesians, Johnson dwells especially on the precepts for family life at the end of the letter. These codes of behavior, not attested in the first Christian generation, all come from Pauline circles:

This is probably because Paul's own proclamation of freedom to women and slaves, combined with his emphatic concern for individual Christian communities (that is house-churches) created significant friction for succeeding generations (p. 340).

Nowadays, one relies on values anchored in Jewish and pagan philosophies. The letter's author bases the marriage institution, not on the social order, but on the order of creation. Creation is reflected in the Church and the Church in the family. "The result for women is thus a retreat from the initial freedom promised them in Paul's preaching and a reassertion of conventional patriarchal morality" (p. 341).

Similarly, Johnson centers her commentary on Colossians on the precepts concerning family life in chapter 3. Christians are watched by the people around them and they must avoid provoking hostility by disrupting traditional social structures. So the spiritual and social equality of the beginnings becomes a cultural liability. The challenge addressed to social structures, characteristic of the earliest Pauline communities, weakens. The familial order is no longer distinguishable from the cultural order. The freedom of the gospel yields to the fear of disregarding social structures (pp. 347–348).

In the pastoral letters, according to Dewey, the writer strives to control women's behavior. A conservative, he prescribes that one should obey the state and that the familial order should reflect that of the Empire. He writes in deliberate opposition to the Paul of old. One must adapt to the values of the surrounding culture and not make any waves. He disapproves of the traditional conduct of women in Pauline communities (1 Tim 2:8-15). They no longer have the right to pray or teach in public. They must be subject to their husbands, and thus the order of the new creation is made subject to that of the old. Women will be saved by motherhood (2:15). We are far from Paul, who advocated celibacy for women! Moreover, whereas in the past some women ministered to widows without being under the authority of a husband, the author wants only "real widows" (5:3), no longer Christian ministers but only women in need. He forbids young widows to go from house to house spreading the word of Christ. To your homes, all of you, under the men's firm rule!

As for the author of Titus, he desires to see the older women teaching the younger ones to love their husbands and children and to be submissive to their husbands (2:1-10). He makes use of women to lead others to interiorize their inferior status and confine their activities to the house. He is constantly preoccupied with controlling the behavior of persons in lower positions. He is ready to sacrifice the freedom in Christ not to antagonize the pagans (2:9).

Finally, in Hebrews, D'Angelo finds little that pertains to women. At the most, one can underline the inconsistency of the churches with their "reinstitution of priestly classes," despite the reinterpretation of the priesthood, a theme to which the author devotes much of his letter (p. 367).

3. The Johannine Literature

John	Gail R. O'Day	pp. 293–304
1–2–3 John	Gail R. O'Day	pp. 374–375
Revelation	Susan R. Garrett	pp. 377–382

According to O'Day, women play a significant role in the Gospel of John. The beginning of Jesus' ministry is due to his mother's urging. In the course of his conversation with the Samaritan woman, Jesus breaks down the barriers separating men and women. Unfortunately, the traditional commentators do not do justice to this woman; they insist on her so-called immorality whereas she shows a singular faith in Jesus and is the first person in the Gospel who has a serious theological conversation with him (p. 296).[10] This woman was a witness who drew her fellow citizens to have their own experience of faith.

In the passage on the adulterous woman, whatever its origin, Jesus deals in the same way with scribe, Pharisee, and woman. The scribes treat her as an object of discussion, but Jesus regards her as a human being equal to others. In chapter 11, the conversation between Martha and Jesus is the theological center of the story of the raising of Lazarus. In the next chapter, the anointing of Jesus by Mary shows that one can love both Jesus and the poor and is an anticipation of the washing of the feet, a participation in the life of discipleship and in the death of Jesus: "Mary is the first person in John's Gospel to live out Jesus' love

10. And Nicodemus in chapter 3?

commandment" (p. 300). At the cross, the mother of Jesus represents his historical life, and the disciple, the Johannine community. At Jesus' death, the continuity between past and future is insured. Finally, on Easter morning, Mary Magdalene is the first disciple of the Risen One.

Several themes in John's Gospel pertain to women. The language of love, the metaphor of the vine, which negates individualism and at the least is nonhierarchical: "There is no bishop branch, elder branch, or church bureaucrat branch with special status in this vine" (p. 303). Even the language on God the Father is essentially relational, "language of intimacy, relationship, and family" (p. 304). The insistence of the church on the "maleness" of this language is a distortion of what it means in John's Gospel.

In the Johannine letters, the first one in particular, the language is quite familial and the accent is placed on the humanity and body of Jesus. This was probably a reaction against Gnosticism with its opposition between body and spirit and its identification of women with the inferior and evil body. The author combats this dualism and affirms "the corporeality of the Christian faith" (p. 375).

In Revelation, the feminine imagery is very important, in particular in the symbols concerning the new Jerusalem, Babylon, and the woman clad with the sun. However, as Garret points out:

> Each of these symbols reflects the male-centered culture of the first century: women are caricatured as virgins, whores, or mothers (p. 377).

This culture set a high value on the control and management of women's sexuality by men. The writer's language is troubling and dangerous. For him, women are thoroughly good or thoroughly bad. The good ones' sexuality is controlled by men; the bad ones' sexuality escapes male manipulation.

4. Other Writings

James	Sharyn Dowd	pp. 368–369
1–2 Peter	Sharyn Dowd	pp. 370–373
Jude	Sharyn Dowd	p. 376

It is especially the first letter of Peter which interests women. In Asia Minor, Christians risk being seen as a counterculture threatening society; for instance, women worship a God different from the one of their husbands or masters. The author seeks both to safeguard Christian identity and to reassure the surrounding society. In his exhortations to married women and women slaves, he insists that they should submit to the social order in obedience to their husbands or masters, but without adopting this order in its entirety since he directs them to remain steadfast in their faith.

This letter poses two questions to the modern reader: the question of the connection between Christian conduct and cultural values and the question of the appeal to remain passive when faced by unjust suffering. Women have been too harmed by these appeals, which were given at a time when there was no other option, for them to still be taken at face value in our day (pp. 370–371).

Two articles close the book, that of Deirdre J. Good, "Early Extracanonical Writings" (pp. 383–389) and that of Amy L. Wordelman, "Everyday Life: Women in the Period of the Old Testament" (pp. 290–396).

Reflections

There is much to learn in this book; however, it does raise some questions.

1. It is obvious that, from the viewpoint of quality, the *WBC* would have nothing to envy in a work with a similar purpose written by men. The women's exegetical commentaries are serious, well informed, and based on results tested for several decades. Of course, because of their North American roots, they reflect a Western perception of the New Testament. And as is the case with the reading of any exegetical study, even the best, there would be many particular points to evaluate and criticize. For instance, the authors of the commentary have only a negative view of power, which for them is synonymous with oppression. There is a certain danger in this idea. Power exists everywhere, and it is inappropriate to ignore it or unconsciously exercise it. Besides, these women, intellectual and belonging to university circles, are not without power.

2. The contents of this book obliges men to confess that their exegesis is not universal. It reflects their prejudices, their unconscious acceptance of a world which in large part they have fashioned in their image, and their inability to see reality with eyes other than their own. Women discover in the Bible realities that men had never noticed and show them to what point their exegesis was limited and conditioned by their masculine approach to reality. Therefore, the reading of this book nec-

essarily leads men to relativize their methods of studying the Bible and calls them to open themselves to other perspectives. One may expect a considerable enrichment of exegesis in the future, which will have to reflect the viewpoints of both men and women. Theology and spirituality will necessarily be affected, without speaking of the ecclesial institution itself. The repercussions of these new readings are absolutely incalculable.

3. These commentaries are a very important cultural and ecclesial revealer. The acuity of their critical scrutiny of the New Testament enables us to glimpse how far women have distanced themselves from their traditional (prefeminist) culture and from that of their churches. Now, it is important to note that the *WBC* was written, not by *one* woman, but by *a number of* women who represent many others as is seen by the titles they cite in their bibliographies. What we have here is a women's movement. North American society has become aware of it to a certain extent, but this cannot be said of all churches, far from it.

4. We cannot read the Bible as these women do unless we have had the experience of an elsewhere which gives another viewpoint on reality. When we reach this elsewhere, there is no turning back. For instance, women have been obliged to learn how to read the Bible by starting from their own selves, to discover the partiality not only of the prefeminist exegesis but also of the Bible itself, which conceals women's perception of both reality and God. There is a word of God to women, spoken millenniums ago, a word which has not yet been heard, a word to which the men who wrote the Bible have not really given testimony. This silence is momentous. It will force a radical reevaluation of concepts such as final word, completed revelation, definitive expressions of the faith, and so on. But one is enabled to pose those questions only if one has travelled elsewhere, far from the place where one was before, when one could not see them because one was prisoner of a certain mindset which was taken for granted and therefore could not be questioned. But having experienced an elsewhere which overturns the reading of reality one was used to and impels one into new paths, one cannot stay put.

5. This is why the movement of women exegetes is so important. It demonstrates that cultures as well as churches will never again be dominated and controlled by men. We are in the midst of a transition to another age of humanity. This does not mean that nothing good has happened up to now. Plato, Jesus, Thomas Aquinas will always remain great lights for humankind, on which their works have left their indelible

mark. But the women's movement powerfully contributes to the revelation of their cultural and religious limitations. Indeed, the very foundations of culture and faith will have to be radically reinterpreted in the years, even the centuries to come.

6. As it is, women's exegesis already poses some quite troubling questions. Here are a few examples. Women's understanding of the New Testament books is diametrically opposed to the traditional reading. The latter sees a continuous progress in the course of the history of the Church: Christological evolution, deepening of theological knowledge, strengthening of the ecclesial institution, commitment of witnesses to the point of martyrdom. The path traced by women's reading goes in the opposite direction. As a general rule, the lot of women goes from bad to worse with the passage of time. The liberation brought by Jesus, expressed up to a point in the undisputed letters of Paul, then Mark, Matthew, and John, is lost to the fear of social anticonformism in Luke's Gospel and Acts, the letters to the Ephesians and Colossians, Timothy and Titus, as well as in the first letter of Peter and Revelation.

The conflict of interpretation is a major one and raises numerous problems. Christological problem: How does one account for the oneness of Jesus and Christ if the latter can reverse the liberating direction of the former and set the Church back on the road of oppression of women? Hermeneutical problem: How does one criticize New Testament writers, such as Luke and the author of the pastorals, for their failure to oppose the cultural pressures of their time when the exegetes of the United States reach their opposite conclusions precisely because they adopt the culture and questioning attitudes of the women of their own society? What is the justification for a critical reading, begun under the pressures of enormous cultural change, to prevail over the obvious meaning of the texts? Institutional problem: If locally there is radical inculturation of the faith, how will the fundamental unity of believers be recognized? Beautiful and unavoidable debates are in store.

It is perhaps not by chance that such questions have been raised in a country made in large part by its history one of the crucibles of humanity. But we must hope that many societies may evolve in such a way that they too may produce the equivalent of the *WBC*.

Three Approaches to the Position of Women in the Q Document: Hal Taussig, Luise Schottroff, and Amy-Jill Levine

◆────────────────────────────────────◆

Jean-François Racine

Introduction

The research into the social milieu where the Jesus movement originated gives great importance to the Q document, understood as one of
the first documents produced by this movement and in all likelihood
one source of the Gospels of Matthew and Luke.[1] Two models of social
milieu have been proposed, one by Gerd Theissen and the other by
Burton L. Mack.[2] Theissen's model can be summarized as follows: The

---

1. In accordance with the system adopted by the International Q Project (henceforth IPQ), the passages of Q are quoted in the order they appear in Luke's Gospel.
This in no way implies a preference for Luke as to the original formulation. [The
quotations from Q are taken from Burton L. Mack, *The Lost Gospel: The Book of Q and
Christian Origins* (New York: Harper-Collins, 1993). The numbering of the Q seg-
ments in Mack's text are given in square brackets after the author's references for Q,
which follow the Lucan parallels as given in John S. Kloppenborg, *Q Parallels: Syn-
opsis, Critical Notes, and Concordance* (Sonoma, Calif.: Polebridge Press, 1988). Ed.]

2. Gerd Theissen, *Le christianisme de Jésus: Ses origines sociales en Palestine*, trans.
B. Lauret, Relais Desclée 6 (Paris: Desclée, 1978); Burton L. Mack, "The Kingdom
That Didn't Come: A Social History of the Q Tradents," in *Society of Biblical Literature
Seminar Papers*, vol. 27 (Missoula, Mont.: Scholars Press, 1988) 608–635. It must be
noted that Theissen does not use only Q to develop his model. Nevertheless, one
cannot deny that certain passages from the Q document occupy an important place
in this model, in particular the instructions on the mission (Q 10:2-12) [QS 20-21], on
family ties (Q 9:60) [QS 19], and on the rejection of reprisals (Q 6:27-36) [QS 9-10]. As
for Mack, his reconstruction is based on the studies of Kloppenborg devoted to the
literary genre of the document. See John S. Kloppenborg, *The Formation of Q: Trajec-
tories in Ancient Wisdom Collections,* Studies in Antiquity and Christianity (Philadelphia: Fortress Press, 1987).

members of the movement are divided into two overall categories. The first one is made up of itinerant charismatics, without home, money, or family, who announce the *eschaton,* equivalent to the advent of the reign of God. The second is made up of sympathizers in the local communities; these are sedentary. They listen to the itinerant preachers and assure them of shelter and food.

Mack's model is vastly different. He discerns at least two different forms of the social milieu of the Jesus movement, corresponding to the strata of the Q document identified by John S. Kloppenborg. The first stratum of the Q document (Q1) belongs to the *instruction* genre of the *sapiential* type. There are six discourses: Q 6:20b-49; 9:57-62 and 10:2-16, 21-24; 11:2-4, 9-13; 12:2-12; 12:22-34; 13:24-30 [QS 7-14; 19-25; 26-27; 35-37; 39-40; 47-48]. This stratum reflects a social configuration in which the Q community is made up of small groups meeting in houses, so that we can speak of a true social network being formed as new contacts are established. At this first stage of the movement, prophetic language is used very little or not at all. The theme discussed at these meetings is not so much an appeal to repentance as an explanation of the new lifestyle. The second stage (Q2) is akin to the *chriae* genre (for instance, *Lives and Opinions of Famous Philosophers* by Diogenes Laertius) of the *prophetic* type. The material of this second stratum is blended with sapiential instructions. This stratum reflects social circumstances in which the members of the Q community have met with opposition and rejection on the part of their fellow citizens upon whom they invoke God's judgment. The third stratum (Q3) is essentially constituted by the story of the temptation Q 4:10-13 [QS 6]. In this stratum, the document takes on the character of a *bios* ("life"), that is, biographical, genre. This addition aims at showing the moral fiber of the hero, Jesus in this case. The social milieu reflected by the third stratum has not yet been explored. However it is noteworthy that the document is hellenized by the creation of the Jesus myth.[3]

3. The stratification of the Q document proposed by Kloppenborg has been criticized among others by Richard A. Horsley, "Questions about Redactional Strata and the Social Relations Reflected in Q," in *Society of Biblical Literature Seminar Papers,* vol. 28 (Missoula, Mont.: Scholars Press, 1989) 186–203; John S. Kloppenborg, "Logoi Prophētōn? Reflections on the Genre of Q," in *The Future of Early Christianity: Essays in Honor of Helmut Koester,* ed. Birger A. Pearson, George W. E. Nickelsburg, and Norman R. Petersen (Minneapolis: Fortress Press, 1991) 195–209; Richard A. Horsley, "Wisdom Justified by All Her Children: Examining Allegedly Disparate Traditions in Q," in *Society of Biblical Literature Seminar Papers,* vol. 33 (Missoula, Mont.: Scholars Press, 1994) 733–751. In this article, Horsley claims that Kloppenborg has established the stratigraphy of the Q document on the basis of an erroneous dichotomy between the sapiential and apocalyptic genres. This dichotomy would be used by

One common point of the models describing the social milieu of the Jesus movement, and hence of the Q community, is that they insist on the countercultural character of the movement. However, little research has been done on the way this countercultural aspect may have been expressed in the life of half its potential adherents, the women. Hal Taussig, Luise Schottroff, and Amy-Jill Levine have separately studied the condition of women which the Q document reveals. Their conclusions are rather different if one takes into account the ways in which each one envisions the social development of the Q community, the importance each one gives to certain passages of the document, and their personal theological concerns. I propose to summarize these three approaches and to evaluate them from a methodological viewpoint. When this is done, I shall identify certain directions which to me hold more promise for a feminist approach to the Q document.

1. Hal Taussig

Taussig's purpose is twofold.[4] On the one hand, he wants to explore the question of Sophia as mother-goddess of Jesus, and on the other, he wants to demonstrate that in all likelihood women were present among

---

numerous specialists of the New Testament literature for cataloguing purposes (Horsley, "Wisdom," 733–735). However, when reading Kloppenborg, one notes that he establishes his stratigraphy principally according to literary criteria. These strata are called "sapiential" or "prophetic" only after they have been identified. On this point, see Kloppenborg, *Formation of Q*, 98–99; and especially, by the same author, "Formative and Redactional Layers in Q," paper presented at the 123rd Annual Congress of the Society of Biblical Literature in Boston, December 5–8, 1987, p. 19. Kloppenborg recognizes that the qualifiers "sapiential" and "prophetic" are imperfect; they indicate only a relative proximity of the redactional strata to sapiential literature and prophetic literature. On this last point, see John S. Kloppenborg, "The Formation of Q Revisited: A Response to Richard A. Horsley," in *Society of Biblical Literature Seminar Papers*, vol. 28 (Missoula, Mont.: Scholars Press, 1989) 210. One will also note that Kloppenborg is more prudent than Mack in the way he qualifies the literary strata. He appears to be reluctant to use the qualifier *apocalyptic* to describe the language of the second stratum and prefers to speak of symbolic eschatology. On this point, see John S. Kloppenborg, "Symbolic Eschatology and the Apocalypticism of Q," *Harvard Theological Review* 80 (1987) 287–306. For a summary of the different positions concerning the apocalyptic character of Q, see Arland D. Jacobson, "Apocalyptic and the Synoptic Sayings, Source Q," in *The Four Gospels, 1992*, 3 vols., Festschrift Frans Neirynck, ed. Frans van Segbroeck and others, Bibliotheca Ephemeridum theologicarum Lovaniensium 100 (Leuven: Leuven University/Uitgeverij Peeters, 1992) 1:403–421.

4. Hal Taussig, "Sophia's Children in Q," a paper presented at the 124th Annual Congress of the Society of Biblical Literature in Chicago, November 19–22, 1988.

the disciples of the Jesus movement. These two aspects of the project are complementary since the existence of a Sophialogy in Q could supply clues to the role of women in the community. In order to realize his plan, Taussig has recourse to the analogy existing between the Cynic movement and the Jesus movement.

Women and Sophialogy

Let us begin with Sophialogy. Jack Suggs' work has shown how Jesus and John the Baptist could be seen as the last of a long series of Sophia's messengers, especially on the basis of the exegesis of Q 7:33-35 [QS 18] (Matt 11:18-19).[5] James Robinson has even maintained that in Q, Jesus sees himself as the child or the messenger of Sophia.[6] Elisabeth Schüssler Fiorenza has followed this lead, stating that Q presents Jesus as the messenger of a God recently discovered as Wisdom, calling her disciples to form communities of equals. Taussig dwells at length on one of the corollaries of Schüssler Fiorenza's thesis, that is, the connection between the feminine gender of Sophia and the presence of women in the Jesus movement.[7]

Nevertheless, Taussig reproaches Schüssler Fiorenza with having put forward few arguments to justify the connection between Sophia

5. Jack M. Suggs, *Wisdom, Christology, and Law in Matthew's Gospel* (Cambridge, Mass.: Harvard University Press, 1970).

6. James M. Robinson, "Jesus as Sophos and Sophia," in *Aspects of Wisdom in Judaism and Early Christianity,* ed. Robert L. Wilken, (Notre-Dame, Ind.: University of Notre-Dame Press, 1975) 12.

7. Elisabeth Schüssler Fiorenza, *In Memory of Her: A Feminist Theological Reconstruction of Christian Origins* (New York: Crossroad, 1983). The two following quotations briefly sum up Schüssler Fiorenza's thought on the Jesus movement as a community of equal disciples in which there are women: "To sum up, the Palestinian Jesus movement understands the ministry and mission of Jesus as that of the prophet and child of Sophia sent to announce that God is the God of the poor and heavy laden, of the outcasts and those who suffer injustice. As child of Sophia he stands in a long line and succession of prophets sent to gather the children of Israel to their gracious Sophia-God. Jesus' execution, like John's, results from his mission and commitment as prophet and emissary of the Sophia-God who holds open a future for the poor and outcast and offers God's gracious goodness to *all* children of Israel without exception" (p. 135). "In the discipleship of equals, the 'role' of women is not peripheral or trivial, but at the center, and thus of utmost importance to the praxis of 'solidarity from below'" (p. 152). In his study, "Feminine Wisdom in Q?" in *Women in the Biblical Tradition,* ed. George J. Brooke, Studies in Women and Religion 31 (Lewiston, N.Y.: E. Mellen Press, 1992) 112–128, Taussig has brought into question the exclusive character of the figure of *Sophia* by quoting Philo, *Fuga* 48–52, where Sophia is treated as a masculine figure.

and the existence of a community of equal members. He intends to correct this deficiency.

The Cynic Movement, Women, and Q

The first thing Taussig wants to do is gather a few arguments in favor of the presence of women in the Q group. To this end, he bases his arguments on the analogy between the Q group and the Cynic movement. Indeed, certain writings mention women having adopted this mode of life.[8] The studies of Leif E. Vaage, Mack, and Francis G. Downing among others have underlined the similarity between Cynic literature and the Q document, which is an incentive for postulating a kinship between the two movements.[9] The hellenization of Galilee in the first

---

8. "I admire you for your eagerness in that, although you are a woman, you yearned for philosophy and have become one of our school, which has struck even men with awe for its austerity. But be earnest to bring to a finish what you have begun. And you will cap it off, I am sure, if you should not be outstripped by your husband, and if you frequently write to me, your benefactor in philosophy. For letters are worth a great deal and are not inferior to conversation with people actually present." Pseudo-Diogenes 3, *Letter to Hipparchia*, in *The Cynic Epistles: A Study Edition*, ed. Abraham J. Malherbe (Missoula, Mont.: Scholars Press, 1977) 95.

"You did well when you changed the name of the city and, instead of Maroneia, called it Hipparchia, its present name, since it is better for you to be named after Hipparchia, a woman, it's true, but a philosopher, than after Maron, a man who sells wine." Pseudo-Diogenes 43, *Letter to the Maroneans*, in *The Cynic Epistles*, 173.

"Hipparchia, the sister of Metrocles, was also captivated by the teachings [of the Cynics]. Both were natives of Maroneia. She developed a passionate attraction for Crates' teachings and lifestyle and paid no attention whatsoever to her suitors, their wealth, their nobility, or their beauty. Crates was everything for her. She even threatened her parents with commiting suicide if she was not allowed to marry Crates. Her relatives implored Crates to talk her out of her decision; Crates did everything he could, but, in the end, unable to dissuade her, he stripped himself of his clothes in front of her and said, 'Here is your husband-to-be and all his possessions; take your decision accordingly, because you cannot be my mate unless you adopt also my mode of life.' The young woman chose, and taking the same costume as he had done, she began to go about with Crates, to live with him [or: to make love to him] in public, and to accompany him to the meals." Diogenes Laertius, 6.96-97, in *Les Cyniques grecs: Fragments et témoignages*, 2nd ed., ed. Leonce Paquet, Philosophica 35 (Ottawa: University of Ottawa, 2nd ed. 1988) 113–114.

9. Taussig, in "Sophia's Children," 4, mentions the work of Kloppenborg, *The Formation of Q*, pp. 310–315; 324–325; Leif E. Vaage, "Q: The Ethos and Ethics of an Itinerant Intelligence" (Ph. D. diss., Claremont Graduate School, 1987); and Burton L. Mack, *A Myth of Innocence: Mark and Christian Origins* (Philadelphia: Fortress Press, 1988) 53–77; Mack, "Kingdom That Didn't Come," 608–635. We can add to this list the

century reinforces the possibility that the Cynic movement influenced the Jesus movement. Given the parallelism of the two movements, the presence of women in the Cynic movement leads Taussig to regard as likely the presence of women in the Jesus movement. However, he admits that there is in the Q document no trace of women having occupied preeminent positions.[10] In fact, some of the allusions to women in Q show them either engaged in domestic tasks, such as the making of bread (Q 13:20) [QS 46], or in maternal cares, attested by the mention of John the Baptist as born of a woman (Q 7:28) [QS 17].[11]

The social model proposed by Gerd Theissen would confirm this state of affairs since, implicitly, the first category of followers gathered men and the second could include women.[12] In contrast, the model offered by Kloppenborg and Mack reconciles the two functions of announcing the reign and seeing to the material support of the community since in such a model these two functions may be discharged by the same persons establishing a social network through contacts between houses. As Taussig remarks, this last model potentially grants a greater role to women in the expansion of the movement at the first stage of its existence reflected by Q1.

A Cynic Sophia as Mirror of Women's Condition

The figure of Sophia appears in the second stratum of document Q (Q2). From the model proposed by Kloppenborg and Mack, this stratum would correspond to a phase dominated by conflicts between the members of the Jesus movement and their fellow citizens. Taussig speculates whether the figure of Sophia which appears in Q2 resembles the figure of a Cynic woman.[13] The answer is yes because Taussig holds that the two experience contempt and rejection. As a proof, Taussig adduces Q 11:49-51 [QS 34]:

> For this reason the wisdom of God said, "I will send them prophets and wise men, some of whom they will kill and persecute," in order to hold

work of Francis G. Downing, especially, *Christ and the Cynics: Jesus and Other Radical Preachers in First-Century Tradition,* 2nd ed., JSOT Manuals 4 (Sheffield, England: JSOT Press, 1993).

10. Taussig, "Sophia's Children," 10.

11. Ibid., 3. Taussig does not consider the allusion to the Queen of the South (Q 11:31), which represents a woman engaged neither in domestic work nor in a mother's duties nor in any family situation.

12. Schüssler Fiorenza, *In Memory of Her,* 146–151.

13. Taussig, "Sophia's Children," 11: "Does Sophia in Q look like a woman Cynic?"

> this generation accountable for the blood of all the prophets shed from the foundation of the world, from the blood of Abel to the blood of Zechariah who perished between the altar and the sanctuary. Truly, I tell you, this generation will be held accountable.[14]

He also adduces Q 13:34 [QS 49]:

> O Jerusalem, Jerusalem, killing the prophets and stoning those who are sent to you! How often would I have gathered your children together as a hen gathers her brood under her wings, and you refused.

Taussig endorses the theory of Claudia Camp according to which the portrait of Sophia is a mirror of women's situation.[15] Therefore, he postulates that the rejection suffered by Sophia reflects that suffered by the members of the Jesus movement and could possibly allude to the participation of women in the movement.

However, Taussig hesitates to describe the Q community as a community of equal disciples for lack of evidence supporting the presence of women in the Q document and because of the paucity of data gleaned in the Cynic literature. However, the mere fact of being able to reconstruct such a community through a coherent social model could be an indication of the important role played by women in the Jesus movement.[16]

Evaluation of Taussig's Approach

The merit of Taussig's research is to have detected the potential of the model offered by Kloppenborg and Mack for exploring women's role in the Q community. Indeed, it is incontestable that women occupied an important place in domestic life. A model of expansion of the movement based on a network of social relationships between houses cannot fail to grant them a role in the expansion of the Q community.

The analogy with Cynic women proves to be accessory and could even weaken the argument. Thus, the small number of references to Cynic women and the fact that they mention only Hipparchia limits the

---

14. In Q 11:49 [QS 34], the text of Matthew (23:34) does not say that it is Wisdom who is speaking. One must note that the IQP has also chosen Luke's formulation as most probably reproducing the original text of Q. See M. C. Moreland and James M. Robinson, "The International Q Project: Work Sessions 6–8 August, 18–19 November, 1993," *Journal of Biblical Literature* 113 (1994) 498.

15. Claudia Camp, *Wisdom and the Feminine in the Book of Proverbs,* Bible and Literature Series 11 (Decatur, Ga.: Almond Press, 1985).

16. Taussig, "Sophia's Children," 13–14.

effectiveness of this analogy. Moreover, it is sometimes very difficult to date Cynic writings so that one cannot really know whether the quoted passages reflect the Cynicism of the fourth century B.C.E. (when the movement arose) or that of the third century C.E. (that is, the probable time when Diogenes Laertius compiled his work).[17] In truth, even if the Cynicism of the first century strongly resembles the Jesus movement, the place occupied by women is perhaps insufficiently documented to prove useful for an exploration of their role in the Q community. Besides, despite numerous similarities between the two movements, differences remain concerning not only their general orientation but also their lifestyle. The concept of the reign of God, on which the whole Jesus movement rests, has no equivalent among the Cynics. The two movements differ also in the description of the dress of their members.[18] In fact, it is far from proven that all the elements of the Cynic movement find their parallels in the Jesus movement.

If the rejection of the figure Sophia in Q can reflect the rejection endured by the members of the Jesus movement at the hands of their fellow citizens, nothing indicates that the rejection of Sophia alludes more specifically to the rejection of the women who were part of the movement. So if one examines Taussig's demonstration, the comparison between the rejection and contempt suffered by Sophia and Cynic women has no foundation since nothing indicates that Cynic women ever met with contempt and rejection. Moreover, we have seen that the parallelism with Cynicism does not deserve serious consideration when it comes to the description and ethos of the members of the Jesus movement. Therefore, by using the figure of Sophia and parallelism with Cynicism, Taussig does not succeed in strengthening Schüssler Fiorenza's description of the origins of Christianity as a community of equal disciples. When these two elements are eliminated, nothing much remains of Taussig's theories. Nevertheless, we believe that his work is of interest because it enables us to make explicit the feminist

---

17. Robert Genaille in his introduction to Diogenes Laertius, *Vie, doctrines et sentences des philosophes illustres,* 2 vols., trans. and ed. Robert Genaille, Texte integral 56, 77 (Paris: Garnier-Flammarion, 1965) 1:5, states that it is not possible to know exactly when Diogenes Laertius lived. One must place his dates between 200 and 500 C.E. Genaille chooses as the most probable the beginning of the third century. But the Cynic letters seem to have been written during the imperial period, up to the third century. On this point, see Marie-Odile Goulet-Cazé, "Le cynisme à l'époque impériale," in *Aufstieg und Niedergang der Römischer Welt: Geschichte und Kultur Roms im Spiegel der neueren Forschung,* vol. 36, pt. 4 (New York: DeGruyter, n.d.) 2805.

18. For a more complete description of the differences between Q and the Cynic writings, see Christopher M. Tuckett, "A Cynic Q?" *Biblica* 70 (1989) 349–376.

potential contained in the model of expansion of the Jesus movement which Kloppenborg and Mack present.

2. Luise Schottroff

Like Taussig's article, Schottroff's book pursues two complementary directions.[19] On the one hand, she finds in Q traces of women's participation in the community. On the other, she seeks to demonstrate that one of the major interests of the document is to include women in its readership. However, these characteristics of Q do not change its fundamentally androcentric nature.

Q: An Androcentric Document

Apart from the Queen of the South (Q 11:31) [QS 32], the women mentioned in Q belong to the domestic class (wheat grinding, Q 17:35 [QS 60]; bread making, Q 13:20-21 [QS 47]). They are the object of transaction, either in marriage (Q 16:18; 17:27 [QS 56; 60]) or in divorce (Q 16:18 [QS 56]). The family conflicts spoken of in Q happen especially between sons and their fathers (Q 9:59-60 [QS 19]). In spite of the important role of women in domestic tasks, notably in food preparation, it is the father who distributes this food: bread (or egg) and fish (Q 11:11-12 [QS 27]).

Q and Patriarchal Structure

For all its androcentric perspective, Q challenges the patriarchal structure. Schottroff detects several signs of this contestation, including Q 17:26-27 [QS 60], which seems to explain the punishment of the flood by the persistence of this structure, summarized by the routine of eating, drinking, and getting married with all the arrangements attendant upon marriage. The "instruction" on divorce also runs counter to the patriarchal structure since in Q 16:18 [QS 56], divorce is considered a fact which Jesus does not seek to prohibit. It is the second marriage which is forbidden, which makes little sense for a woman in a patriarchal society, except if this structure is replaced by another in which women do not have to depend any longer on men for their livelihood.[20]

19. Luise Schottroff, *Itinerant Prophetesses: A Feminist Analysis of the Sayings Source Q*, trans. J. Reed, Institute for Antiquity and Christianity Occasional Papers 21 (Claremont: Institute for Antiquity and Christianity, 1991).
    20. Ibid., 9–10.

Another sign of contestation is found in Q 12:52-53 [QS 44], which declares that belonging to the Jesus movement is a cause of chronic family conflict which threatens the patriarchal order.

Q and the Presence of Women

One can notice that the family divisions mentioned in Q 12:52-53 [QS 43] involve not only men but women as well: mother against daughter and daughter against mother, mother-in-law against daughter-in-law and daughter-in-law against mother-in-law. This presupposes their presence in the Q community since they rebel against the patriarchal structure. The impression that indeed women were part of the community is reinforced by a certain esteem shown to women's work, juxtaposed three times to men's work.

Men's Work	*Women's Work*
Q 13:18-19 [QS 46], sowing the mustard seed[21]	Q 13:20 [QS 46], bread making
Q 17:34 [QS 60], men working in the fields[22]	Q 17:35 [QS 60], women grinding wheat
Q 12:24 [QS 39], neither sow nor harvest	Q 12:27 [QS 39], neither spin nor weave

Not only is this recognition of the value of women's work exceptional in this sort of society, but there is more: the parable of the yeast compares divine activity to the work of women. One is naturally led to believe that this recognition reflects women's participation in the expansion of the Jesus movement.[23] If the Q community questions the patriarchal structure, the inclusion of women in the "mission" would represent one aspect of the new ethos. Theissen's model proves inadequate because it does not correspond to this new ethos. In fact, Theissen describes an organization in which men who are itinerant prophets

21. Here *anthrōpos* designates a man as indicated by the following saying.

22. Here Schottroff chooses Matt 24:40 rather than Luke's text, contrary to IQP; see James M. Robinson, "The International Q Project, Work Sessions 12–14 July, 22 November, 1991," *Journal of Biblical Literature* 111 (1992) 508.

23. Other examples of this juxtaposition of men and women in Q are brought forth by A. J. Batten, "More Queries for Q: Women and Christian Origins," *Biblical Theology Bulletin* 24 (1994) 44–51 (especially 47–48). Examples of this are the linking of the Queen of the South and the inhabitants of Nineveh on the day of judgment as well as that of the man looking for his sheep and the woman for her drachma. In Batten's opinion, these pairings of man/woman demonstrate the intent of the document to address both men and women.

rely for their subsistence on communities that are patriarchal in structure.[24]

And Sophia in All This?

Whereas Taussig saw the figure of Sophia in Q as a reflection of women's condition, Schottroff refuses this correlation. She admits that sapiential themes are present in Q, but regards them as marginal and of slight relevance since they are subordinated to the dominant message of Q which is the gospel of the poor.[25] Besides, Schottroff remarks that "in the writings we call Wisdom literature (Wisdom of Solomon, Sirach, Proverbs, and others), the gospel announced to the poor does not play any part. Rather, these writings focus on the wise and pious man *[sic]* and are interested in how the paterfamilias will be able to establish a prosperous patriarchal household *[Haushalt]*."[26] She deems that Q reveals its convictions on this topic in Q 10:21 [QS 24]: "I am grateful to you, father, master of heaven and earth, because you have kept these things hidden from the wise and understanding and revealed them to babies. Truly I am grateful, father, for that was your gracious will." Schottroff affirms that, by offering the revelation to infants *(nēpioi)*, that is, to persons without education, among whom women predominated,[27] Jesus here rebukes in a sarcastic manner those who pretend to be wise. Such an opinion would be an attack against the patriarchal structure since Wisdom, in the Jewish context, aims at perpetuating and strengthening this structure.

Evaluation of Schottroff's Approach

Schottroff's interpretation of passages such as Q 12:52-53; 13:20-21; 16:18 [QS 43; 46; 56], supports the belief that women were present and active in the Q community. It is true that this feminine activity can imply a new lifestyle different from that of the typical patriarchal structure. This is the reason Schottroff seems to want to reject Theissen's model. In fact, it might be surprising that she only widens this model by keeping the categories of itinerant prophets (a function now discharged by women also) and sedentary supporters found in Theissen. The support group's mode of life remains fundamentally unchanged and is justified by the fact that it makes possible the existence of the first category, that of the itinerant preachers. As Mack says, the existence

24. Schottroff, *Itinerant Prophetesses*, 9.
25. Ibid., 13–14.
26. Ibid., 13.
27. Ibid., 14.

of two categories of members with opposed lifestyles raises difficulties for anyone who attempts to explain the relationships between the two groups.[28] In the present case, the group of itinerant prophets—men and women—seems to be free from the patriarchal structure, but must count for its subsistence on the resources of supporters whose prosperity largely depends on this structure; such a dependence amounts to an implicit confirmation of the wholesomeness of the system. It seems to us that Schottroff would be better off if she completely rejected the dichotomy supporters/itinerant prophets and adopted a model in which the functions are undifferentiated, that is, in which the proclamation of the gospel is not incompatible with the production of material goods. In other words, Schottroff would be well served by adopting the social model proposed by Kloppenborg and Mack.[29]

A certain ambiguity also remains in Schottroff's article concerning the relationship between Sophia and the sapiential literary genre. Schottroff seems to regard Q as being prophetic in character because its dominant theme is the gospel announced to the poor. This conclusion appears justified to us, the more so as the author rightly remarks that the appearances of Sophia (Q 7:35; 11:49 [18; 34]) are of the prophetic type. Nonetheless, one can wonder whether Schottroff clearly perceives the distinction between Sophia and the sapiential literary genre and the distinction between the sapiential literary genre aiming at maintaining a traditional social structure and the use Q makes of this genre to deliver its message.

The stratigraphy proposed by Kloppenborg lays emphasis upon the distinction between Sophia and the *instruction* genre of the sapiential type.[30] Q1 is organized according to the *instruction* genre and the prophetic "personage" of Sophia enters only in Q2, that is, in the prophetic stratum of the document which imparts to the whole of Q a prophetic tone.

If Schottroff is right in affirming that Jewish sapiential writings, such as the Wisdom of Solomon, Sirach, Proverbs, and others, tend to perpetuate the patriarchal structure, the use of the sapiential literary genre does not necessarily endorse this tendency. As a comparison, the *catechism* literary genre, originally destined to transmit a religious doctrine in a fixed way, has sometimes been used to spread a doctrine completely foreign to the religious sphere.[31] The first stratum of Q (Q1)

28. Mack, "Kingdom That Didn't Come," 608.

29. See above, pp. 99–101.

30. See Kloppenborg, *Formation of Q*.

31. It is enough to cite Lydia Maria Child, *Anti-slavery Catechism*, 2nd ed. (Newburyport, Conn.: C. Whipple, 1839) or Editorial Staff of the Review of Reviews, eds.,

makes use of the *instruction* literary genre of the sapiential type, but the message it contains and intends to spread contradicts many points in traditional Jewish wisdom. Therefore, it is not desirable to elude, as Schottroff does, Sophia and the sapiential aspect of Q, for they appear incompatible with the dominant message of the document: the gospel announced to the poor. Kloppenborg's and Ronald A. Piper's studies have shown that an important part of this good news announced to the poor is done in the instruction genre.[32] Let it suffice to mention, among other passages, the Beatitudes (Q 6:20b-49 [QS 2-14]), the words on trust in prayer (Q 11:9-13 [QS 27]) and on useless anxiety (Q 12:22-24 [QS 39]).

Despite these few remarks, Schottroff's book is an important contribution to the exploration of the feminist potential of Q. She convincingly shows that certain passages, such as Q 12:52-53; 13:20-21; and 16:18 [QS 44; 46; and 56] call into question the patriarchal structure of first century Palestine.

3. Amy-Jill Levine

Amy-Jill Levine takes for granted that there are in Q several redactional strata mirroring different social situations.[33] She holds that the second stratum (Q2) clearly shows the presence of women in the Q group. However, the paucity of references to women in Q2 makes it difficult to determine their role.

Q1, Instructions Given to Marginal People

One can call marginal a group of persons who have relinquished money, shoes, and staff (Q 10:4 [QS 20]). This marginalization is a choice because the members of the group have freely renounced these possessions. Moreover, this marginal position stands out the more as the group questions the existing social order and wants to substitute another one in which the just and sinners are equal before God (Q 6:35

Two Thousand Questions and Answers about the War, 2nd rev. ed. (New York: The Review of Reviews Co., 1918). One can find numerous examples of these pseudo-catechisms in Raymond Brodeur and others, *Les Catéchismes au Québec 1702–1963* (Sainte-Foy: Université Laval, 1990) 357–363.

32. Kloppenborg , *Formation of Q,* 171–244; Ronald A. Piper, *Wisdom in the Q-Tradition: The Aphoristic Teaching of Jesus,* Monograph Series, Society for New Testament Studies 61 (New York: Cambridge University Press, 1989).

33. Amy-Jill Levine, "Who's Catering the Q Affair? Feminist Observations on Q Paraenesis," in *Paraenesis: Act and Form,* ed. Leo G. Perdue and John G. Gammie, Semeia 50 (Atlanta: Scholars Press, 1990) 145–161.

[QS 9]) and in which the principle of reprisals is abolished (Q 6:27-35 [QS 9]). Levine recognizes that there remains a paradox in this marginality because this group must rely on the support of the dominant social system not only to survive but also to define itself.

The fact that there are two categories of members—that is, the itinerant beggars and the sedentary supporters—casts doubt on the existence of a community of equal disciples because the difference in modes of life contradicts the principle of equality. If this equality exists, it must be within each category.[34]

According to Levine, it is not certain that this group of marginalized people included women. For instance, there is nothing in the instructions that indicates their presence. True, the instructions concerning clothing and food can be addressed to women as well as to men, but those concerning forced labor (Matt 5:41), the possibility of becoming sons of God (Q 6:35 [QS 9]), the metaphor of master-disciple (Q 6:40 [QS 11]), that of the builder of a house (Q 6:48-49 [QS 14]) seem rather to apply to men. However, as Levine observes, the absence of women in Q1 does not necessarily mean their absence from the group. There are other important questions, such as ethnic differences, political opinions, friendship, that are not treated either. But their absence does not mean they were unimportant to the members of the group.[35]

Q2, Women and Conflicts

The only text which Levine sees as proving the presence of women in the Q group is Q 12:52-53 [QS 43]. That passage shows that women are implicated in the family conflicts caused by adherence to the Jesus movement. However, this does not mean that women were protagonists in these conflicts. As in the case of Q1, the author thinks that they may be mentioned not for themselves but as family members and that their role is always restricted to that of supporters.[36]

Because of the attestation of the presence of women in Q2, it would be possible to retroactively extend this presence to Q1. Although plausible, this presumption is not supported by texts. Levine refuses to use a hermeneutics of suspicion as proposed by Schüssler Fiorenza: according to this approach, the silence of the texts on the topic of female membership can be due to its being kept hidden.[37] Levine observes that this

---

34. Ibid., 150.

35. Ibid., 152.

36. Ibid., 152, 156.

37. Elisabeth Schüssler Fiorenza, *Bread Not Stone: The Challenge of Biblical Interpretation* (Boston: Beacon Press, 1984) 111–112; Schüssler Fiorenza, *In Memory of Her* 101–102.

silence can reflect a state of affairs in which women's role was not of great importance. The gospel is addressed to the poor, which in Schottroff's eyes, would indicate the inclusion of women in the Jesus movement. Levine contests the value of this argument; she points out that Q 6:20; 9:58; and 10:21 [QS 8; 19; and 24] use a rhetoric of weakness rather than one of gender (masculine or feminine). She adduces two reasons to explain the omission of the concept of gender in this rhetoric: "Either women of the culture were not characteristically poor and weak, in which case their presence in the rhetoric would be inappropriate. Or, the women were so marginalized, but were not recognized as being such within the cultural imagination."[38]

Finally, Levine questions the idea that the use of Sophia and the images associated with it would demonstrate the important role played by women in this movement (as Taussig declares). The use of Sophia in Q2 could simply indicate that the Q community was at ease with this figure because of (1) the use of the sapiential genre in Q1 and (2) the desire to affirm the connection between Q1 and Q2. Thus, the use of the Sophia theme can be seen as supporting equally well the masculinization of the figure of Sophia and the feminization of the figure of Jesus.[39]

Evaluation of Levine's Approach

When compared with Taussig's and Schottroff's approaches, Levine's is minimalist, which acts as a damper. We must agree with her when she says that the absence of women in the texts can be interpreted in several ways. It can reflect either the result of a willful obfuscation of their presence or of the slight importance granted them.

Levine also shows clearly how equivocal is one of the rare explicit testimonies to the presence of women, Q 12:52-53 [QS 43]. The possible hypothesis that women's role was only one of support owes much to the fact that Levine adopts Theissen' model according to which there were two categories of roles in the community.

Conclusion

The three studies we have considered differ in their portrayal of the social development of the Q community, the importance they give to the figure of Sophia, and their theological goals. Certain directions taken by these studies seem to hold more promise for the elaboration of a feminist perspective of the Q document.

38. Levine, "Who's Catering the Q Affair?" 154.
39. Ibid., 155.

One can wonder up to what point Theissen's model, adopted by Schottroff and Levine, limits women's participation in the expansion of the movement. The existence of two categories of members, each with its own tasks, almost unconsciously implies a division by sex because the imagination more easily attributes an itinerant lifestyle, that is, the outside world, to men, and the domestic infrastructure, that is, the inside world, to women. On the contrary, the development model proposed by Kloppenborg and Mack, and adopted by Taussig, offers because of its flexibility better possibilities for exploring women's roles in the Q community. In a way, this model breaks open the dichotomy—men/ preaching/outside world versus women/domestic support/inside world—and suggests a pattern in which the two worlds are no longer separated and in which the contributions of men and women tend to be undifferentiated. Moreover, this model better reflects the rural social character of first century Palestine where women routinely helped men in field work and economic transactions (purchase and sale of goods).[40] The expansion of the Jesus movement through a social network linking houses is also more likely in the context of a countryside where hamlets and villages were often separated by more than an hour's travel on foot.[41]

Schottroff makes a major contribution by pointing out that several times Q joins men's work and women's work. This avenue is success-fully followed by A. J. Batten, who supplies other examples of this juxta-position of men and women.[42] In our opinion, this type of juxtaposition is an indication that Q addresses equally men and women. Another sign of this inclusiveness in Q could be Q 12:52-53 [QS 43], but Levine's critical observation that women are mentioned perhaps only because they are family members calls for caution. Nonetheless, it remains that Q 12:52-53 [QS 43], as well as Q 9:60 [QS 19] and 14:26 [QS 52] (10:37 in Matthew's text), weakens the patriarchal structure by attacking one of its fundamental values, family unity. However, we must not forget that, as Schottroff reminds us, Q still adheres to an androcentric formulation.

However, these few allusions to women show that an egalitarian social ethos is also at work in Q. This ethos gains by being set within a wider perspective in order to reveal its significance. This perspective is

---

40. See Kathleen E. Corley, "Jesus' Table Practice: Dining with 'Tax Collectors and Sinners,' Including Women," in *Society of Biblical Literature Seminar Papers*, vol. 32 (Missoula, Mont.: Scholars Press, 1993) 453.

41. See John S. Kloppenborg, "Literary Convention, Self-Evidence, and the Social History of the Q People," in *Early Christianity, Q and Jesus*, ed. John S. Kloppenborg and Leif E. Vaage, Semeia 55 (Atlanta: Scholars Press, 1991) 89.

42. See above, n. 23.

that of the historical, sociological, and anthropological studies on the condition of Mediterranean women. These studies question a certain image of the Mediterranean societies in antiquity as uniformly patriarchal. In fact, women's participation in public life as well as their influence on domestic life are now well documented.[43] About the first century, these Mediterranean societies seem to have known a certain emancipation of women. According to Kathleen E. Corley, who synthesizes several studies on the subject, women had begun to be present at public banquets as early as the end of the Republic and the beginning of the Empire.[44] One of the goals of Augustus' laws making marriage and remarriage obligatory was to curb this emancipation.[45] Bernadette J. Brooten's book on the role of women in the leadership of synagogues also questions a certain view of Jewish religious life as being solely men's business.[46] Finally, certain passages from Paul's letters (Phil 4:2-3; Rom 16:1-2, 3) allude to women sharing in the building of the Christian communities of the Hellenistic world.[47] Placed in such a context,

43. See among others, Bernadette J. Brooten, *Women Leaders in the Ancient Synagogue: Inscriptional Evidence and Background Issues*, Brown Judaic Studies 36 (Chico, Calif.: Scholars Press, 1982); Bernadette J. Brooten, "Jewish Women's History in the Roman Period: A Task for Christian Theology," *Harvard Theological Review* 79 (1986) 22–30; Corley, "Jesus' Table Practice"; Kathleen E. Corley, *Private Women, Public Meals: Social Conflicts in the Synoptic Tradition* (Peabody, Mass.: Hendrickson, 1993); Sarah B. Pomeroy, "Women in Roman Egypt: A Preliminary Study Based on the Papyri," *Aufstieg und Niedergang der Römischer Welt*, vol. 10, pt. 1 (1988) 707–723.

44. See Corley, *Private Women*, xv–xvi, 53–66.

45. *Lex Iula de maritantibus ordinibus* in 18 B.C.E. and *Lex Papia Poppaea nuptialis* in 9 B.C.E. See also Eva Cantarella, *Pandora's Daughters: The Role and Status of Women in Greek and Roman Antiquity*, trans. Maureen B. Fant (Baltimore: John Hopkins University Press, 1987) 122, 143.

46. See Brooten, *Women Leaders*. This study is based on inscriptions discovered in the synagogues of Palestine and the Mediterranean Basin to affirm that leadership positions in the synagogues were open to women. One must note that all these inscriptions were found in the synagogues of the Diaspora. Moreover, they date from the Roman and Byzantine periods.

47. Concerning Rom 16:1-2, see the article by C. F. Whelan, "Amica Pauli: The Role of Phoebe in the Early Church," *Journal for the Study of the New Testament* 49 (1993) 67–85. Whelan explores the possible meaning of "protectress" *(prostatis)* in the framework of the voluntary associations existing in the first century. Olivette Genest, "Lectures féministes de la Bible," in *Entendre la voix du Dieu vivant: Interprétations et pratiques actuelles de la Bible*, ed. Jean Duhaime and Odette Mainville, Lectures bibliques 41 (Montréal, Médiaspaul, 1994) 320, also remarks that we must understand the term *prostatis* "with the fullness of meaning it has in Jewish and Greco-Roman literature, in which it designates leaders, presidents, governors, superintendents, and influential women."

the hypothesis that Q is addressed as much to women as to men and that women take part along with men in the task of spreading the Jesus movement becomes much more credible as still another sign of a widespread movement.

Who Is Misogynist: Paul or Certain Corinthians?

Note on 1 Corinthians 14:33b-36

◆————————————————————————◆

Michel Gourgues

The text of 1 Cor 14:33b-36 is often adduced as one of the proofs of the antifeminism in the New Testament. Is there anything left to say about this passage, which is a frontal attack on the sensibility of contemporary female and male readers? Without intending to review the whole history of its exegesis, I want to briefly present here a particular exegesis of this passage. Formulated almost fifteen years ago and re-fined since then, this original explanation has not yet succeeded in gaining the attention it deserves. But before all else, it is helpful to re-view for the readers the dead ends to which the other, better known ex-planations lead.

1. Beyond the Dead Ends

Literally translated, the text in question reads as follows:

33b   . . . As in all the assemblies of the saints,

34   women should be silent in the assemblies, for they are not permitted to speak, but should be subordinate, as the law also says.

35   If they want to know something, let them ask their husbands at home, for it is shameful for a woman to speak in an assembly.

36   What is this! Has the word of God originated with you? Or are you the only ones it has reached?

The difficulties raised by these verses are well-known. To begin with, they support the persistent accusation of the antifeminism with which

Paul is charged and which for a large part springs from these very
verses. True, these problems, as exegesis has observed for a long time,
reside above all at the level of Pauline thought itself. That women are
reduced to silence in the Christian assemblies indeed contradicts what
has been said a little before in the same letter (11:5), where it was taken
for granted that women had the right to pray and prophesy in the same
cultic setting. Moreover, repeating, as it seems, conceptions already traditional in Christianity, Paul will affirm that "there is no longer male
and female; for you are all one in Christ Jesus" (Gal 3:28b).

One might think that while affirming the fundamental equality of
men and women before God, Paul and the first Christian communities
maintained the patriarchal order predominating in the society of the
time in the same way they proclaimed the equal dignity of master and
slave, all the while tolerating slavery. However, here in 1 Cor 14:34,
what is discussed is not the silence and submission of women in society at large but *in the Christian cultic assembly*. Was this not running
counter to their theological convictions?

The listing of attempts to explain the passage under study has been
done again and again.[1] It will be sufficient to cite a few of them. Ac-

1. One finds examples of this in many studies of this passage published in the
last twenty years and listed here in chronological order: André-Marie Dubarle,
"Paul et l'antiféminisme," *Revue de Sciences Philosophiques et Théologiques* 60 (1976)
261–280; Neal M. Flanagan and E. H. Snyder, "Did Paul Put Down Women in 1 Cor
14:34-36?" *Biblical Theology Bulletin* 11 (1981) 10–12; Gerhard von Dautzenberg, "Zur
Stellung der Frauen in den paulinischen gemeinden," in *Die Frau im Urchristentum,*
ed. Helmut Merklein and Karl Müller, Quaestiones disputatae 95 (Freiburg: Herder,
1983) 182–224; David W. O'Dell-Scott, "Let the Women Speak in Church: An Egalitarian Interpretation of 1 Cor 14:33b-36," *Biblical Theology Bulletin* 13 (1983) 90–93;
Elisabeth Schüssler Fiorenza, *In Memory of Her: A Feminist Reconstruction of Christian
Origins* (New York: Crossroad, 1983) 230–233; Jerome Murphy-O'Connor, "Interpo-
lations in 1 Corinthians," *Catholic Biblical Quarterly* 48 (1986) 81–94; David W.
O'Dell-Scott, "In Defense of an Egalitarian Interpretation of 1 Cor 14:34-36: A Reply
to Murphy-O'Connor's Critique," *Biblical Theology Bulletin* 17 (1987) 100–103; W.
Munro, "Women, Text and the Canon: The Strange Case of 1 Corinthians 14:33-35,"
Biblical Theology Bulletin 18 (1988) 26–31; R. W. Allison, "Let Women Be Silent in the
Churches (1 Cor 14:33b-36): "What Did Paul Really Say, and What Did It Mean?"
Journal for the Study of the New Testament 32 (1988) 27–60; Brendan Byrne, *Paul and the
Christian Woman* (Collegeville, Minn.: The Liturgical Press, 1989) 59–65; Antoinette
Clark Wire, *The Corinthian Women Prophets: A Reconstruction through Paul's Rhetoric*
(Minneapolis: Fortress Press, 1990) 135–198, 229–232; L. Boston, "A Womanist Re-
flection on 1 Corinthians 7:21 and 1 Corinthians 14:33-35," *Journal of Women and Reli-
gion* 9–10 (1990–1991) 81–89; Craig S. Keener, *Paul, Women and Wives: Marriage and
Women's Ministry in the Letters of Paul* (Peabody, Mass.: Hendrickson, 1992) 70–100;
J. H. Petzer, "Reconsidering the Silent Women of Corinth—A Note on 1 Corinthians

cording to the hypothesis which remains the most widespread[2]—
although accepted as a last resort—this text would not go back to Paul
himself. It would have been added afterwards by one or several disciples whose thinking was less permissive than Paul's and closer to
that of 1 Tim 2:11-15 for example. But this hypothesis does not stand up
before the data of textual criticism. Although sometimes displaced and
put after v. 40 in more recent manuscripts, vv. 34-35 are well attested in
the most important and oldest manuscript tradition.[3] In view of this, is
it not arbitrary to postulate a later interpolation?

Beside current positions like the one just mentioned, there are, at
the opposite pole, isolated attempts at a solution, often ingenious, not
to say ingenuous! For instance, in order to reconcile 1 Cor 14:34-35 with
1 Cor 11:2-16, one will assume that in the first passage, the command to
be silent concerns only married women whereas in the second, the
right to pray and prophesy is granted only to unmarried women.[4] Or
else, it is proposed that fearing that the Christian community be identified with certain marginal cults known in Corinth and giving a more
important place to women, Paul would have held up as a model the
usage of the Palestinian Judeo-Christian communities.[5] These hypothe-
ses are not much more satisfactory than those mentioned above.

2. Echo and Rejection of a Corinthian Position

The original solution to which I alluded above holds that in 1 Cor
14:35, Paul echoes a restrictive position current in the Corinthian community and that in 14:36, he rejects this position while expressing his

---

14:34-35," *Theologia Evangelica* 26 (1993) 132–138; D.-J. Nadeau, "Le problème des
femmes en 1 Co 14, 33b-35," *Études Théologiques et Religieuses* 69 (1994) 63–65.

2. From the study of Gottfried Fitzer, *Das Weib schweige in der Gemeinde* (München:
Kaiser, 1963) down to the 1990 commentary of Jerome Murphy-O'Connor, "The
First Letter to the Corinthians," in *The New Jerome Biblical Commentary*, ed. Raymond
E. Brown, Joseph A. Fitzmyer, and Roland E. Murphy (Englewood Cliffs: Prentice
Hall, 1990) 811ff.

3. See Bruce Manni Metzger, *A Textual Commentary on the Greek New Testament*,
2nd ed. (New York: United Bible Societies, 1975) 565. For an examination of the text
from the viewpoint of textual criticism, see E. Earle Ellis, "The Silenced Wives of
Corinth (1 Cor 14:34-35)," in *New Testament Textual Criticism: Its Significance for Exegesis*, ed. Eldon J. Epp and Gordon D. Fee (Oxford: Clarendon Press, 1981) 213–220;
see also Petzer, "Silent Women of Corinth."

4. Curiously enough, it is this position that Schüssler Fiorenza supports in *In
Memory of Her*; she seems to be unaware of the interpretation we are going to out-
line, one which would be grist for her mill!

5. Nadeau, "Le problème des femmes," concurs with this interpretation.

own mind. Advanced by several authors[6] since 1981, this hypothesis has not yet, to my knowledge, been the object of commentaries[7] and it seems still unknown in French-speaking circles.[8]

But good arguments can be brought forth to support it. It will be useful to list those which appear the strongest to me, whether from Paul's text itself or the studies mentioned in the notes.

1. The orders to remain silent in 14:34-35 contradict not only 1 Cor 11:5 but also what was just said before in 14:31:

> "For you can *all* prophesy, one by one, so that *all* may learn and *all* be encouraged."

In this sentence, the last two *pantes* ("all") almost certainly include the women in the community; it must be the same for the first *pantes*. Thus, one cannot see how Paul, in vv. 34-35 would impose silence on those he has just encouraged in v. 31 to prophesy.

2. Nothing in vv. 34-35 suggests that this is Paul's opinion. For instance, he does not say, "I do not permit them [*ouk epitrepō*]"[9] but "they are not permitted [*ouk epitrepetai*] to speak."

3. It is true that in certain manuscripts, one reads, "Let *your* women [*gynaikes hymōn*]" instead of "let women [*gynaikes*] be silent in the as-

---

6. See in particular, Flanagan and Snyder, "Did Paul Put Women Down?"; O'Dell-Scott, "Defense of an Egalitarian Interpretation"; Allison, "Let Women be Silent." For all this, Allison does not abandon the interpolation hypothesis: 1 Cor 14:34-36 would have been excerpted from another letter of Paul to the Corinthians, and v. 33b would have been written for the purpose of integrating the excerpt into the text.

7. There are some exceptions like Charles H. Talbert, *Reading Corinthians: A Literary and Theological Commentary on 1 and 2 Corinthians* (New York: Crossroad, 1987) 92ff. The explanation is discarded in Carol A. Newsom and Sharon H. Ringe, eds., *The Women's Bible Commentary* (Louisville: Westminster/John Knox, 1992) 328; and another explanation, totally unverifiable, is adopted: vv. 34-35 would have been a gloss written in the margin of Paul's text and subsequently inserted into the text by scribes, sometimes after v. 33, sometimes after v. 40.

8. For instance, there is no mention of this hypothesis in Daniel Marguerat, "Saint Paul contre les femmes? Essor et déclin de la femme chrétienne au premier siècle," in *Le Dieu des premiers chrétiens,* 2nd ed., Études bibliques 16 (Geneva, Labor et Fides, 1993) especially 139–141.

9. As will be the case in 1 Tim 2:12: *didaskein de gynaiki ouk epitrepō* ("I do not permit any woman to teach"). This restrictive position, like some others in the Pastoral Letters, seems to demonstrate that a gradual hardening with regard to women occurred in the communities.

semblies." In this case, one could legitimately see here Paul's order or wish expressing his personal position rather than a Corinthian opinion. But in fact the short reading ("women"), attested in the best manuscripts, is preferable.[10]

4. The restrictive position expressed in v. 34 is based on the Law—in this case Gen 3:16, it seems. Now this way of basing Christian practices solely on the ancient Law is not Paul's custom; rather, it would suggest to us the practice of the Judeo-Christians inside the community.[11]

5. In 1 Cor, it is not rare for Paul to echo an opinion of his correspondents before criticizing it. In certain passages, like 1:12; 7:1; 15:12, 35, Paul expressly states that he is speaking of some of the Corinthians' opinions or statements: "each of you says," "concerning the matters about which you wrote," "how can some of you say?" In other places, like 6:12-13, he does not specify anything, but merely cites statements known to the readers in order to immediately refute them.[12]

The example of 1 Cor 6 is particularly illuminating. In vv. 12a and 13a, Paul makes a reference to the Corinthians' argumentation, to which he responds in vv. 12b and 13c. Convincing clues favor this interpretation of the text:[13]

(a) First of all, the very structure of v. 13, in which the Corinthians' position and Paul's are presented under a strictly parallel form:[14]

10. Metzger, *Textual Commentary*, 565ff.

11. A passage like 7:12 shows the existence of Judeo-Christians within the community in Corinth. One could be tempted to attribute to them the position expressed in vv. 33b-34 and to see there a firm intent to perpetuate in the Christian communities the usage of the Synagogue as far as women were concerned. This idea could be supported by the phrase in v. 33b, "as in all the churches of the saints," if this last term, as is sometimes the case in the Corinthian correspondence (see 2 Cor 8:4; 9:1, 12), designated the members of the Palestinian communities. But *hagioi* ("saints") has more often a wider meaning: see 1 Cor 1:2; 6:1; 16:15; 2 Cor 1:1; 13:12 among others.

12. See also 10:23; and perhaps 2:15; 8:1, 4, 8. See Murphy-O'Connor, "Interpolations in 1 Corinthians"; rather surprisingly, this author refuses to see a Corinthian slogan in 14:34-35, without giving decisive reasons, in my opinion.

13. Already suggested by writers like Charles F. D. Moule, *An Idiom Book of New Testament Greek* (Cambridge, England: Cambridge University Press, 1953) 196–197, this interpretation has been convincingly defended by Murphy-O'Connor, first in an article, "Corinthian Slogans in 1 Cor 6:12-20," *Catholic Biblical Quarterly* 40 (1978) 391–396, and later on more briefly in his commentaries *1 Corinthians*, N. T. Message 10 (Wilmington: Michael Glazier, 1979) 49–54, and "First Letter to the Corinthians," 804.

14. The parallelism stands out still more clearly in Greek: v. 13a: *ta brōmata tēi koiliai, kai hē koilia tois brōmasin, ho de theos, kai tautēn kai tauta, katargēsei* ("'Food is

v. 13a	v. 13b-14
"Food is meant for the stomach and the stomach for food," and God will destroy both one and the other.	The body is meant . . . for the Lord, and the Lord for the body. And God raised the Lord and will also raise us. . . .

(b) The affirmation "the Lord is for the body" in Paul's response, which is otherwise very difficult to understand, is perfectly explained by Paul's wish to give his response a form exactly parallel to that of the objection.

Perhaps the same pattern is also in 6:18, in which the first part of the verse could be a reference to the Corinthians' statement, followed by Paul's answer:[15]

v. 18a	v. 18b
Every sin that a person commits is outside the body	but the fornicator sins against the body itself.

Here too, this supposition would allow us to understand v. 18a, which is hard to comprehend if it is seen as Paul's opinion. The two statements are contradictory and it is to palliate this contradiction that certain translations (like the TOB for example)[16] render v. 18a thus: "Every *other* sin a person commits is outside the body," adding a word ("other") which is not in the text. On the contrary, if v. 18a quotes an opinion held by some Corinthians, it enables us to be even more precise in identifying the idea to which verses 12 and 13 already alluded. The Corinthians accepted the existence of sin, but they conceived it only in relation to the interior realm of the mind, motives, and intentions, and they refused to connect it with purely external acts involving just the body. A purely physical act—like eating or engaging in fornication—accomplished without evil intent in no way amounts to a sin *(hamartēma)*.

---

meant for the stomach and the stomach for food,' and God will destroy both one and the other") parallel to v. 13c-14: *to de sōma . . . tōi kyriōi, kai ho kyrios tōi sōmati, ho de theos ton kyrion ēgeiren kai hēmas, exegerei* ("The body is meant . . . not for fornicaion but for the Lord, and the Lord for the body. And God raised the Lord and will also raise us by his power"). Verse 12 similarly juxtaposes the Corinthians' affirmation and Paul's response: "'All things are lawful for me,' but not all things are beneficial. 'All things are lawful for me,' but I will not be dominated by anything."

15. See Murphy-O'Connor, "Corinthian Slogans," 392ff.

16. Nouveau Testament, 2nd ed., Traduction Œcuménique de la Bible, (Paris: Cerf/Les Bergers et les Mages, 1979) 503.

6. Lastly, various elements of 14:36 suggest that it is precisely Paul's position in reaction against the Corinthians'. One sign of this is that the particle "or" *(ē)* used at the beginning of an interrogative sentence often serves to introduce a refutation or a protest.[17] Verse 36 is therefore in disagreement with the affirmations of vv. 34-35, which prohibits seeing in them the opinion of Paul himself.[18]

7. Still, in v. 36, we note that in the end the masculine gender is used ("the *only* ones," *eis hymas monous*), about which the least one can say is that these words are not addressed only to women! Is it not more normal to see here a reference to certain men in the community who were eager to limit the women's right of speaking in the cultic assemblies and from whom Paul would demand by what right they claimed to control the gift and use of God's word?

Speaking of this interpretation—in vv. 34-35, Paul is referring to a Corinthian "slogan" which he refutes in v. 36—Jerome Murphy-O'Connor writes, "If we speak only of pure possibility, we can only agree. But the true question is the following: Which of the two possibilities—the Corinthian slogan and the post-Pauline interpolation—is the more probable?"[19] In my opinion, there is no doubt about the answer when one considers the convergence of the clues we have just enumerated in favor of the first possibility.

For his part, Murphy-O'Connor favors the second possibility because, as he notes, when in the first letter to the Corinthians, Paul contests a position held by his correspondents, there is no impassioned

---

17. Grammars and lexicons dealing with this particle characterize it as a "disjunctive conjunction" (for instance Félix-Marie Abel, *Grammaire du grec biblique, suivie d'un choix de papyrus,* 2nd ed. [Paris: Gabalda, 1927] 344; Joseph Henry Thayer, *A Greek-English Lexicon of the New Testament,* 19th ed. [Grand Rapids: Zondervan, 1978] 275) or else as an "exclamation expressing disapproval" (Henry George Liddell and Robert Scott, *A Greek-English Lexicon,* 9th ed. [Oxford: Clarendon Press, 1961] 761). Thayer, *Greek-English Lexicon,* is even more precise: "before a sentence contrary to the one just preceding, to indicate that if one be denied or refuted the other must stand." O'Dell-Scott, "Let the Women Speak," 91, thinks he finds in 1 Cor 11:22 a similar use of the particle *ē.* But is not this a different case, the more so as the author seems to read this particle in v. 22a (in which one has *mē*) whereas it comes at the beginning of the second question asked in v. 22?

18. Murphy-O'Connor, "Interpolations in 1 Corinthians," 92, admits it, but since he continues to see an interpolation in vv. 34-35, Paul's reaction of disagreement expressed in v. 36 concerns, according to him, the situation spoken of in vv. 26-33. This position has been criticized, especially by Talbert, *Reading Corinthians,* 93.

19. Murphy-O'Connor, "Interpolations in 1 Corinthians," 91.

reaction comparable to that expressed in v. 36.[20] But is it a well-founded assumption to consider Paul bound by such uniformity in the expression of his reactions and feelings?

A similar argument opposed to the "Corinthian slogan" hypothesis rests on the length of vv. 34-35. When elsewhere in 1 Cor—let us recall the examples of 6:12, 13-14, 18 cited above—Paul refers to an opinion of his correspondents and then turns it down, the opinion or statement in question is briefly expressed.[21] This is true. But why would Paul be obliged to adhere always to the same response pattern, especially if he actually refers to the text of a letter received from the Corinthians (see 1 Cor 7:1)?

To sum up, among all the solutions which have been proposed, is not the "Corinthian slogan" the one which best explains the many difficulties posed by the interpretation of 1 Cor 14:33b-36 without raising other difficulties in as great a number?

---

20. Ibid., 92.

21. There is a note agreeing with this in *Women's Bible Commentary*, 328. Wire's observation, in *Corinthian Women Prophets*, 229ff., stating that Paul's habit is to make clear that the objection he is refuting is that of his correspondents is valid only if one takes into account (as she does) 6:10, 13 and 10:23.

Love As Subjection, the Christian Ideal for Husbands and Wives

A Structuralist Study of Ephesians 5:21-33

◆ ———————————————————————————— ◆

Marc Girard

A fair number of Christians today would not need much prompting to tear up the six or so pages from Scripture in which an apostle dares to exhort women to have an attitude of "subjection"![1] At least in our Western milieux, it is now hardly possible to read these passages within the Sunday liturgy without provoking unmistakable reactions: for certain men, a faint "macho" smile and, for others, a feeling of hidden malaise; for the women, a more unanimous reflex, perhaps like frustration or even a burst of anger barely repressed.

And yet, what if Paul and Peter had been poorly understood? Is there not in these texts a word from God to rehabilitate or, at least to submit to more impartial judicial proceedings?

We must concede that one needs quite a dose of courage—or naivete —to address this delicate problem of New Testament hermeneutics in the wake of so many others, both devil's advocates and defenders. From among all the incriminated texts, we shall choose only one, the weightiest, not to say the only really weighty one from the theological viewpoint, the one usually singled out to be convicted as an example: Eph 5:21-33.

As calmly as possible in the context of a social and ecclesial debate causing tempers to flare wildly, we shall attempt to base our analysis on a methodological foundation which we deem to be strong and trust-

---

1. 1 Cor 14:34; Eph 5:22-24; Col 3:18; 1 Tim 2:11; Titus 2:5; 1 Pet 3:1, 5-6. One could remark with humor that in the Bible the number six very often symbolizes imperfection, if not evil and sin!

worthy, that is, structuralist criticism.[2] This means that before project-
ing onto the ancient text a whole gamut of emotions and contemporary
rational criticisms, we shall strive to examine the text technically so
that it may reveal to us—like the x-ray of a bone—the articulations of
thought which form its solid skeleton. Only after being enlightened by
this examination, shall we pose the hermeneutical question: How are
we to separate, when appropriate, the gangue of expressions too intimately linked with a given culture from the precious gold which reflects the light of God's transcultural design? On the strong basis of this
twofold approach, we shall finally try to show the pastoral consequences of Paul's theology[3] on the couple, man and woman.

1. Structuralist Heuristic

In the chart on page 127, the text of Eph 5:21-33 is arranged according to its structure in order to facilitate its analysis.[4] From the thematic
viewpoint this text is part of a larger subsection which treats of the mutual relations between husband and wife (5:21-33), parents and children (6:1-4), masters and slaves (6:5-9). Everybody agrees on this; the
only catch is that some commentators attach 5:21 to the preceding
verses. But our analysis will immediately and frankly reject this option
on the strength of a rather solid structuralist argument.

The Large Inclusion (vv. 21 and 32-33)

To begin with, we are placing ourselves at the first level of analysis,
that of the maxi-structure. Verse 21 responds to vv. 32-33 so as to define
the boundaries of the pericope. What we have here is a genuine inclusion A . . . A. Formally, the pattern is made clear by the twofold occurrence of the idea of "fear" (*phobō* . . . *phobētai*) in vv. 21 and 33: we shall
have to explain the biblical meaning of this term later on.

2. On the method, see Marc Girard, "L'analyse structurelle," in *Entendre la voix
du Dieu vivant: Interprétations et pratiques actuelles de la Bible,* ed. Jean Duhaime and
Odette Mainville (Montréal: Médiaspaul, 1994) 149–159.

3. As is the rule in studies of synchronic exegesis, we do not enter at all into the
debate on whether Paul is the author of Ephesians. On this question, the reader will
consult, if need be, the specialized books and commentaries.

4. [The translation of Eph 5:21-33 used in the following analysis is the author's.
Ed.]

²¹ (Be) *subject* to one another in the **FEAR** of Christ

²² (Thus) *wives* to (their) own *husbands* as to the Lord.	²⁵ *Husbands, love* (your) *wives* as also *CHRIST* has loved the *CHURCH* and delivered himself up for her.
²³ For a husband is *head* of his wife, as also *CHRIST* (is) *head* of the *CHURCH*, himself savior of the *BODY*.	²⁶ *in order that he might sanctify her*, having purified her through the bath of water in the word,
	²⁷ in order that he might present her to himself, glorious, the *CHURCH*, having neither stain nor wrinkle nor anything of the (kind), but *so that she may be holy and irreproachable.*
²⁴ But as the *CHURCH* is *subject* to *CHRIST, SO* also, *wives* to husbands, in everything.	²⁸ *IN THE SAME WAY* they must, *husbands, love* their *wives* like their (own) *BODIES*; the one *loving* his *wife* loves himself.
	— — — — — — — — — — — — — — — —
	²⁹ No (man), indeed, has ever hated his (own) *flesh*, but he feeds (it) and keeps it warm,
	as also *CHRIST* (does for) the *CHURCH*, ³⁰ for we are members of his *BODY*.
	³¹ "This is why he will leave, the man, father and mother, and will attach himself to his *wife*, and they will be, the two of them, (oriented) to (form) one (single) *flesh*."

³² This mystery is great: I say (it) (concerning) *CHRIST* and (concerning) the *CHURCH*.

³³ This is why you also, one by one, (let) everyone LOVE his WIFE as (he loves) himself, in order that the WIFE might **FEAR** (her) HUSBAND!

The marker placed at the beginning and repeated at the end of the inclusion determines the overall framework of Paul's discourse. From the viewpoint of the meaning, one can already note that vv. 21 and 33 are the only ones in the whole pericope to address interpersonal relationships in their mutuality: strictly speaking, "to be subject to one another in the fear of Christ" echoes "to love his wife and fear her husband." From this structuralist relationship, vv. 21 and 33, one can infer a sort of semantic equivalence, in Paul's thought, between subjection, love, and fear. It goes without saying that we shall return to this topic.

The First Section: Address to Wives (vv. 22-24)

Let us now proceed, for a moment, to the second level of analysis, that of the intra-sectional structuring.

1. Verses 22-24, even 21-24, form a plainly evident **chiastic construction:**

> X   *hypotassomenoi,* "subject" . . . *Christou,* "Christ" . . . *hai gynaikes tois idiois andrasin,* "wives to (their) own husbands" (vv. 21-22)
>
> Y   *kephalē,* "head" (v. 23a)
>
> Y   *kephalē* (v. 23bc)
>
> X   *hypotassetai . . . Christō . . . hai gynaikes tois andrasin* (v. 24)

2. The use of the intra-sectional inclusion [X . . . X] confers on the idea of subjection the status of *dominant idea* of the section. At first sight, one could be inclined to restrict the import of this dominant idea to the attitude of the wife toward her husband (vv. 22-24b). But the initial marker of inclusion X . . . X obviously includes v. 21 (initial marker A of the large inclusion); this inclusion goes beyond the thematic framework and specific subject of the first section, as if to temper, stylistically and theologically, what odious and excessive connotations the unilateral affirmation of the subjection wife → husband could convey; for the author of the letter, the "subjection of wives to husbands" is to be inserted into the framework of the more general morality of the mutual subjection of Christians to one another. Here we have a fundamental point of exegesis. Paul writes *hypotassomenoi* (in the masculine) and not *hypotassomenai* (in the feminine)!

Besides, we see that Paul himself softens the verbal forms when he speaks of wives. Is it through respect? delicacy of feelings? absence of pressure from circumstances in the circle he was addressing? Be that as it may, the only imperative in the whole section (v. 21) is addressed to couples (and even probably to all Christians, including the unmarried).

And when in either of the markers [X . . . X] Paul explicitly directs his morality of "subjection" to wives, he implies the verb *hypotassein* within an elliptical sentence (v. 22)[5] or relegates it to a subordinate clause within a comparison (v. 24). It is as if Paul, whether intentionally or intuitively, was averse to saying in an explicit, rough, and lapidary way, "Wives, be subject to your husbands!"[6] So much for the dominant idea.

   3. The *subdominant idea* is found of course at the point YY (v. 23). Here again, there is a statement which, at first sight, is shocking with its reduplication of the word "head." What we have here is a *māšāl* (comparison), a sort of theological proverb seeking to define the relation husband → wife in comparison with the relation Christ → Church. In our own minds and languages, the word "head" immediately and spontaneously suggests one or the other of the four following ideas: intelligence (the brain), the authority of the leader, and as a consequence, superiority, precedence.

   This bodily *symbolism,* which is rather universal, is not absent from the text. Brought up in pure and stringent Judaism, Paul lives in a society pretty well dominated by masculine power. But the theological accent is not placed there. Here the word "head" means first of all responsibility. As a proof, v. 23c contains only the image of salvation effected: in the comparative transposition centered around the word "head," "husband" is equivalent to "Christ . . . savior," "wife" to "Church . . . body [of Christ]."

   It is also possible that Paul speaks here in the manner of a *midrash.* In his ancestors' language, *rōʾš,* corresponding to the Greek *kephalē,* expresses the idea of "first" place. Not first with the meaning of primacy, domination, honor, but simply of chronological priority. In the Yahwistic account of creation, the man is created before the woman, in the first place.[7] Now, the writer strives to demonstrate in his poetical dramatization that man and woman share an identical and equal nature. In view of the fact that in the second section of our passage (v. 31) Paul quotes the last verse of the Genesis story verbatim,[8] one can legitimately infer that there is already an implicit reference to it in v. 23a.

---

   5. For the textual criticism, we follow the option of Kurt Aland and others on the basis of the preponderant witnesses (especially P[46] and B) even though a larger number of manuscripts repeat the verb *hypotassein* in v. 22.
   6. In this, he substantially softens the preceding formulation of 1 Cor 14:34 and Col 3:18.
   7. See Gen 2:7-23.
   8. Gen 2:24.

The Second Section: Address to the Husbands (vv. 25-31)

Let us pursue the analysis at the second level, the intra-sectional one. Here, the structuralist method enables us to immediately see two subsections forming a unit by themselves (vv. 25-28 and vv. 29-31). In a first phase, we shall consider each of the two separately (therefore on the third level). Having done this, we shall be better equipped to demonstrate the consistency of vv. 25-31 as a whole.

1. The entire second section concerns husbands. It begins with an *imperative subsection* (vv. 25-28) composed according to a concentric symmetry with a twofold relation:

> X   *hoi andres agapan tas gynaikas kathōs . . .* , "husbands love (your) wives" (v. 25)
>
> Y   *hina autēn hagiasē,* "in order that he might sanctify her" (v. 26)
>
> Z   (v. 27ab)
>
> Y   *hina ē hagia,* "so that she may be holy" (v. 27c)
>
> X   *houtōs . . . hoi andres agapan tas . . . gynaikas* (v. 28)

The moral exhortation is essentially found in the inclusion X . . . X (vv. 25 and 28). Here Paul does not at all hesitate to use the verb in the imperative (v. 25a) or in the indicative, which is the explicit terminology of deontology, of "duty" (v. 28a). He counsels and even commands married men to love their wives. The order is accompanied by a twofold comparison. In the initial marker of the inclusion, the theological comparison rests on Christ's example in his quasi-conjugal relationship with the Church, a model of love and self-giving (v. 25bc). Now, precisely for Paul—later on we shall draw an important ethical conclusion from this—"to love" and "to deliver oneself for" form a hendiadys, that is, the expression of one single idea by two equivalent, synonymous terms which clarify and complete one another.[9] In the last analysis, the love of Christ for his Church can be defined only by reference to the exemplary mystery of the cross: self-renunciation, self-emptying *(kenōsis),* to the point of the total sacrifice of his breath and blood. In the same way, this must be true of a husband's love for his wife. In the marker closing the inclusion, Paul illustrates his moral lesson with another comparison, more down to earth, or let us say more psychological: he must love his wife as one loves one's own body (v. 28bc). By adding, "The one who loves his wife loves himself," he particularizes, in the domain of conjugal relationships, the "second commandment" enunciated by Jesus in a

9. See also Eph 5:2.

general perspective, "You shall love your neighbor as yourself" (Matt 22:39 and parallels, quoting Lev 19:18). This hardly veiled Gospel reminiscence could imply that in Paul's thought, the wife is for her husband the closest "neighbor" among neighbors.

As to the portion of the text [Y Z Y] (vv. 26-27) placed between the initial and final markers of the inclusion X . . . X, its only function is to develop the theological comparison (v. 25bc) by joining it to a final sentence with three parallel members (triple *hina*, "in order that"). For what purpose did Christ the lover give himself to the Church, his bride? Essentially to "sanctify" it (dyad Y . . . Y). The verb *hagiazein* (v. 26) and the corresponding adjective (v. 27c) certainly bear the mark of the Hebrew root *qdš*: elected, united in marriage with Christ, the Church finds itself set apart, separated, for a mission of fruitfulness; it shares in the transcendent status, "wholly other," of its divine spouse. For the essential characteristic which differentiates what is "wholly other" (God, the world beyond, eternal life, and so on) from the realities of this world is the absence of imperfection and evil. This is why, in order to become the spouse of the Transcendent, the Church needs to be delivered from its imperfection, its sin, its evil, in other words, to be "purified . . . through the bath of water in the word" (v. 26); the water which reabsorbs and the breath which carries sounds symbolize the Holy Spirit, the origin of the more-than-life and the process of its transmission; one understands how the Church, immense and universal womb set apart for a mission of fruitfulness, thus gives birth for its spouse to a multitude of "reborn" sons and daughters, especially through the sacramental channel of baptism. Let us go back to the triple parallel enunciations (vv. 26-27): not first holy but "sanctified," the Church by its mystical union with Christ, its spouse, becomes holy (v. 26), glorious, immaculate, forever young (v. 27ab), and freed from all that could be a cause of reproach (v. 27c). Among the three final propositions [YZY], one emerges at point [Z]) (v. 27ab). It takes on a somewhat special semantic value with regard to the other two. Why, one could ask, did Paul want to concentrate attention precisely on it? For two reasons in our opinion. The first is in reference to the nuptial theme: according to custom, on the wedding day the bride was "presented" to the man "in splendor," that is, sumptuously dressed and adorned with heavy jewels.[10] The other is due to the occurrence of the word "Church," around which, in fact, the whole of the small theological development of vv. 26-27 is organized.

---

10. *Endoxon*, "glorious," renders the Hebrew *kᵉbuddâ*. The root *kbd*, originally evoked the idea of weight, heaviness, no less than that of radiance.

2. Then comes an *explanatory subsection* (vv. 29-31) within the structure of the section addressed to husbands. Here, Paul leaves aside the
imperative style and the tone of moral exhortation in order to go deeper
into the second point of the comparison he has just introduced (cf. v.
28b). The thought unfolds on the pattern of concentric construction:

> X   *sarka*, "flesh" (v. 29ab)
>
> Y   (vv. 29c-30)
>
> X   *sarka* (v. 31)

The inclusion X . . . X contains the purely psychological and biological part of the argumentation. One can reconstitute Paul's reason-
ing rather simply by having recourse to a syllogism:

- nothing is more natural than loving one's own body (v. 29a) as is
  shown by the care one takes in feeding and protecting it (v. 29b);

- now it is said in Genesis that woman and man come to form "one
  flesh" (v. 31b);[11]

- therefore—the affirmation is naturally inferred from the argument—
  nothing is more natural for a man than loving his wife; what v. 28 already had stated and what v. 33a will repeat again.

Point Y (vv. 29c-30) bases the argument on a deeper justification,
theological, or more exactly, Christological in nature. The married man
must take care of his wife as he does his own flesh, patterning his behavior on Christ the bridegroom in his constant solicitude for the
Church. Here Paul subtly passes from the word "flesh" *(sarx)* to the
word "body" *(sōma):* we who form the Church, "we are members of
[the] body" of Christ; in other words, through the mystery of an eternal
marriage, we become with him "one flesh" (see v. 31b).

3. The two subsections addressed to spouses (vv. 25-28 and 29-31)
are not simply juxtaposed but form a *homogeneous whole*. The proof of
this is the inclusion. It would be possible to consider the occurrences of
the word *gynē*, one in the beginning, the other at the end of the section
(vv. 25a and 31a), as forming an inclusion. But it is better to take vv. 32-
33 as the final marker of the inclusion, even though these verses go beyond the section, and to hold onto the key expression *agapan tas gynaikas
(tēn gynaikan)*, "to love his wife" (vv. 25a and 33a), because these words
best express the essential import of the section directed to husbands.[12]

11. See Gen 2:24.
12. One could add the pair "Christ . . . Church" (vv. 25b and 32) which has a
crucial importance in Paul's argumentation in support of the moral exhortation.

One should not be surprised at the placement of the final marker of the inclusion beyond the end of the section: first, this phenomenon is frequent in biblical writing; and especially second, the inclusion of the first section, as we have seen, also proceeds by going beyond its limits (in this case the initial marker is placed before the inclusion). Therefore, there is a rather astonishing stylistic symmetry in the two intersectional inclusions, as shown in the following diagram:

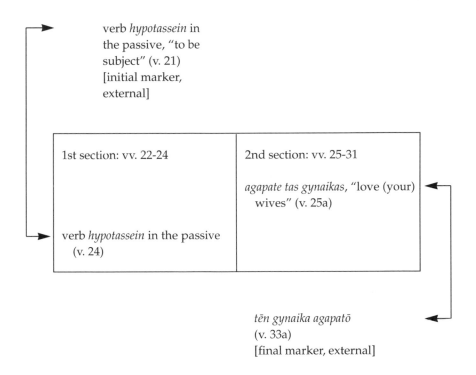

Let us add one last observation. From the thematic viewpoint, the phrase *hōs heauton* "as himself" in v. 33a recalls v. 28.

The Parallelism of the Two Sections (vv. 22-24 and 25-31)

The two sections framed by the markers of the large inclusion A . . . A not only follow one another but form a true diptych. This arrangement comprises, at the very least, the entire first section and first subsection of the second section, in brief, the two sides of the moral exhortation as such. In order to better illustrate the relationships between the two, let us pick out the pertinent elements of the text:

²¹ (Be) subject . . . ²² (Thus,) *WIVES TO (THEIR) OWN HUSBANDS.* . . .	²⁵ᵃ *HUSBANDS,* love (your) *WIVES*
²³ᵃᵇ *AS ALSO CHRIST* (is) head of the *CHURCH*	²⁵ᵇᶜ *AS ALSO CHRIST* has loved the *CHURCH.* . . .
²³ᶜ himself savior of the *BODY.* ²⁴ . . . *SO* also, *WIVES TO HUSBANDS.* . . .	²⁸ *IN THE SAME WAY* they must, *HUSBANDS,* love their wives like their (own) *BODIES.* . . .

1. To begin with, we can describe the *structuralist formula* of the diptych as follows: (BCD)$^\alpha$ // (BCD)$^\omega$. The bipolarity bride → bridegroom [α] and bridegroom → bride [ω] aims at synthesizing, that is, expressing in its totality the reality of conjugal relationships in conformity with the Christian ideal.

2. The *first segment* of the correspondences [B$^\alpha$ // B$^\omega$] is based on the repetition of the words *gynaikes* and *andres*, "wives" and "husbands." It contains Paul's ethical exhortation to wives (v. 22) then to husbands (v. 25a): "subjection" for the former, "love" for the latter. From the analysis of the great inclusion, we have already sensed the interchangeability of the two terms.

3. The *second segment* [C$^\alpha$ // C$^\omega$] is based on the repetition of *(kat)hōs kai ho Christos . . . tēs (tēn) ekklesias (-an)*, "as also Christ . . . the Church." It introduces on both sides the theological justification: Christ the spouse is "head of the Church" (v. 23ab); he "loved the Church" and "delivered himself up for her" (v. 25bc).

4. The *third segment* [D$^\alpha$ // D$^\omega$] is again based on the words *gynaikes* and *andres*, thus reiterating (to form the intra-sectional inclusion) the contents of the first segment. But it contains also two more recurrences: *houtōs*, "as also," which, at the end of the Christological affirmation, brings back the text to the moral exhortation; then *sōma*, "body," according to a semantic tension between the purely biological meaning (v. 28a) and the metaphorical sense (v. 23c). We shall come back to this point.

5. Up to now, in our analysis of the diptych we have omitted the second subsection of the discourse addressed to husbands (vv. 29-31). As we have seen, it is simply an addition supplying a scriptural basis for

the comparison introduced in v. 28. However, one remarks a striking *parallelism between point YY of the first section* (v. 23) *and point Y of the explanatory subsection* (v. 29):

²³ . . . *AS ALSO CHRIST* (is) head of the *CHURCH,* himself savior of the *BODY.*	^{29c} . . . *AS ALSO CHRIST* (does for) the *CHURCH,* ³⁰ for we are members of his *BODY.*

Here again three expressions recur: *ho Christos, tēs (tēn) ekklesias (-an),* and *sōma*. But this time, "body" has only the metaphorical meaning and applies to the Church in both places. This structuralist relationship confirms what we have already suggested when speaking of the symbolism of the "head." This word evokes above all, not superiority and domination, but responsibility in relation to life ("savior") and sustenance (provider of food, well-being, and protection).

Determination of the Global Structuralist Formula

All these critical considerations, from both the formal and semantic viewpoints, lead us to determine in a more authoritative manner the structuralist formula of the whole pericope: $A/(BCD)^{\alpha}//(BCD)^{\omega}/A$. We can now condense into one diagram the major articulations of the text:

A
love-subjection-fear in general
(v. 21)

$(BCD)^{\alpha}$ *love-subjection in the wife* **(vv. 22-24)**	$(BCD)^{\omega}$ *love-self-giving in the husband* **(vv. 25-31)**

A
love-self-giving in the husband and love-respect in the wife
(vv. [32 and] 33)

Complements of Micro-Structuralist Analysis

It is advantageous—even on the theological plane—to study at the most microscopic level the mechanism of certain phrase constructions: specifically, vv. 21-22, 23, 24, 25, and 28.[13]

13. We have analyzed the ternary parallelism of vv. 26-27 above, p. 131.

1. *vv. 21-22* are organized as follows:

[a] Subject	[b^{whole}] to one another	[c] in the fear of Christ
	[b^{part}] wives to (their) own husbands	[c'] as to the Lord

The theme of the two members of the sentence is subjection [a]; the attitude of subjection prescribed to wives in particular is placed clearly within a general exhortation actually addressed to all Christians [b^{whole} //b^{part}] in the essential and explanatory framework of the spiritual relationship of every believer with Christ [c//c'].

2. In perfect conformity to the classical model of the *māšāl, v.23ab* places what is compared and the point of comparison in parallel:

For	[a] a husband	[b] is	[c] head of his wife	
As also	[~a] Christ		[~c] head of the Church	[d] himself savior of the body

It is evident that v. 23c, which is supremely important from the theological viewpoint, adds the [d] element to the parallelism; one can speak of an addendum.

3. Then comes *v. 24* which is also a perfect *māšāl:*

But as	[a~] the Church	[b] is subject	[~c] to Christ	
so also	[a] wives		[c] to husbands	[d] in everything

As in v. 23ab, it is the twofold analogy wives ~ Church and husbands ~ Christ which structures the parallelism; the only difference is that the two terms of the comparison reverse the order they had in v. 23ab, this merely for stylistic reasons. As in v. 23c, two words [d: "in everything"] are an addendum to the parallelism: they add a note of totality which intensifies the malaise of contemporary readers.

4. In *v. 25*, Paul continues with the same analogy, even though the addressee is different:

as also	[a] husbands	[b] love	[c] (your) wives
	[~a] Christ	[b] loved	[~c] the Church
		[b'] and delivered himself up	[~c'] for her

The structuralist formula illustrates two literary characteristics: first, of course, the form of the *māšāl;* then the important hendiadys formed by the pair "to love" and "to deliver oneself up," which determines in all clarity the specific, unique kind of love which Christian ethics promotes.

5. In *v. 28*, the parallelism is a little less strict from the literary viewpoint; it is not much more than a purely formal repetition:

In the same way	[a] husbands	[b] love their wives	[c] like (they love)
they must			their (own) bodies;
	[a'] the one	[b] loving his wife	[c'] loves himself

The first member of the sentence, in the plural, enunciates a "duty" of marital love based on natural self-love; the second member, in the singular, takes up the same idea under the form of a sapiential principle, of a saying, of a proverb drawn from common experience.

2. Contextual, Theological, and Moral Hermeneutic

In this study we are pursuing an essentially exegetical objective with all the required methodological rigor. We must be clear. We are not seeking first and foremost to defend Paul's teaching or to champion at all cost an egalitarian ideology by striving to base it on Eph 5:21-33. It would be rash, naive, and futile to want to completely exonerate the apostle of any tendency to hierarchize the roles within the couple, society, and the Church. Paul's thought—this is a truism—bears the mark of his milieu and his time. But one question immediately arises: Must we explain by cultural limitations the whole content of his moral challenge, including the theological justification on which it is based? Let us attempt to distinguish, with as much finesse as possible, the elements of the text which are due to the contingent context—and which, as a consequence, cannot in any way be normative for us today—and the deeper transcultural elements, those which still illuminate, and always will, the "mystery" of conjugal life (see v. 32) and which express in some way an incontrovertible aspect of God's thought and plan.

The Cultural Limits of the Pauline Discourse

Two ropes, in a manner of speaking, bind Paul's argumentation in some way: the one concerns the structure of social relationships as they were in his society; the other, the way of interpreting the Hebrew Scriptures current at the time.

1. It was a mark of ancient cultures to subordinate certain social groups to others. The whole formed by Eph 5:21–6:9 presupposes and

maintains this *non-egalitarian scheme:* the relations husband → wife, parents → children, masters → slaves squarely fit into a social relation of dominant over dominated. And this is true despite the toning-down which Paul repeatedly brings to his discourse in order to make the de-ontology (the teaching of moral responsibilities and duties) reversible, that is, bilateral.

Paul does not directly challenge these social structures—which had been firmly rooted in his milieu for centuries and would remain so for many centuries to come—but which at bottom are contingent and mu-table. However, he occasionally relativizes them. For instance in the matter of conjugal relations:

> — For the wife does not have authority over her own body, but the hus-band does; likewise the husband does not have authority over his own body, but the wife does (1 Cor 7:4).

> — But I want you to understand that Christ is the head of every man, and the husband is the head of his wife, and God is the head of Christ. . . . Indeed, man was not made from woman, but woman from man. . . . Nevertheless, in the Lord woman is not independ-ent of man or man independent of woman. For just as woman came from man, so man comes through woman (1 Cor 11:3, 8, 11-12).

> — There is no longer Jew or Greek, there is no longer slave or free, there is no longer male and female (Gal 3:28).

In the same vein, with regard to the institution of slavery, let it suffice to reread the note to Philemon.

2. In Eph 5:21-33, Paul explicitly refers to the Yahwistic story of crea-tion (v. 31). We have even suggested the possibility of another reminis-cence (23a), still more obvious after the reading of 1 Cor 11:3, 8, 11-12! This conviction that man was created before woman—whereas scien-tific paleobiology could argue to the contrary—is the consequence of a somewhat *fundamentalist reading* of Scripture, which modern exegesis with its methods easily succeeds in reevaluating. At least as we have interpreted it, the symbolism of the "husband-head," even though one should not abusively harden it by reading it in terms of authority, su-periority, and total power, is akin to this historicizing interpretation which takes the data of Genesis at face value without submitting them to the test of literary criticism.

The Sociological Context of the Pauline Exhortation

A structuralist study like ours enables us to visualize, as if by x-ray, the articulations of the text and thought. Now, one realizes at first sight that the second part of the diptych, addressed to husbands (vv. 25-31), is much more developed that the one directed to wives (vv. 22-24). Moreover, we have noted that the imperative form, or its equivalent, the verb "must," is frequent in the exhortation to husbands while it is softened by ellipses (vv. 22 and 24b) and relegated in the sentence preceding the section (see v. 21) addressed to wives.[14]

How are we to interpret these data? The places where the imperative form is used certainly betray sensitive spots in conjugal relationships which required Paul's energetic and theologically well-founded admonition concerning the mutual subjection of men and women (v. 21) and the love husbands must lavish on their wives (v. 25; see also v. 28a). In fact, in Paul's time, the "husband" still had the attitude reflected by the corresponding Hebrew word *baʿal* (literally "lord," "master," "ruler"). For his part, Paul turns this attitude upside down in two passages:

— He commands husbands to "love" and "to deliver themselves up" (the hendiadys *agapan kai heauton paradounai* in v. 25). This is a complete reversal of the sexual conjugal relationship in which the wife passively delivers her body to her husband.

— With supreme audacity, Paul extends to all Christians, men and women, the duty of passive "subjection" (participle *hypotassomenoi* in v. 21), with the etymological meaning of "to go along with, to place oneself under," here again reversing, implicitly, the classical schemes of the most ordinary and natural position for the practice of sexual relations.

Furthermore, Paul seems to present wives' subjection less as an exhortation than as a statement of fact (vv. 22 and 24b). This is probably why he does not insist and does not feel obliged to use the imperative mode. He is content with justifying such an attitude, then socially accepted, by a Christological argument. We believe that one can conclude that, in Paul's time, women accepted without too many protests or rebellion this type of conjugal relations, characterized by their subjection.

The Theological Pearls of the Pauline Argumentation

We believe we can find in our passage from Paul five transcultural affirmations concerning Christian marriage, that is, points of theology which have the value of a timeless doctrine.

1. First is the idea of the *salvation* of the couple. It is in v. 23c that the word *sōtēr* is explicitly used.

14. See pp. 128–129.

Now, as we have seen, on the stylistic level, this little fragment of a sentence looks like an addendum to the otherwise perfect internal parallelism of v. 23ab.[15] One thing is certain, one cannot see there an addition, a gloss, a later interpolation. Three reasons oppose this supposition:

— The first reason, stylistic, is based on the use of an identical construction at the end of v. 24.

— The second reason, maxi-structuralist, is due to the undeniable relationship of vv. 23abc and 29c-30, in which one finds the only two metaphorico-symbolic uses of the word *sōma*, "body" of Christ (= Church).[16]

— The third reason, thematic, rests on the recurrence of the theme of soteriology, from one end of our passage to the other (vv. 23c, 25c, 26-27, 29c).

Everywhere in the text, the savior is Christ. Still, the following question arises: From the comparative transposition of v. 23, can one infer that the husband is the savior of his wife as Christ is "savior of the body"? This would be possible if in the sentence structure, Christ saved in virtue of being "head of the Church." But the stylistic discontinuity observed between v. 23ab and 23c renders this hypothesis untenable. The analogy between husband and Christ is founded on the word "head," the only common denominator between the two; in fact, this analogy is valid merely on the sociological plane (responsibility in the order of family and social relationships). The idea of "salvation," added here to give Christological (see v. 25bc) and ecclesiological (see v. 30) depth to the whole statement, cannot in any way be transposed to the plane of conjugal relationships.

Let us say in conclusion that within the married couple, neither is the "savior" of the other. According to the usage of antiquity, it was the husband's duty to provide food and clothing for his wife (see v. 29 together with v. 28). But there is a vast difference between insuring someone's quality of life and giving someone life (= saving)! Both parties are therefore gratuitously saved. In other words, "savior of the body" in its entirety, Christ is the sole savior of the husband, the wife, the couple, and the family as a domestic church.

2. Another theological pearl, the *holiness* of the couple. Here again, Paul explicitly applies the theme to the bride-Church (vv. 26-27). Set apart (this is the original meaning of the Hebrew *qādôš*) by immersion

15. See p. 136.
16. See pp. 133–135.

into the "bath" of faith and the "word" placed in her, the Church appears radiant, endowed with unfading youth and unsullied moral integrity. By being believers and children of the bride-Church, Christian couples receive the fruits of sanctification generated by this marriage of Christ with humanity.

3. As to the idea of the *newness* of the couple, Paul borrows it from Genesis: "He will leave, the man, father and mother, and will attach himself to his wife" (v. 31ab). Only here, this idea is enriched by the profound mystery of the marriage of the Risen One with the Church. To begin at the incarnation: the Bridegroom leaves the Father's house (heaven) in which he enjoyed transcendent relationships (intra-trinitarian) in order to contract unheard-of relationships with humankind based on total self-giving. And this leads him to the cross, a paroxysmal experience of self-sacrificing love (v. 25bc).

4. The scriptural quotation continues: "and they will be, the two of them, [oriented] to [form] one [single] flesh" (v. 31c).[17] This is how the ancient author to whom Paul refers comments upon the exclamation he attributes to Adam after Eve arises: "This at last is really a bone of my bones and a flesh of my flesh." This expression is holistic and of the bipolar type which expresses the totality of the person with two complementary terms: bones, symbol of stability, and flesh, symbol of fragility. In the thought of the Yahwist theologian, this was a means of underlining the perfect unity and identity of nature shared by the man and the woman. Whereas Adam had given names to animals, a sign of his superiority and power over them, the woman has no other name than that of the man, in the feminine form (*ʾiššâ*). Here again, Paul endows the sacred text with a singular depth of meaning. The *unity* of the husband and wife is based on the exemplar Christ ⇆ Church: a community of flesh and fruitfulness, of course, but equally a community of purpose and destiny.

5. All this can be summarized by a feature which is a synthesis, the *sacramentality* of the couple. Obviously, one cannot say that Paul is the creator of this term itself, but Eph 5:21-33 actually establishes the foundation for the theological reality of marriage as a sacrament.

One does not expect to find, hardly veiled in the text, a very strict theoretical framework in matters of symbolism. In his reflection, Paul always accents *the symbolized*, that is to say, the union "as-matrimonial"

---

17. *Kai esontai hoi dyo eis sarka mian.* Our paraphrase seeks to render the rich nuances of the text.

of Christ with the Church. This idea is most clearly brought out in two places in the pericope under study.

> — The apex is certainly in v. 32 in which Paul defines this relation Christ ↔ Church as "a great mystery" *(mystērion mega)*. St Jerome has translated this by the Latin word *sacramentum,* which goes beyond what the Greek text strictly means. For Paul, it is the "symbolized" (Christological-ecclesiological) which is the "mystery," and not the human, observable, and tangible "symbolizing," which refers to it and suggests it (the couple—in today's theological terms, we would say by mode of sacrament). As for Jerome, when speaking of "sacrament," he places himself rather on the side of the "symbolizing," in the same vein as the quotation from Genesis in the preceding verse.

> — The other striking expression using spousal symbolism is in v. 27a: on his wedding day, Christ "present[s] her to himself, glorious, the Church." The expression recalls clearly, but freely, the ritual in use in Jewish weddings in which the task of presenting the bride was incumbent on a relative or a friend of the bridegroom.[18]

In fact, to define the relation husband ↔ wife in comparison with the relation Christ ↔ Church, Paul does not strictly adhere to the literary categories of symbolic transposition, but rather uses the analogical, comparative, or metaphorical style. This happens four times:

> — in v. 23, on the basis of the twofold use of the word "head";
> — in v. 24, on the basis of the idea of "subjection" (owed to the "head");
> — in v. 25, from the viewpoint of the husband's "love";
> — in v. 29, from the viewpoint of the care one takes of one's own "flesh."

Therefore, it would appear at first sight that we have a simple exemplarity, at least in vv. 24, 25, and 29, which strictly speaking pertain more to ethical exhortation than to symbolic theology. Paul successively recommends three attitudes: to wives, subjection; to husbands, self-giving love and care in providing for the material and affective needs of their wives. One probably could extrapolate and include v. 23, especially if the word "head" must be understood in a moral and sociological sense (responsibility) rather than as an anthropological and philosophical observation on the respective natures of man and woman.[19]

18. See p. 131.
19. See p. 129.

By sacramentality of the couple we mean the creatural potential—which the relation husband ↔ wife possesses as "symbolizing"—to evoke the mystery of the relation Christ ↔ Church (or God ↔ Israel, God ↔ humanity). Strictly speaking, this sacramentality of the couple does not quite belong to the literal exegesis of Eph 5:21-33 but rather to the reinterpretation and deeper theological examination of the text. But one is easily led there even within an intra-biblical theology since this sacramentality was already explicitly revealed in the Old Testament: clearly in the conjugal experience of the prophet Hosea (Hos 1–3), which is manifestly a "symbolic action in the most technical meaning of the term. The same is true of certain allegories, as that in Ezekiel 16 or even those in the Song of Songs, at least at the stage of the canonical utilization of this text in Judaism and later on in Christianity. In itself, the union of the created couple (the "symbolizing") calls for what is beyond itself: the union of the uncreated with the created at the very heart of history (the "symbolized"). In other words, if God created humans "male and female" (Gen 1:27) "as [his] image and [his] likeness" (Gen 1:26), it is not only in order that humans "multiply and fill the earth and subdue it" (Gen 1:28), but in order that they may discover through their own conjugal experience the secret cipher hidden there, a mystery of infinite love, an eternal plan of communion, fruitfulness, and salvation.

The Moral Scope of the Pauline Challenge

Let us return to the level of what is observable. What sort of ethics derives from Paul's exhortations to wives and husbands? Three explicit terms crop up in this respect, "subjection," "love," "fear." One can legitimately add the sense of responsibility, inferred from the interpretation we have given of the word "head."

1. Logically, we are obliged to treat the first two terms together, since they are placed in a strict parallelism in the maxi-structure.[20] Therefore, we shall speak of a conjugal ethics of *love-subjection*.

At the end of our technical analysis, let us recall the principal points arrived at: on the one hand, women's subjection is inserted into the wider framework of the mutual subjection enjoined on all Christians (v. 21); on the other hand, "subjection" (vv. 22, 24) and "self-giving love" (v. 25) are equivalent and interchangeable up to a certain point.

20. For the large inclusion, see pp. 126, 128, and for the diptych, see pp. 133–135.

(a) In order to clarify through semantics the first of these two points, an analysis of the biblical theme of "subjection" will be helpful, starting from the uses of the verb *hypotassein*. The Septuagint does not yield much that can serve our purpose.[21] The New Testament proves a bit more productive. Out of a total of thirty-seven occurrences of *hypotassein*, fourteen interest us more particularly because they deal with social status, either in general or within the ecclesial community.[22] This analysis enables us to list the main groups of persons called "submissive": in society, wives to their husbands, servants to their masters, the civil population to the heads of the state; in the Church, the "women,"[23] the young, and the whole community to the spiritual leaders.

Nowhere, whether in the Church or in civil society, is there any question of advocating an autocratic power or of recommending blind and total obedience. In every occurrence, or nearly every occurrence, one could, without weakening or betraying the text, translate the word "subjection" by "respect." To sum up, in social, socio-ecclesial, and moral matters, that is, in the sphere of human relationships, *hypotassein* never has the very strong meaning of constraint and domination that it has in theological and Christological enunciations. One example will suffice to illustrate this: Luke 2:51. In Jesus, God (the Son) does not find

21. The 27 occurrences of *hypotassein* translate some ten different Hebrew terms. Most often, what is meant is military and political subjection (21 times); 5 times, the religious subjection of humans to God; once, the subjection of animals to humans.

22. Here is how the occurrences are divided:

—Cosmic meaning: the universe "subjected" for a time to futility (twice), then to Christ (12 times); the demons "subject" to the power of the Twelve (twice).

—Ecclesiological meaning: the Church subject to Christ, her head (once).

—Religious meaning: "non-subjection" to God (twice); subjection to God (once).

—Christological meaning: the eschatological Christ "subject" to God (once).

—Anthropological meaning: the "inspirations of the prophets subject to the prophets" (once).

—Social meaning: women "subject" in conjugal life (4 times without counting 2 occurrences where the word is grammatically implied); slaves or servants "subject" to their masters and mistresses (twice); the people "subject" to magistrates and legitimate political authorities (4 times); Jesus, having come of age, "subject" to his parents (once).

—Socio-ecclesial meaning: the young (once) and the entire community (once) "subject" to church leaders; women "subject" during community worship (once).

—Moral and spiritual meaning: Christians "subject" one to another (once).

23. 1 Cor 14:34, which, as Michel Gourgues notes in the preceding chapter, is perhaps simply a quotation recorded and then criticized by Paul. However, see also 1 Tim 2:11, which uses the noun rather than the verb *hypotassein*.

it demeaning to be "subject" to human beings, Mary and Joseph. And yet, at that time Jesus is no longer a child but a male Jew who has just reached the legal age of majority. All the more reason, therefore, for humans not to find it demeaning to be "subject," one to another (Eph 5:21), without regard for social status or sex.

From a more thematic viewpoint, Paul's affirmation is not all that unusual. In his exhortations concerning communal ethics, he advises Christians "not to think of [themselves] too highly" (Rom 12:3), "to regard others as better than [themselves]" (Phil 2:3), following the example of the self-emptying *(kenōsis)* to which Christ himself assented (Phil 2:5-8). There is in this passage the foundation of a Christian ethics and spirituality—absolutely inescapable—of subjection.[24]

(b) Let us take a further step. Can we claim that for Paul, subjection is the Christian form of every love? Are the two terms perfectly interchangeable from the ethical viewpoint? It is important to introduce distinctions and nuances.

On the one hand, the maxi-structuralist analysis of Eph 5:21-33 demonstrates two things. First, there is a strict relation between vv. 21 and 33 although separated because we are dealing with an inclusion: the proof of this is the repetition of the word "fear" (noun and verb); but more globally, "[to be] subject to one another" is parallel to "to love one's wife" + "to fear one's husband."[25] Afterwards, we showed the strictest parallelism between "wives subject to their husbands" (vv. 22, 24) and "husbands loving their wives" on the model of Christ, who "delivered himself up" (vv. 25, 28). The hendiadys "to love" and "to deliver oneself up for" attests to this modelling of husbands on Christ because the paradigm, at once human and divine, "subjected himself in everything" (see v. 24b) at the hands of his adversaries and assassins.

On the other hand, Paul could not properly, at least because of his own culture, reverse the two terms without falsifying his thought and even offending those to whom his message was addressed. He would never have been tempted to write, "Husbands, be subject to your wives and you, wives, love your husbands and deliver yourselves up for

24. See also Gal 5:13.

25. From a more technical viewpoint, how shall we qualify the relation? We do not think that it is a relation of pure and simple equivalence, of synonymity, but a relation of the general (v. 21) to the particular (v. 33): what is true on the plane of relationships within the whole community applies even more so to the married couples who are part of it. We must not forget the logical sequence (and even grammatical, in view of the participle *hypotassomenoi,* which refers to the preceding verse) between vv. 21-33 and vv. 19-20 which deal with the community worship.

them." Concerning the latter, he would have accomplished nothing, except to encourage a de facto situation which already excessively exposed women to exploitation by men. As for men, Paul could not, lest he arouse resistance or fall into ridicule, exhort them to subject themselves to their wives because of the social stereotypes and perhaps also—we alluded to this above—because of the sexual stereotypes in the matter of conjugal relations.

To summarize, even though the terms "subjection" and "love" in their concrete contextual meaning are not perfectly interchangeable, they nonetheless express the same conjugal ethics of selflessness, of self-renunciation for the benefit of the other spouse.[26]

2. Paul also outlines a conjugal ethics of *fear*. Structurally, the word is a weighty one: it is used twice and by itself determines the large inclusion, which formally unifies the whole pericope and gives it its dominant semantic color.

For us today, this word does not raise any fewer problems than the word "subjection," far from it. But we must understand it in its biblical sense. Especially in v. 21, it has the full meaning of the root *yr'* in the Hebrew Scriptures. To fear God is not first of all to feel a morbid dread of God, but to develop towards God a religious attitude, full of respect and adoration, as well as an awareness of one's ethical and cultic duties. For Paul, the mutual subjection of believers must be practiced "in the fear of Christ," that is, with the full consciousness that such subjection is the consequence of the baptized persons' membership in the ecclesial community. So at the end of the pericope, Paul has no scruples about speaking of the wife's "fear" for her husband; we must understand the term as respect, veneration, always within the framework of human relationships completely renewed and deepened by the experience of faith in Christ.

This said, let us agree on one point: the majority of commentators do not give sufficient attention to the fact that, formally, Paul does not make "fear of the husband" an imperative, a command. Besides, as we have seen in our study of the first section (vv. 22-24), Paul does not give any order to women anywhere; he avoids all imperatives.[27] Likewise, in v. 33, the very form of the sentence limits the recommendation only to the man (use of the subjunctive): "[let] everyone love his wife . . . in order that the wife might fear [her] husband." The respect shown by

26. "If one wishes, perhaps one could say that Paul enjoins on the wife 'subjection in love' and on the husband 'love that subjects itself.'" Angelico Di Marco, "Ef. 5, 21–6, 9: Teologia della famiglia," *Rivista Biblica* 31 (1983) 197.

27. See pp. 128–129.

the wife to her husband is not the object of a formal order; it appears rather as a consequence of the effort made by the husband to practice self-giving love, the love which "delivers itself up."

Finally, in spite of slightly different semantic nuances, the words "subjection," "love," and "fear" complete one another and support one another in order to define new conjugal mores—running counter to the prevailing mores—which must be the specific mark identifying Christians.

3. Let us come to the last point: the conjugal ethics of *responsibility*. It rests on the twofold use of the word "head" in v. 23, with the precise meaning which we have emphasized.[28] At the surface of the text, one cannot doubt that the term applies exclusively to the husband and stems from the example of Christ, "head of the Church."

A similar idea recurs in vv. 28-29. When one melds the elements under syllogistic form, one perceives even more clearly Paul's argumentation:

— he who loves his wife loves his own body (v. 28b);

— he who loves his own body cares for it (v. 29ab);

— therefore, he who loves his wife must take care of her (implicit conclusion).

Up to now nothing more down to earth in the way of marital responsibility!

The introduction of the Christological paradigm certainly contributes to deepen the ethical reflection, but at the expense of continuity by a break in the argumentation:

— he who loves his own body takes care of it (v. 29ab);

— Christ takes care of his Church (v. 29c) which is his own body (v. 30);

— however, Christ has not taken care of his own body since "he gave himself up" for his Church to the point of suffering the horror of the cross (v. 25bc)!

The human ethic of responsibility entails the husband's duty to "feed" his wife and "keep her warm." However, the ethic of responsibility transfigured by faith in Christ can go to the point of exacting a total self-renunciation according to the example Jesus gave us. Such could be the summit of the moral demands of marriage as a sacrament.

---

28. See p. 129.

Let us now tackle the crucial question: Does the responsibility of this "head" within the life of the couple fall to the husband alone? According to the sociological and cultural schemes, Paul would have probably answered yes. But in our opinion, his theology does not necessarily imply such a hard line. In order to demonstrate this, we must go somewhat deeper into the point of comparison so that any possibility of sophism may be avoided. In reality, there is no dichotomy between the head and the body. By nature, the "head" is integrated into the "body" so that the divine "savior of the body" (v. 23c) is by the same token savior of the head. Moreover, men as "heads," as well as women—whether married or not—are part of the "body" of Christ (v. 30) and not part of the head. Finally, if it is equally true that "Christ is the head of the Church" which is his "body" (v. 23bc) and "the husband is head of his wife" (v. 23a), no one would state that the wife is the body of the husband-head. As we have said, within the strict exactitude of the micro-analysis, the parallelism of the sentence is limited to v. 23ab; formally, v. 23c is an addendum.[29] Therefore, it is possible, if not to demonstrate, at least to show to what degree the attribution of the family leadership to the husband rather than to the wife derives more from Paul's cultural baggage than from his theological insight.

Anyhow, v. 29 explicitly mentions two concrete signs of love as responsibility: to provide food and comfort. Now even in ancient societies, this twofold task was shared by man and wife. The former earned and brought the food, but it was the latter who prepared it to nourish her husband and children. The same applies to the clothes and the heating of the home, including the radiance of affective warmth. . . .

3. Pastoral Consequences

We would not want to end this study of a key text on Christian marriage without someway reaching into the contemporary life experience of married couples. Nowadays, this experience is subject to violent crises, a fact which obliges us to revise classical approaches.

The Interchangeability of Roles within the Couple

For some decades now, the concrete praxis of conjugal life has seriously brought into question not only Paul's cultural schemes but also his very theology. We shall limit ourselves to three observations.

29. See pp. 136 and 139–140.

First, the vertiginous increase in the number of women who are "heads" of the family. In itself the phenomenon is not completely new. Formerly, it happened that widows became heads of the household although the oldest son often assumed the responsibility of the family welfare in the place of his dead father. What is new is the magnitude of the phenomenon. Not only widows but more often wives, deserted by their husbands or having freed themselves from a suffocating marriage, fully assume the role of "head." In the majority of cases, the diagnosis of the disease reveals, at the root, the absence or insufficiency of love as subjection, love as self-giving (see Eph 5:21-22, 25, 33) in favor of the absolutized love-of-one's-own-flesh (see 28b, 29).

A second important social change is the number of women who now work outside the home and supply a second salary, in certain cases more substantial than the husband's. This results in a weakening of the traditional metaphorical attribution of the word "head," especially if it is defined, as we have done, in terms of responsibility. In many cases, we are forced to consider a twofold image of the "head": the one responsible for the other, the other for the one, and both together for the children; thus, the clearer delimitation of respective roles that obtained formerly is somewhat blurred. In such a context, one will be helped by the nuances we have brought to the subject, concerning the transposition of the word "head" from the Christological sphere to the socio-conjugal sphere.[30]

Finally, in certain countries the refinement and modernization of collective conventions regarding work have entailed entirely new clauses in relation to paternity leaves: at the birth of a child not just the mother is taken into account but the couple; the two spouses can, without loss of wages, share a certain number of weeks at home with the baby. All this fits in well with our structuralist reading of the diptych in Eph 5:21-33, according to which love as subjection (vv. 21-24) and love as self-giving (vv. 25-33) are two practically interchangeable terms.[31]

The Specificity of the Roles Within the Couple

Notwithstanding the preceding observations, psychology tends to demonstrate that there exists within the parental couple certain gender-specific contributions in the process of the integration of the child's personality. Beyond outrageously caricatured stereotypes—the macho father, authoritarian provider, image of strength, conquest, ability to deal with the exterior world, and the gentle mother, submissive, sensitive,

30. See pp. 147–148.
31. See pp. 145–146.

image of protection, affection, mercy, and intimate relationships—every child must have the irreplaceable experience of two distinct relationships, with the father and with the mother. In this domain, the anthropological and psychological sciences can enlighten theology and help it to eventually define in a more refined and transcultural way the symbolism man-Christ and woman-Church, without falling into simplism or ideology.

The Indissolubility of Christian Marriage

Within our social context, in which separations and divorces are proliferating like an epidemic, the New Testament texts enjoining the stability of marriage act as a killjoy or douse like a cold shower. However, the command goes back to Jesus himself, who in this disagrees with Moses and the rabbis of his time.[32] No pericope brings to this doctrine a more profound theological justification than Eph 5:21-33. As we have seen, from one end of the text to the other, Paul understands conjugal love (the "symbolizing") only in relation to the mystery of Christ (the "symbolized").[33] Under at least three aspects, he adds considerable depth to the theological content of Genesis 2:24, which he quotes verbatim. From the hermeneutical viewpoint, Paul innovates by revealing the profound and hidden meaning (typological) of the ancient text (see Eph 5:31-32). From the properly Christological viewpoint, the purpose of the unity of the human couple is to reflect, symbolize, and strive to reproduce the unity of the Risen One with humanity, his bride. But from the moral viewpoint, this purpose of unity and stability soon becomes unrealizable if one does not conquer the natural instincts of domination ("to subject" rather than "to be subject to"), egotism (the love that grasps, possesses, and draws all things toward itself rather than the love that gives and "delivers itself up for").

And so it is indispensable that the concrete man and woman who come together to share one destiny have, at the root of their union, a minimum understanding of symbolization. Hence the importance for the Church to maintain and develop a pastoral ministry caring for couples who are badly matched, in order to free them from null and void marriages, that is, asymbolical marriages. Prolonging these marriages ends over time in fostering hellish situations gravely destructive not only to the couple but also to the children born to them.

---

32. See, among others, Matt 19:1-9.
33. See pp. 141–142.

The Holiness of Christian Marriage

To a world in which many trivialize conjugal infidelity, the paradigm of Christ, who, in his nuptials with the Church, makes it holy, can offer weighty matter for reflection . . . and conversion. Already Genesis 2:24 presented the conjugal relation as marked by breaking apart.[34] Paul prefers the language of setting apart and purification.[35] One can draw from Eph 5:26-27 three practical corollaries for married couples, three fruits of genuine love as self-giving (alias love-subjection or love-fear):

— to "purify" oneself without ceasing by plunging into the bath of the "word" proclaimed in the ecclesial assembly Sunday after Sunday;

— never to let mutual love be affected by "stain" or "wrinkle" or grow old;

— not to give one's spouse grounds for reproaches by giving him or her a love which is imperfect, disappointing, and opposed to the Christological model.

Conclusion

As elsewhere in his letters, Paul does not batter down the walls built by the culture and usages of his time. But this in no way prevents him from being a foremost herald in proclaiming the newness of the message and experience of the Risen One.[36] The meticulous study of Eph 5:21-33 will have enabled us to detect some limits to Paul's way of expressing himself but above all to sense and taste the immeasurable theological and spiritual force that drove him, an apostle and a pastor.

It would be a loss to remove from public reading and sophisticated theological reflection a biblical text so powerful and masterfully structured,[37] one which better than any other paves the way for a Christian theology of sacramental marriage. In recent exegesis, the trend is to insist on the idea of mutual subjection and subordination of the two spouses.[38] But in general, recent exegesis fails to show, as we have felt it

34. See pp. 140–141.

35. See p. 141.

36. See Michel Bouttier, *L'épître de saint Paul aux Éphésiens* (Geneva, Labor et Fides, 1991) 242: "[From the familial code in force], the submission remains, but the motive is turned upside down."

37. This, contrary to what C. Leslie Mitton asserts, *Ephesians,* New Century Bible Commentary (Grand Rapids, Mich.: Eerdmans, 1981) 210.

38. For instance, Markus Barth, *Ephesians,* The Anchor Bible 34A (Garden City, N.Y.: Doubleday 1974) 608–610, 700–720; M. Huftier, "Sur les droits de la femme,"

was useful to do, how this viewpoint is based on the strictest structuralist composition of the pericope.

For us there remains at the end of this research a troublesome point which calls for further study: the symbolism of the "head" and the "body." We probably have here a useful clue, indeed, an irreplaceable and unavoidable one, not only for refining further the theology of the couple and family but also for submitting to a much more systematic analysis the whole problem—how relevant today—of the access or non-access of women to ordained ministries. The Christian practice of ministries will never be sufficiently clarified by relying solely on anthropological and sociological considerations, although these are useful. Equally insufficient is a demonstration based only on the technical exegesis of scriptural passages, none of which, we must admit, directly deals with these questions. The solution resides, at least in our opinion, in the emergence of a true symbolic theology which would know how to reconstruct in their mysterious unity the plane of created nature and the plane of nature potentially perfected in Jesus Christ "savior of the body" which is the Church (Eph 5:23). It is there, in this "great mystery," among all others, (5:32) that the Christian couple, in the process of incessant growth, finds its true dignity, its fullness of meaning, and the sources of the still unknown ethics of freedom which is its own.

Esprit et Vie 89 (1979) 561–568; Di Marco, "Ef. 5, 21–6, 9," 189–207; E. Fuchs, "De la soumission des femmes: Une lecture d'Éphésiens 5, 21–33," *Le Supplément* 161 (1987) 73–81; Robert W. Wall, "Wifely Submission in the Context of Ephesians," *Christian Scholar's Review* 3 (1988) 272–285; J. R. Beck, "Is There a Head of the House in the Home? Reflections on Ephesians 5," *Journal of Biblical Equality* 1 (1989) 61–70; G. F. Wessels, "Ephesians 5:21-33 'Wives, be subject to your husbands. . . . Husbands, love your wives,'" *Journal of Theology for South Africa* 67 (1989) 67–76; John E. Toews, "Paul's Radical Vision for the Family," *Direction* 19 (1990) 29–38; and so on.

The Authority of the Bible Challenged by Feminist Hermeneutics

◆────────────────────────────────────◆

Gérald Caron

I have chosen to present this study for two main reasons, one hermeneutical, the other much more personal.

The question of the authority of the bible is more than ever on the agenda. More specifically, it is the value of biblical tradition itself (or of certain of its parts) which is under the closest scrutiny. People continue to study the bible,[1] to refer to it, to consult it, and even to be nourished by it. For a great number of persons, it is still sacred scripture and remains an eminent guide for one's spiritual journey. But one no longer has the same reverential attitude, one approaches it in a different manner, one feels more freedom in assessing the world it reflects, and of course, completely in harmony with the modern mentality, one dares to question it to the point of doubting its usefulness for today's world. This explains in large part why the bible's authority has become one of the most pressing and timely questions for biblical hermeneutics. Today, many symptoms reveal that reading the bible causes increasing malaise. It would be irresponsible to ignore it and, even more, to minimize its importance.

Now, on the more personal plane. First, as a Christian who continues to be nourished by scripture but also as an interpreter always seeking to facilitate more and more the experience of the word of God, I do not escape the increasingly troubling questions which modern society asks of the Christian tradition, originating in scripture. Since these questions also prove to be my own, it seems urgent to me to know how to approach them and, if possible, answer them. How can I safeguard the

1. In this study, the words "bible" and "church" will not be capitalized because their authority has been called into question [note in the French edition]. [In the interest of consistency, the words "scripture" and "scriptures" will also not be capitalized. Ed.]

authority of the word of God and at the same time develop a critical sense or, better still, a hermeneutical principle that enables me to read the scriptures in a way which respects my personal integrity? This dilemma is not as simple as it appears. Speaking of my own journey, it took me years to be able to assert and maintain (in all serenity) that such and such a passage of scripture is not or is no longer word of God either for me or for the community to which I belong. Therefore, I squarely and consciously place myself within today's way of approaching the problem, a way which is at the very core of the debate on the authority of scripture. In my opinion, this way is particularly well presented by contemporary feminist criticism.

I have divided my article into four parts. First, I shall try to pose the problem clearly as it is raised by feminist criticism. Second, I shall come to the important question of the place attributed to the experience of women in feminist hermeneutics and its consequences for the manner of perceiving scripture. In my third part, I will attempt to identify what is at stake in this discussion and its considerable effects on the elaboration of what could be termed a new model of authority. I shall end by presenting some elements of reflection in view of attempting a tentative first evaluation or first assessment of the current debate.

1. The Problem

The questioning of the bible's authority, or of certain portions, is not a new phenomenon. The names of Marcion and Luther are often mentioned in this regard. But closer to us, the rise of modern biblical criticism and historico-critical methods has been the first true challenge to the traditional way of regarding the bible. It goes without saying that such a revolution profoundly affected traditional theological discourse on the inspiration as well as on the authority of the scriptures.[2] This sort of "relativizing" of the bible did not happen without conflict, and what has been called the "battle" for the bible still goes on in certain evangelical milieux, clearly illustrating the often violent debate caused by this new way of approaching the biblical text. Over the past twenty, thirty, or even forty years, the work of initiating hundreds of students into historico-critical methods has no doubt given many teachers the

2. Although these concepts have become technical terms to designate a specific domain of the faith, they are not synonymous. Whereas the first one tends to designate the unique character of the Scriptures, the second stresses more the effect of these writings on the believing community. As the title suggests, the problem which I intend to deal with pertains to the second concept.

opportunity of reliving their own "rite of passage." From the Catholic side, although the solution finally adopted at Vatican II proved quite liberating in some respects, it has not resolved all the problems, as I shall attempt to show at the very end of this study.[3]

Today's debate is resolutely downstream from the discussion generated by modern criticism, and due in large part to the attacks mounted by both liberation theologians and feminist criticism. One can say that in both cases, the initial impetus for critical reflection came from underprivileged and oppressed classes, and it is precisely this new perspective which later gave rise to a quite different way of regarding and reading the bible. In general, people are agreed on a radical critique of any reading which favors or maintains the status quo, but feminist criticism goes much farther by attacking not only the interpretation of the text but the value granted the biblical text itself. No longer is the problem simply to reconcile the bible's authority with the sort of questions raised by a historico-critical approach to the text or even with a reading falsified by some ideology (often unconscious) of the interpreter. What is questioned today, and in a radical manner, by this new type of criticism is the biblical text itself with its content, whether theological or ethical.[4]

Rosemary Radford Ruether's well-known study *Faith and Fratricide*, published in 1974, is a striking example of this. This sensational book raised and continues to raise troubling questions from ethical as well as Christological viewpoints, touching the very essence of the New Testament. The experience of the Holocaust has made us sensitive to such an extent that it is more and more difficult to ignore a language which has certainly nurtured, if not created, Christian anti-Semitism. But the calling into question goes much farther than mere language; it is aimed at the very contents of the New Testament. The challenge is gigantic, and to know how to respond is not simple. How are we to reconcile our vision and understanding of scripture with the certitude of having to deal with texts which appear plainly "immoral" to an increasing number of Christians of both sexes?[5]

---

3. See the Dogmatic Constitution on Divine Revelation, *Dei Verbum*, of Vatican II, no. 11: ". . . it follows that the books of Scripture must be acknowledged as teaching firmly, faithfully, and without error *that truth which God wanted put into the sacred writings for the sake of our salvation*" [emphasis added]. Vatican Council II, *The Documents of Vatican II*, ed. Walter M. Abbott (New York: Herder and Herder, 1966).

4. See Bruce C. Birch and Larry L. Rasmussen, "The Nature and Role of Biblical Authority," in *Bible and Ethics in the Christian Life* (Minneapolis: Augsburg, 1989) 145–147.

5. See Sandra M. Schneiders, *Beyond Patching: Faith and Feminism in the Catholic Church* (New York: Paulist Press, 1991) 53.

The challenge to the Jewish and Christian scriptures by recent feminist criticism runs along the same lines. As I have already pointed out, this new criticism stems from the community of the underprivileged, and in the case of feminist criticism, these underprivileged are above all women and their lived experience. Under the influence of the feminist movement, whose first goal is to promote the emancipation and liberation of women, many women learned to name this lived experience in terms of oppression, subordination, sexism, and violence. The bible had played—and continues to play—too important a role in Christian and Jewish consciousness to escape for long the critical eye of feminist researchers.[6] Thus, the bible was very rapidly accused of being one of the most insidious instruments, and for certain persons even the principal instrument, used in this operation of discrimination and exploitation. Rather than offering or dispensing a liberating message for both women and men, it is now perceived as a text that strengthens the solidly entrenched patriarchal and hierarchical system, maintains the statu quo, and so continues, under the banner of the word of God, to perpetuate the oppression of women. It is sufficient to mention here the well-known passage of 1 Tim 2:9-15 or that of Eph 5:21-32, up to very recently the favorite text at wedding celebrations.[7]

That the bible very rapidly became the "battlefield" of feminist studies is not surprising. As we just mentioned, it is accused of perpetuating the oppression, the bondage, and even the suppression of women. And it took little time to identify the real culprit. Born in an androcentric culture and in an essentially patriarchal system of values, the bible is the product and reflection of these. What is more, not only was the bible written by men and for men, but it was canonized by men; this is a fact fraught with heavy consequences, as is increasingly recognized. And up to a very recent past, this bible was the quasi-exclusive property of an authority exercised solely by men.

This recent awareness of the androcentric and patriarchal character of the bible is without doubt one of the most significant contributions of the theological criticism inspired by feminism. Once one's eyes are opened, it becomes more and more difficult to ignore and especially to remain insensitive to the disastrous effect which the androcentrism of the text and the patriarchal structures it supports have had of women's lives. They have been not only marginalized, reduced to silence, but in some way made invisible. This is true not only of the biblical texts

6. Already in the nineteenth century, Sojourner Truth, Anna Julia Cooper, and Elizabeth Cady Stanton, who edited *The Woman's Bible,* 2 vols. (New York: Arno Press, 1972 [© 1895–1898]), were very critical of certain claims found in the Scriptures on the subject of women.

7. On this, see Marc Girard's analysis in the preceding chapter.

themselves but even more of the manner in which they have been used to better control women. For many women and men today, it is useless, to paraphrase Radford Ruether, to talk of liberation if one is not prepared to include in it the liberation from patriarchal institutions, which are the true perpetrators of the oppression of women.

It is possible to speak of a certain consensus concerning the androcentrism of the biblical text and the patriarchal culture which as a rule it presupposes and supports. However, there is less agreement concerning the way of evaluating the importance of this historical phenomenon and more particularly the impact of such a reading on what response to make to certain claims of scripture. For instance, for the trend called "loyalist,"[8] the problem lies not at the level of the biblical text but rather at that of its interpretation. This said, we cannot underestimate the fact that the great majority of feminist criticisms goes far beyond this. They suspect, and even reject, not only the tendentious and often abusive interpretations given to one or another biblical passage in the course of centuries but a part of the text itself. As Sandra Schneiders has aptly stressed in her interesting little book *Beyond Patching*, the problem does nor reside outside but at the level of the text, that is, *in* it.[9] For several interpreters today, this very text has become "dangerous," it is a true "danger to health"[10] and must be handled with care, it speaks with "forked tongue."[11] All these are as many expressions of a state of affairs about which one does not have the right to remain silent.

Faced with this challenge, the women who persist in considering the bible as sacred have no way of returning to the past. Therefore, if the text itself is the defendant, if, as ideological feminist criticism maintains, the androcentrism of the bible and its patriarchal ideology are largely responsible for the oppression of women, for their marginalization, for their demonization, or simply for their suppression, it becomes impossible to ignore any longer the question of the *value* of this tradition. How can such texts, oppressive and tendentious for a part of the community, be regarded as normative? Could the God of the Jewish

---

8. On this terminology, see Carolyn Osiek, "The Feminist and the Bible: Hermeneutical Alternatives," in *Feminist Perspectives on Biblical Scholarship*, ed. A. Yarbro Collins (Chico, Calif.: Scholars Press, 1985) 93–105.

9. See Schneiders, *Beyond Patching*, 38.

10. Apparently, this expression was coined by Susan Brooks Thistlethwaite, who would have used it after a particularly arduous day spent at work on the *Inclusive Language Dictionary*. See Sharon H. Ringe, "The Word of God May Be Hazardous to Your Health," *Theology Today* 49 (1992) 371.

11. See Robin Scroggs, "How We Understand Scripture When It Speaks with Forked Tongue," in *The Text and the Times: New Testament Essays For Today* (Minneapolis: Fortress Press, 1993) 109–124.

scriptures, the God of Jesus Christ, be an oppressive, patriarchal, sexist, and racist God? Is there a word of God, some Good News for today's women? In brief, is it possible to escape the dilemma faced by feminist research: having to choose between remaining faithful to scripture, not without unmasking its patriarchal structure and exposing its fundamentally patriarchal character, and denying it any normative value and any authority?[12] Is there still any way to preserve the bible's authority or is one obliged to do anything, even to reject it, in order to neutralize the harmful effects it had and continues to have on women? In the last analysis, can one continue both to regard the bible as a sacred text and respect one's own integrity?

These incisive and disturbing questions are far from insignificant and to attempt an answer is not, despite appearances, a simple task. These questions present in all their acuteness the current debate on the authority of scripture as it is affected by feminist criticism. For the feminists of the current called "reformist" or "liberationist," who will be given special attention in the following pages, it is indispensable to find satisfying answers to these questions if one hopes to safeguard the normative character of the bible for the communities for whom it is sacred scripture.[13] For these circles, it is simply impossible to justify in any way the patriarchal discourse of oppression and domination. Nothing can approve of such a discourse, not even recourse to the bible.[14] The question is therefore the following: On what criteria does feminist criticism rely for selecting what can finally be accepted, rejected, or simply ignored, and so safeguard the authority of scripture? This will be the object of our second part.

2. The Place of Women's Experience in the Debate

First of all a few remarks. For rather obvious reasons it seems to me, I shall limit my field of research. This will not take into account the im-

---

12. See P. Milne, "The Patriarchal Stamp of Scripture: The Implications of Structuralist Analysis for Feminist Hermeneutics," *Journal of Feminist Studies in Religion* 5 (1989) 34.

13. "The patriarchal character of scripture is certainly not absolute, but it is so significant that the authority of scripture must be *redefined*." See Ellen K. Wondra, "By Whose Authority? The Status of Scripture in Contemporary Feminist Theologies," *Anglican Theological Review* 74 (1993) 93.

14. See Letty M. Russell, "Authority and the Challenge of Feminist Interpretation," in *Feminist Interpretation of the Bible,* ed. Letty M. Russell (Philadelphia: Westminster Press, 1985) 140.

portant "rejectionist" current for whose members the bible as well as Christian culture are rejected as irrecoverable.[15] I shall also overlook any fundamentalist approach and to a certain point any evangelical approach which tends to refuse the idea or the mere suggestion that the bible may present any problem or which considers its patriarchal and androcentric character an integral part of revelation.[16] In the first case, the irremediably patriarchal character of the bible is the cause of its rejection; in the second case, there is simply no possibility of any sort of debate on the authority of the bible.

The debate takes place elsewhere. As I just said, it chiefly engages theologians belonging to the "reformist" or "liberationist" current. Although this group, the most numerous, recognizes the presence of oppressive elements in both the bible and Christian tradition, it does not reject either one. Contrary to Mary Daly or Carol Christ for instance, the members of this group remain convinced that the word of God, as it reaches us in the bible and through tradition, is not intrinsically an oppressive word but, on the contrary, is *recoverable* for all who know how to free the text and its traditional interpreters from the ideological prejudices that rule them and to "liberate women from the disastrous consequences of these same prejudices."

Let us come now to the topic of my second part. According to Katherine Doob Sakenfeld, the feminist discussion on the authority of scripture is closely linked with the *place* granted women's experience in the appropriation of the biblical testimony.[17] As we shall see, this place indeed plays a central role here. The importance accorded to scripture and tradition will inevitably depend upon the value attributed to women's experience. Certain feminists of this current attribute a quasi absolute authority to women's experience, thereby placing the norm and authority outside the bible. Others equally sensitive to women's oppression and to the significant part the bible and tradition have had in this oppression nevertheless refuse to divest the bible of its traditional authority. Rather, they seek to identify a tradition or a central

15. Besides, the feminist current in general does not understand why so many women who call themselves feminists continue to accord importance and worth to a book, the bible, which exhibits so many prejudices toward women.

16. Whether one sees the problem in the interpretation that has been given to the bible or whether one reaffirms its absolute authority by unequivocally declaring that the teaching found in it, for instance on the silence imposed on women in the Christian assembly (1 Cor 14:33-35 and 1 Tim 2:15) or the subjection "in everything" of wife to husband (Eph 5:22-24; and also 1 Tim 2), has the force of divine law and therefore one must submit to it.

17. Katherine Doob Sakenfeld, "Feminist Perspectives on Bible and Theology: An Introduction to Selected Issues and Literature," *Interpretation* 42 (1988) 6–7.

principle which could in some way "authorize" their struggle for equality and the process of liberation to which they are committed. One must say that in this category it is not always easy to see the exact relation between this hermeneutical key or canon and the role attributed to women's experience. Finally, for others it is a very different conception of revelation and of the way in which this revelation is accessible in the scriptures that leads them to see in women's experience an important criterion of discernment for rightly evaluating the oppressive or liberating elements present in the biblical text.

The importance accorded women's experience in feminist theology does not have to be proved here. The only thing I want to do is stress that obviously one must include under this expression the biological, cultural, and even historical experience of women. But just as obviously, one must say that it is their more properly "feminist" experience which is the point of departure for feminist theology.[18] By this, I mean the experience of the androcentric and patriarchal structure of society, responsible in large part for the tragedy of a humanity unable to develop its full potential in men and women called to grace and freedom. It is this pivotal experience that impels many women to fight against everything that hinders this full development, in particular the patriarchal discourse on what it means, in the last analysis, to be a human being.

This same experience has for some time led a good number of women to call into question the bible's authority. Seen through feminist lenses, the bible no longer appears so clearly as the message of liberation it was traditionally recognized to be. Instead, for many women today it is to a great extent a message of subordination, enslavement, and even violence.

Feminists cannot ignore this experience, fundamental to their approach.[19] Unavoidably it affects everything they touch, including the bible. In a certain way, it becomes an important criterion for determining what in the bible, as well as in tradition, contributes to perpetuat-

18. The definition given by Radford Ruether is especially illuminating: ". . . that experience which arises when women become critically aware of those falsifying and alienating experiences imposed upon them as women by a male-dominated culture," and not simply any experience of a person who happens to be female. This is the experience of struggle to affirm and determine oneself as a woman, against the coercions of patriarchal culture. See Rosemary Radford Ruether, "Feminist Interpretation: A Method of Correlation," in *Feminist Interpretation of the Bible,* 114.

19. "Whether or not feminists choose to discuss the issue, it is pressed upon them every time they propose an interpretation or perspective that challenges a dominant view of scriptural authority and interpretation." Russell, "Authority and Challenge," 137.

ing the oppression of women and therefore must be set aside. The result is that for some feminists only the sections of the bible which affirm the total equality of men and women and eschew every patriarchal and hierarchical idea can be regarded as having a normative value for the faith community. Indeed, the bible is full of stereotypes of women, of caricatures, revealing silences, and masculine perceptions of women's world. In other words, women's experience becomes an important criterion for evaluating the revelatory merit for women of a given theology or given passage, for deciding what is or is not word of God, what is or is not normative. No doubt an important criterion. But is it decisive?

If there is in feminist theology a sort of consensus on the essential role played by women's experience as it is defined above, there is no agreement on the weight that should be accorded to this experience and on the place given it in the process of evaluating the bible. Exactly what is its relation to biblical and Christian tradition? Must we consider it a criterion of discernment or rather a norm somewhat approximating a biblical "canon" or, finally, the unique norm?

Let us begin with the most radical position, that of the Catholic exegete Elisabeth Schüssler Fiorenza, whose reputation is well established. What distinguishes this theologian from many other researchers is precisely the absolute value she attributes to women's experience in her theology. Convinced that the bible is a fundamentally androcentric and patriarchal book written by men and for men, moreover, a book which continues to perpetuate the oppression of women through hierarchical institutions, Schüssler Fiorenza draws the conclusion that one simply cannot make of it (or continue to make of it) the central norm of Christian faith. For her, there is one single norm that can adequately help women to triumph over this oppression and facilitate their self-determination. This norm is outside the bible, in the community of women struggling for their liberation, a "women-church" which claims the right to occupy the central place in the Christian community.[20] For

---

20. It is interesting to compare the different definitions given of this "women-church." For instance, Elisabeth Schüssler Fiorenza: "the movement of self-identified women and women-identified men in biblical religion," *Bread Not Stone: The Challenge of Feminist Biblical Interpretation* (Boston: Beacon Press, 1984) xiv; Ruth C. Duck: "those engaged in living out a discipleship community of equals and in moving toward freedom from patriarchal models of self and church," *Gender and the Name of God: The Trinitarian Baptismal Formula* (Cleveland: Pilgrim Press, 1991) 88; Mary Hunt: "a global, ecumenical movement made up of local feminist base communities of justice-seeking friends who engage in sacrament and solidarity," "Defining 'Women-Church,'" in *Liberation Theology: An Introductory Reader,* ed. Curt Cadorette and others (Maryknoll N.Y.: Orbis, 1992) 207–208.

Schüssler Fiorenza, there is one single authentic criterion permitting the rating of biblical texts according to whether they are useful or not to the cause of women (and of all those who are oppressed) and to their fight against oppression. Only the passages which correspond to this criterion become "word of God" and "paradigms of liberation" for the Christian community, not, it must be noted, because they are part of the bible, but because they are declared such by "women-church."[21] As one can see, Schüssler Fiorenza does not place revelation in the bible or in the tradition of a patriarchal church but actually in the *ekklesia* of women.[22] It is this "new magisterium"[23] which confers on the texts their normative character,[24] not the reverse.

As has been pointed out, Schüssler Fiorenza seeks to redefine the bible's authority by no longer looking on it according to the traditional model of the *archetype* which identifies the bible with a document of the past, containing an immutable and eternal revelation, but rather as a *historical prototype* which, like every prototype, serves as a model for building and improving what is needed in the present.[25] To want at all costs to locate in the bible the norm of revelation is, in her opinion, to continue to make of it an archetype. The bible is more a resource to utilize than an authority to follow. Without a doubt, Letty M. Russell is right when she says that Schüssler Fiorenza refuses to go on playing the "game of authority," that is, she refuses to submit the feminist norm

21. See Elisabeth Schüssler Fiorenza, "The Will to Choose or Reject: Continuing Our Critical Work," in *Feminist Interpretations of the Bible,* 132.

22. "The locus or place of divine revelation and grace is therefore not the Bible or the tradition of a patriarchal church but the *ekklesia* of women and the lives of women who live the 'option for our women selves.'" See Schüssler Fiorenza, "Will to Choose or Reject," 128. As Claudia Camp observes, "What makes Schüssler Fiorenza different, and it is an important difference, is her insistence on the authority of women over the Bible." See Claudia Camp, "Feminist Theological Hermeneutics: Canon and Christian Identity," in *Searching the Scriptures: A Feminist Introduction,* ed. Elisabeth Schüssler Fiorenza, vol. 1 (New York: Crossroads, 1993) 159.

23. I am borrowing the expression from Pamela Dickey Young, *Feminist Theology/Christian Theology: In Search of a Method* (Minneapolis: Fortress Press, 1990) 24.

24. Elisabeth Schüssler Fiorenza, "Emerging Issues in Feminist Biblical Interpretation," in *Christian Feminism: Visions of a New Humanity,* ed. Judith L. Weidman (San Francisco: Harper and Row, 1984) 35–36.

25. "To read the Bible not as an unchanging archetype but as a structuring prototype is to understand it as an open-ended paradigm that sets experience in motion and makes transformation possible," Elisabeth Schüssler Fiorenza, *But She Said: Feminist Practices of Biblical Interpretation* (Boston: Beacon Press, 1993) 149. See also *In Memory of Her: A Feminist Theological Reconstruction of Christian Origins* (New York: Crossroad, 1983) 32–33; and *Bread Not Stone,* 61.

to a higher biblical authority permeated through and through with androcentric and patriarchal notions.

There remains one question to ask: Does Schüssler Fiorenza still accord any sort of authority to the Christian bible? The answer she offers in *Bread Not Stone* and confirms in *But She Said* will have to suffice for the time being. First, she categorically refuses to leave the bible in the hands of anyone interested in maintaining the status quo or its patriarchal ideology; second, in the name of feminist solidarity, she recognizes the important role and influence the bible continues to have in the world and in particular in the lives of many women.[26] In the end, the question for Schüssler Fiorenza and many other feminists is no longer so much to know whether the bible continues to have authority as to make sure it still can be of use to and stand as a sacred text for an *ekklesia* of women who totally rely on their vision of a world liberated from any oppression.

This position has given rise to a whole gamut of reactions, both positive and negative, which would no doubt be interesting to look at. But I lack the time to dwell on this and readers will have to wait for a critical essay. It is enough for me to say that such a position has at the very least the merit of clearly outlining the debate.

It is not the importance granted to the particular experience of women but rather the *place* it occupies in theology which distinguishes the position of a large number of feminists from that of Schüssler Fiorenza. Indeed, an important group of feminist theologians refuse, more or less radically, to abandon the bible's authority in favor of this experience and, to a certain degree, subordinate it to a principle exterior to the bible.[27] By considering scripture as the preeminent locus of revelation, these researchers still have to face the same problems originating in the androcentric and patriarchal character of the bible (and of the Jewish and Christian traditions born of it). They must find a means of "recuperating" or "reforming" the bible in order to safeguard its authority. They discover this means in a theme, a tradition, a text, in brief, in a central principle which will enable them to distinguish in the bible and tradition life-giving elements which liberate from everything that

---

26. See *Bread Not Stone*, 28. See also *But She Said*, 137: "A critical feminist theological rhetoric does not seek to fashion theological arguments to explain why it is important for feminists to read the Bible or to remain Christians. Instead, it critically explores the socio-symbolic worlds of the Bible and their theological meanings and moral values, because countless women still read and value the Bible as sacred Scripture."

27. In *But She Said*, 146–149, Schüssler Fiorenza says that their hermeneutics is of the "canonical" type.

oppresses and destroys. Whatever the name given to it, this "canon"[28] or this hermeneutical principle will become the "rule" or the "judge" of everything, of all that "disfigures or constrains"—for instance, the numerous texts which accept or even prescribe the subordination of women—and of all that liberates and affirms, for instance the Christian charter of Gal 3:28.

This strategy is not new by any means since it goes back at least to Marcion. The Reformation used it; modern historical criticism made it even more necessary. And as is proved by some recent studies on the bible's authority, not necessarily emanating from feminist circles, it seems indispensable to face the numerous and often difficult theological and ethical questions posed by the contemporary world. From the specifically feminist side, what is sought is a general message of liberation applicable to women. Such a strategy, as Schüssler Fiorenza points out in her book *But She Said,* precisely serves to maintain the normative unity of the bible,[29] and this explains the qualification of "neo-orthodoxy" which she gives to the theological (apologetic) approach of theologians such as Rosemary Radford Ruether and Letty M. Russell.

These two theologians are indeed often mentioned as representative of this approach. But what is most interesting in their work is their way of integrating the hermeneutical principle with the feminist principle.

As is generally recognized, the thought of Radford Ruether has undergone a considerable evolution on this point. In the 70s, she saw the bible as essentially proclaiming a message of liberation perceived more particularly, but not exclusively, in the tradition of the prophets and that of Jesus, the ultimate word of God.[30] This tradition presents an often radical criticism of the established system by siding with the underprivileged and oppressed classes, contests the status quo, and proclaims a different vision of society founded on peace and justice. For Radford Ruether, this prophetico-messianic testimony, which she uncovers at the core of the bible, becomes in some way the norm, the rule, or else the "canon" permitting the evaluation of the authority of the rest of the bible. Whatever contradicts this message deserves to be censured and sometimes judged as being squarely opposed to revelation.

28. This approach or strategy is often labeled a "canon within the canon."

29. Schüssler Fiorenza, *But She Said,* 140–142.

30. "I identify myself as a Christian in terms of what I would call the 'prophetic messianic core' of biblical faith. This I see as the norm for judging both Scripture and tradition," quoted by Young, *Feminist Theology,* 37, from Rosemary Radford Ruether, in *Theologians in Transition,* ed. James M. Wall, The Christian Century "How My Mind Has Changed" Series (New York: Crossroad, 1981) 164.

Radford Ruether's thought undergoes an important development in her subsequent writings from the 80s on. Today, she tends to advocate the necessity of establishing a correlation between this biblical tradition and a feminist principle called the "full humanity of women," a correlation which in all likelihood can be the product only of the lived experience of women within the women-church.[31] If we must believe Radford Ruether, this principle has priority over her previous norm or biblical canon. Indeed, in a particularly interesting contribution to the book edited by Russell on feminist biblical hermeneutics, she seems to confirm the absolute necessity of such a correlation in order for the bible to effectively become a source of liberation for women.[32] It is the same principle—at the heart of the feminist theology of liberation—which leads her to look elsewhere than in the bible for other texts which can make women's experience more visible.[33]

Like Radford Ruether, Russell sees in women's experience as defined above one of the norms for the evaluation of all biblical and religious tradition. Nevertheless, being a committed Christian, she is incapable of abandoning a tradition into which she was born. But, and this is significant, it is less the biblical text than her personal experience of the word of God in Jesus Christ which supplies her with her hermeneutical key. She discovers there a divine promise, revealed in Jesus, to restore creation, a promise that stimulates and as it were "authorizes" her own quest for justice and liberation. As she herself finds it important to stress, it is her own history which led her to this hermeneutical key, a history marked by seventeen years of her life spent in sharing the difficult lot of a poor multiracial community in a Protestant parish in East Harlem. For Russell, the bible is more than a prototype, it is a sort of "memory of the future," a "memory" which, thanks to what we can already glimpse and anticipate of the divine initiative in biblical history as well as in our own history, opens wide the doors to a new life.[34] By suggesting a new model of authority, which she calls "authority of partnership," to replace the "authority of domination," Russell clearly indicates that the Christian community needs a sacred text which must

31. According to Schüssler Fiorenza, "its goal is not simply the 'full humanity' of women, since humanity as we know it is male-defined, but women's religious self-affirmation, power, and liberation from all patriarchal alienation, marginalization, and oppression." See "Will to Choose or Reject," 126.

32. See Rosemary Radford Ruether, "Feminist Interpretation: A Method of Correlation," in *Feminist Biblical Interpretation*, 117.

33. For a criticism of Radford Ruether's position, see Schüssler Fiorenza, *But She Said*, 148.

34. See Russell, "Authority and Challenge," 139.

function as a "scenario" opening onto life.[35] For her, what is at work is a "configuration of the sources" that seek to enrich the way in which God makes God present to each one of us.[36]

Although this type of approach is not irreproachable from the strictly feminist point of view,[37] I prefer to emphasize here the genuinely distinctive criticism offered by Carolyn Osiek in her analysis of the various feminist currents. Indeed, she wonders whether Radford Ruether and all the critics who appeal to the hermeneutical key of "canon within the canon" are not finally, in their effort to discern what belongs or does not belong to the revealed data, guilty of identifying in an almost simplistic manner two qualities of the text: its character of revelation and its normative value due to its authority.[38] As if the word of God had come to us in the bible under the form of "quasi-propositions" easy to spot![39]

Sandra Schneiders offers the same sort of criticism to the approach of Schüssler Fiorenza,[40] but in her case, readers have a wide open access to what I would call the hermeneutic foundation of such a criticism. Quite recently Schneiders has articulated a theory of interpretation of the biblical text which allows her not only to safeguard the unique place of scripture but also to discern in it a source of hope for the very persons whose oppression it has legitimized.[41] For Schneiders, the true

---

35. Ibid., 138.

36. Ibid., 146.

37. See the critique of Schüssler Fiorenza in *But She Said,* 147–148.

38. Although closely related, these "affirmations of faith" are different, as Sandra Schneiders aptly demonstrates in her recent work, *The Revelatory Text: Interpreting the New Testament as Sacred Scripture* (New York, Harper-Collins, 1991) 44–59. Whereas the term "revelation" (and this applies also to "inspiration") expresses the idea of a God who communicates with us through the contents or the testimony of these books, the terms "authority" and "normativeness" refer to the same contents, but envisaged in their relation to the readers. It is in virtue of this authority accorded the bible that the believing community recognizes in it a normative value, a value of norm, of rule, or of "canon" for faith. The determination of the biblical canon did one thing, establish these writings as an official norm for the faith and practice of the church. For another excellent presentation of these different concepts, see the study of T. A. Hoffman, "Inspiration, Normativeness, Canonicity, and the Unique Character of the Bible," *Catholic Biblical Quarterly* 44 (1982) 447–469.

39. See Osiek, "Feminist and the Bible," 104.

40. Schneiders' criticism appears in *Horizons* 19 (1992) 306–307, in response to the "Review Symposium" on her book *The Revelatory Text.*

41. See Schneiders, *The Revelatory Text.* For what follows, see especially Schneiders' important article "Feminist Ideology, Criticism and Biblical Hermeneutics," *Biblical Theology Bulletin* 19 (1989) 3–10.

question is not of the exegetical order but clearly of the hermeneutical order. Her ideas are worth examining, even if very briefly.

In agreement with most feminists on the fact that the problem is at the level of the text, Schneiders directs her whole attention to the text as text and to the human endeavor which any interpretation necessarily is. Following contemporary hermeneutics in the tradition of Hans-Georg Gadamer and Paul Ricœur, she looks at the text, not in a positivist way as a kind of box containing the meaning intended by the author, but rather as "a mediation of meaning taking place in the act of reading." Somewhat like a judge who, in order to decide on his verdict, relies on both past decisions and current perceptions concerning justice, the hermeneut of today must interpret this "witness" of God's revelation, which the bible is, by the lights of both the past and the present. Basing herself on Ricœur's theory of the distancing which happens when one passes from oral discourse to written and of the supplement of meaning that goes with this passage, Schneiders places the true referent of the biblical text, not in the experience of the past, but rather in the readers' experience created by the text and, in a way, projected before them. Here is where the true referent of the text is—the reality it proclaims, its "truth"—not in the historical world of Paul or John to which of course the text naturally refers. In the New Testament perspective, this "world" has a name, and according to Schneiders it is "the world of discipleship."

If it is true that the interpretation of a text culminates in its appropriation or its augmentation by the reader, this text can, thanks to a certain autonomy gained when it became written text, create not only what Gadamer called an "efficacious historical consciousness" but also lenses through which the text itself will be subsequently judged. In the same way the Declaration of Independence served to create a people finally able to decide that slavery was incompatible with the vision of freedom and equality intended by this foundational document, the Hebrew and Christian scriptures have created a community which is beginning to realize the incompatibility of the patriarchal system— simply assumed by the biblical authors—with the liberating purpose of the sacred text. Therefore, it is the true referent of the text which demands the repudiation of, for example, all that is oppressive for today's women. In the last analysis, what Schneiders proposes is a "hermeneutics of transformation" and not of "selection" as in preceding approaches. A hermeneutics that takes into account the fact that Christian experience is based on the foundational text and at the same time creatively interprets it.

It is not the importance granted to women's experience in the interpretation of scripture which distinguishes Schneiders' position from

Schüssler Fiorenza's. Although Schneiders attributes to it a somewhat different function, she recognizes that Schüssler Fiorenza has greatly contributed to the debate by rightly making of the experience of the oppressed (women in particular) struggling for their liberation the pre-eminent hermeneutical perspective from which it is possible to recognize from now on the oppressive elements in the biblical text. The major distinction between the two positions is found in their fundamentally different ways of understanding revelation in its relation to scripture. Schneiders rejects every positivist conception of this relation which would tend to compare the biblical text to a sort of "semantic reservoir" of revelation, as if the "witness" of the bible was communicated to us under the form of quasi-propositions. For her, either the whole bible is revelation or else it is no revelation at all. Either one still sees in it holy scripture or one denies it any special mediation of the mystery of revelation. In this respect, the title of her latest book is significant: *The Revelatory Text*. Let this be clear: the bible is not a source of information on God or God's plan for humanity; instead, it is a text capable of stimulating believing readers to dialogue with a God who chooses to communicate in this way.[42]

3. A New Model of Authority

I hope this cursory review, too brief no doubt, of the ways in which feminist theologians today deal with the question of the authority of the scriptures will have served to show the role or rather the important place which women's experience holds in the current debate. There is no doubt that this experience is largely the cause of the questioning of the bible's authority by a certain number among them and, by the same token, of the elaboration of a new type or model of authority more akin to their weltanschauung.

It has been said that the word "authority" makes people nervous.[43] When associated with the bible, it makes women more and more nervous. It is enough to examine the manner in which women have been treated "in the name of the bible," how it has been used though the centuries to marginalize them, subjugate them, legitimize the violence they endured, always in the name of the word of God, to understand their fear, their nervousness, and even their anger. Of course, one can-

---

42. See Schneiders, "Review Symposium," 306–307.

43. See Sharon H. Ringe, "The Word of God May Be Hazardous to Your Health," *Theology Today* 49 (1992) 367. I draw on this article for some of the remarks that follow.

not ignore the enormous positive influence the bible has had on a vast number of people, men and women, of all ages and all colors. But it has also supported the silence and oppression of women, and to widen the debate for a moment, it has served to promote sexism, racism, and the violence worked on women. And all this justified of course by the authority of a text which continues to be regarded as "Holy Scripture"!

As we have seen, many feminist critics are no longer in agreement with such a state of affairs and refuse to submit to an authority that denies their experience as women, and for many among them, even their Christian experience. For several, it has simply become impossible to wholeheartedly trust this so-called word of God and to submit to its authority and its often destructive demands. Not just their health, their very survival is threatened.[44] The only authority they are ready to accept is an authority that nurtures them, affirms them, and opens for them the road to freedom.

This is why such a large number trust their own experience as women as it is now celebrated in the community or the "women-church." This new "magisterium," as it has been called, explains in large part their radical questioning of the way in which the authority of the bible, and any—not to say hierarchical—authority have been traditionally understood and exercised. Indeed, one of the most important and no doubt most exciting questions raised by feminist criticism of these last years is precisely that of knowing whether one can really separate the bible's authority from the community for which it has become scripture. In a word, is it possible to understand the authority of scripture *independently* from the community?

If one has followed the presentation I have just made on the important role attributed by feminist critics to women's experience in the process of biblical interpretation, one already knows the answer. A strong majority answers no. For many among them, it is simply impossible to dissociate their discourse on the authority of the bible from the context of the community which has made of this book its sacred text.

In a way, this is an old debate but perhaps it is not useless to pay close attention to it. The more so since such a viewpoint, as we shall see, agrees very well with certain developments of modern hermeneutics. It would be erroneous to see this new way of perceiving the bible's authority as a "foreign body" landing here from a planet hitherto unknown. I see it rather as the maturation of an awareness which is growing at such a rate that people are rightly beginning to speak of a true hermeneutical turning point.

---

44. See Schüssler Fiorenza, "Will to Choose or Reject," 130.

Without doubt, one of the most significant contributions of the application of modern criticism to biblical texts has been to draw attention to the primordial role played by a large number of Jewish and Christian communities in the formation, elaboration, production, and even selection of the biblical books. As is shown by numerous "rereadings" of the texts themselves, a true "collective activity of interpretation" had been at work before the definitive redaction of each of these books. Indubitably, the establishment of the canon of the bible is still regarded today by many as having brought to an end the production of the bible, but it is more and more obvious that whereas this "material" production of canonical books has indeed ceased, the same cannot be said of the interpretation of these books, of the authority granted to this corpus in the course of centuries in the many communities of interpretation.[45] As someone recently remarked, if one cannot isolate the writing under study either from the work of faith which produced it or from the steps that have contributed to confer upon it a particular status, it would be futile to want to separate it from the long road it has traveled among believing communities.[46] Therefore, both before and after the determination of the canon, the production of the text has continued in faith communities, and as feminist theologians vigorously argue, it is crucial that this interpretive activity go on and moreover belong no longer to just a part of the community but to the whole community.

As I have already noted, such a conception seems to fit in with certain recent developments of contemporary hermeneutics, more particularly with the place given readers in the process of the interpretation of the text and its "production." Not only are readers part of this interpretive process but their reading is unavoidably affected by all that constitutes their own individualities.

It is within this hermeneutic perspective that we must place the attack launched by feminist ideologists against the well-known fortress of historico-critical exegesis, that is, the claim to a totally objective approach to the biblical text. To think it possible to have a neutral and wholly objective exegesis is, in their eyes, a vain dream. Every reading is inevitably affected by the readers' cultural and social baggage, the

---

45. I borrow this vocabulary from David H. Fisher who makes a distinction between what he calls *the work* and *the text* which is nothing else than the way in which the communities have interacted with or interpreted these books in the course of history. See "Work, Text and the Power of Interpretation," *Toronto Journal of Theology* 9 (1993) 177–186.

46. See C. Wackenheim, "Les textes normatifs à l'épreuve de l'interprétation," *Revue des Sciences Religieuses* 65 (1991) 98.

conscious or unconscious presuppositions they bring to their approach to the text. It is no doubt too soon to declare victory, but I believe I am right in saying that the battle has begun well and here and there one can already perceive more or less discreet moves toward retreat on the part of opponents.

Perhaps even more important for our purpose is this realization, increasingly widespread among hermeneuts, that one cannot really speak of the interpretation of a text without readers appropriating this text for themselves in one way or another. This appropriation means that there is an encounter between readers and the text, a dialogue between the two. A genuine dialectic is established between the "world" of the readers and "the literary world" of the text. In the case of the bible, this dialogue ends often enough with an invitation to see things differently, with an appeal to *metanoia*, but one can already foresee that this dialogue may lead also to confrontation.

Therefore, it is not especially surprising to see the canon of scripture itself submitted to questioning by feminist criticism. The Old Testament as well as the New have been written, at least principally, by men, for men, and likewise the process of canonization has been the business of men. As a consequence, men's values and experiences, including their perception of women, have served to define human nature and the reality of things. It follows that even if here or there, in the New Testament for example, one discovers the traces of an anti-patriarchal vision of the Christian experience to which some feminist theologians cling, history has amply demonstrated the influence exerted by those who won the battle of the canon (the "historical winners") in the course of the early centuries. In the eyes of feminist researchers, this canon presents a problem precisely because it does not reflect the identity of the Christian community, whether in the past or today.[47] Hence the question: How is it possible to speak of a text as normative for the whole community since it includes only half of it? It has been written very appropriately, "Whoever says canon says exclusion as well as inclusion." And let us not forget that women are not the only ones to be excluded.

It is finally because of a liberating and inclusive vision of society and the church, founded on respect for human dignity and on women's

47. See Sharon H. Ringe, "Reading from Context to Context: Contributions of a Feminist Hermeneutics to Theologies of Liberation," in *Lift Every Voice: Constructing Christian Theologies from the Underside*, ed. Susan Brooks Thistlethwaite and Mary Potter Engel (New York: Harper and Row, 1990) 287. See also the interesting discussion raised by John Koenig and the honest response of Schneiders in "Review Symposium," 297–300, 307–308.

own experience of God's action as it is celebrated in "women-church," that feminist hermeneutics takes the field against a model of authority largely responsible for the exclusion of women from full participation in the implementation of God's plan. It is not authority as such which is questioned but the model that has been used and the way it has been wielded. The context goes far beyond the question of the bible's authority; it concerns the validity of the established system and also the concept of the faith community. Within the Christian milieu, the debate will finally be ecclesiological in nature and cannot but have serious repercussions on the way we look at the bible.

In her article on the authority of the bible challenged by feminist hermeneutics,[48] Russell maintains that in the communities in which the bible is invested with a unique authority, the model of authority that prevails is essentially a model of *domination*. The description she gives of this model is interesting and worth looking at for a moment. Reality is seen under a hierarchic and pyramidal form where the topmost echelon is invested with a quasi-absolute power. The function of this model is to reinforce the solidly established system of an authority which watches *over* the community and keeps order by respecting the status quo as much as possible. Anything that does not square with the established structures, ideas, or persons is seen as a threat and must of necessity be silenced or eliminated. The mind-set of the people in power is the law and at the same time becomes a source of oppression for all who are subject to this power. As long as this paradigm persists, all decisions reflect the established power. Feminist ideology can only reject such a model of authority which excludes a priori any personal perspective and as a consequence the integrity of persons themselves. (Hence the necessity of demythologizing authority).

Russell asserts that a new model of authority is in the process of emerging and will cause a revolution in our approach to theological as well as biblical data. She defines it as an "authority of partnership." Others, like Sakenfeld,[49] prefer the simpler term of "authority of the community" while still others underline the "dialogic" character of this authority which ultimately expresses itself in the community.[50] Such a model clearly aims at promoting a democratization of authority, at fostering the idea of an authority exercised in a community whose every member, without any distinction, has the right to speak up. This

48. See Russell, "Authority and Challenge," 143ff.
49. See Katherine Doob Sakenfeld, "In the Wilderness, Awaiting the Land: The Daughters of Zelophehad and Feminist Interpretations," *Princeton Seminary Bulletin* 9 (1988) 192.
50. See Schneiders, *The Revelatory Text*, 56–57.

authority does not become a tool of domination but rather a service to the community from which it ultimately receives its legitimacy.

There is much more within this concept. Sakenfeld offers at least two different ways of looking at this new model. For instance, one can consider this "authority of the community" in descriptive terms, that is, one can observe the way in which it was exercised both in the formation of the canon and in the course of centuries of theological reflection based on scripture. However, in a more constructive manner, this new paradigm tends to emphasize the important role played by the community in the interpretation of the bible and more particularly the idea that it is finally in its encounter with the biblical text that the community experiences the word of God. Moreover, according to Sakenfeld, this model also has the advantage of preventing any claim to full possession of the truth by the group in power, whether yesterday or today.[51]

If this new model fully "authorizes" the experience and participation of the entire community in the task of interpreting the scriptures, it seems also to reflect a conception of authority which shows more respect for the very nature of faith and religious commitment. In this regard, it is especially significant to observe to what point several feminist studies on the bible's authority and Christian tradition strive to carefully define the type of authority envisaged in this discussion.[52] Above all, one must distinguish it from any form of coercion and domination. Whatever the way in which this authority expresses itself, its demands will never be, according to Schneiders, absolute and unilateral but relative and "dialogic" instead. In the case of the bible, everything depends on the understanding one has of revelation. Our perception of the bible's authority will necessarily be very different according to whether we have a dynamic vision of revelation understood as a communal testimony of God's self-revelation or if we see in it a depository of well defined propositions which we would be constrained to accept.[53] To me, it is evident that there exists a correlation between the idea one has of the bible understood as revelation and the idea one has of its authority.

---

51. See Sakenfeld, "In the Wilderness," 192–193. For instance, it is in virtue of this model that, as an exegete, Sakenfeld feels obliged "to take serious account of all the factors that led to distinctions between canonical and extracanonical (sometimes therefore lost or even never recorded) viewpoints, and especially to notice whose voices never got into the conversation at all" (p. 193).

52. See the articles of Wondra, "By Whose Authority?"; Ringe, "Reading from Context"; and particularly the discussion of Schneiders in *The Revelatory Text*, 55–59.

53. See *The Revelatory Text*, 55–59.

In the last analysis, this authority originates in God, who is for all believers the ultimate and absolute authority. It is an authority one can experience only through a whole ensemble of human mediations, among which is the bible. There is a danger that will probably continue to exist: that of wanting to attribute to these mediations, human therefore historically and culturally conditioned, the absolute authority reserved for God. Such an enterprise is doomed to failure because we shall never succeed in domesticating the Spirit of God, which alone has the monopoly on truth. If we think this through, we realize that only the immediate vision of God could stop what we have called above the "production" of the text within the faith communities.[54]

This "production" is made possible because a sort of "constant regeneration" of communities—which are at once the creations of this living text and the instruments of its constant renewal and of its historical rereadings—happens.[55] Many women today are absolutely convinced that this "regeneration" is channeled through their experiences of God's action in their lives. And it is on the strength of these experiences that they dare to cast into question the very contents of biblical tradition or, if one wishes, the sort of authority which has been attributed to it in the course of centuries.

4. Some Final Reflections

It is time to conclude. I shall propose two brief reflections which could almost be the first draft of a survey needing completion.

For several years now, the Catholic church and the Protestant churches have come closer in their respective ways of approaching the question of the sources of revelation. As we know, Vatican II has abandoned the doctrine of the "two sources" (scripture and tradition) in favor of a more unified and more dynamic vision of scripture now understood in its fundamental relation to the living tradition of the church. Although scripture still remains the *norma normans* (the ruling norm), it is impossible to isolate its ultimate significance from the readings and rereadings taking place within the life of the church. A similar movement, but in the opposite direction, is clearer and clearer in many Protestant churches. The *scriptura sola* principle is no longer understood independently from the tradition. Without presuming to know the reasons that have led these churches to recognize the eminent role

54. See Fisher, "Work, Text and the Power of Interpretation," 183–184.
55. See Camp, "Feminist Theological Hermeneutics," 162–163.

played by the living tradition of the ecclesial communities in the reading of scripture, we must however note the importance not only of the ecumenical dialogue but also of the impact made by contemporary hermeneutical developments. As Marcel Dumais wrote several years ago, the living tradition of the churches becomes a true hermeneutical key to a better understanding of the bible.[56]

We must rejoice over this. Notwithstanding the encouraging signs which one can discern in the recent document of the Biblical Commission on the interpretation of the bible, the addition of an explanatory note to the evaluation of feminist interpretation invites moderation in this rejoicing.[57] As Catholic feminist theologians, among others, do not tire of repeating, as long as the bible and this living tradition are used to deny access to ordination to half of humanity, there are many reasons to remain skeptical. For a great number among them, the voice of Miriam continues to be heard: "Has the LORD spoken only through Moses? Has he not spoken through us [Miriam and Aaron] also?" (Num 12:4). To talk about the living tradition is to recognize in the experience of all members of the community—itself generated by the "text"—the authentic domain of a reading which ultimately rests on the experience of God in the dailiness of our lives. Some have used the word "dogmatism" to qualify the so-called "power" now claimed for the community and women's experience, and thus one accuses the feminist hermeneutical movement of wanting, when all is said and done, to replace the magisterium with another, that of the community of women. What surprises me most in this sort of accusation is the vocabulary used. This proves that feminist ideology is absolutely right when it so vigorously denounces the illusion of a discourse supposed to be ideologically neutral.

By claiming a central place for the community of women, feminist theologians do not seek to replace one magisterium with another of the same order. Rather, they maintain that this women-church is capable of offering a different vision, more ecclesial and more communal, of authority and Christian experience. A vision made of sharing, respect, exchange, openness, support, apprenticeship, questionings, strayings, research, and discovery. A vision which is already celebrated in the "women's community." I always have appreciated Krister Stendahl's "wisdom." One day, with his usual humor and refreshing turn of mind,

---

56. See Marcel Dumais, "Le caractère normatif des écrits du Nouveau Testament," *Église et Théologie* 10 (1979) 144–145.

57. Pontifical Biblical Commission, "Interpretation of the Bible in the Church," *Origins* 23 (1993–1994) 524.

he made this remark: "One has too often used the authority of the institution and of the bible to put an end to discussion rather than to make it possible; it is a very bad habit."[58]

My second reflection bears on the well-known solution of Vatican II to the problem of the authority of scripture. As I have already mentioned in my introduction, this "definition" was a direct answer to the numerous questions—most of them historical—raised for more than a century by the historico-critical approach to the bible. By specifying that only "the truth . . . put into the sacred writings for the sake of our salvation" bound the Christian conscience,[59] the pastors at the council wanted to offer the Catholic people a criterion to help them separate the biblical message (which God was good enough to put there) from the historical and cultural envelope in which this message had reached us. As Elizabeth Johnson[60] points out, post-conciliar theologians, among whom was an ever increasing number of people with a feminist orientation, soon widened this principle to also include social structures and systems. Convinced that the predominant ideology of the bible (as well as of tradition) is essentially androcentric and patriarchal, feminist criticism places the problem on the level of language as well as on that of the content or teaching of the text itself. Not only does this text silence women, it also legitimizes sexism, racism, classism, slavery, and even violence. Must we regard these "teachings" as part of this "truth . . . put into the sacred writings for the sake of our salvation," or are they historical residues which unfortunately have been "absolutized" during two millennia? Fortunately, we are better equipped nowadays to see them as not belonging to the truth of the salvific message.[61]

This brings us to the one really crucial question: How is one to finally succeed in establishing what in the interpretation of the biblical text is "truth . . . put into the sacred writings for the sake of our salva-

58. See Krister Stendahl, "Ancient Scripture in the Modern World," in *Scripture and the Jewish and Christian Traditions: Authority, Interpretation, Relevance*, ed. Frederick E. Greenspahn (Nashville: Abingdon, 1982) 212.

59. See *Dei Verbum*, no. 11.

60. Elizabeth A. Johnson's response in *Horizons* 20 (1993) 341, to the "Review Symposium" on her book, *She Who Is: the Mystery of God in Feminist Theological Discourse* (New York: Crossroad, 1992).

61. "But the theological question for today is whether these teachings are the truth from God about our salvation or whether they belong to time-conditioned mentalities that can be judged to be unessential to salvific truth, indeed even contradictory to it, *in the light of other central biblical texts*," ibid. The italicized clause clearly suggests the idea of the "canon within the canon" mentioned in the second part of this study.

tion" by resorting to a rule, to a special canon, or else to a magisterium? Whose will be the ultimate decision in the matter of interpretation? For feminist researchers the question is neither abstract nor purely rhetorical; as we have already seen, their survival is at stake.

Having counted women among the groups most notoriously victimized by a systemic oppression in both society and religious institutions, feminist theologians have no other choice than being extremely critical of any structure or system of authority which, to remain in power, relies on a text recognized as androcentric and patriarchal to the core. Must we then adopt the thesis of Schüssler Fiorenza, that is, refuse to continue playing "the game of the authority" of scripture and instead endorse women's testimony to the truth which God has kindly revealed and continues to reveal "for the sake of our salvation"? Does the only way to mount a serious criticism of a text as patriarchal as the bible finally consist in denying it any role in the revelation of the divine mystery?

The model proposed by Schneiders, introduced in the second part of this article, obviously does not answer all questions. However, at this stage of my reflection, it seems to offer not only a means of eliminating a dilemma which I confess I find uncomfortable but also an interesting way of envisioning at least the question of the "truth" of the text. This is already a point of departure. As I have previously pointed out, Schneiders rejects every positivist conception of the bible which makes of it a sort of box containing the definitive meaning intended by its author. On the contrary, she adopts a symbolic approach to the biblical text which locates revelation not in a series of propositions but in the "witness" of the communities expressing themselves through these texts. This truly dynamic understanding of revelation takes into account the fact that this witness is unavoidably limited because it is human, and preempts any attempt at absolutizing it. At the same time, it does not diminish in any way the importance which feminist circles attribute to women's experience; within this perspective, such an experience becomes a powerful and necessary criterion for discerning what is and what is not the word of God, what belongs and what does not belong to the "truth" which God has kindly willed to procure our salvation.[62]

Thus, Francis Schüssler Fiorenza is right when he says that one cannot truly separate the question of the authority of scripture from the still energetically debated question of the meaning of the text. Since this quest for the meaning undeniably has priority, it is within this context

---

62. See Schneiders' final remarks on the occasion of the "Review Symposium" of her book, *The Revelatory Text*, 306–307.

that the problem of the authority of the bible must be resolved.[63] The discussion goes on.

63. "The issue of authority becomes integrated with the issue of meaning. It is no longer simply a question of whether the scriptural text has authority or not. Instead the question of the meaning of the text takes priority and only in the context of the resolution of the issue of meaning can the issue of authority be resolved. Differences in meaning entail differences in authority. Moreover, just as experts as well as popular interpretations of a text differ, so too are there correspondingly different conceptions of authority." See Francis Schüssler Fiorenza, "The Crisis of Scriptural Authority: Interpretation and Reception," *Interpretation* 44 (1990) 358.

Contributors

◆ ——————————————————————————————— ◆

Gérald Caron, Atlantic School of Theology, Halifax, Nova Scotia

Aldina da Silva, Faculté de théologie, University of Montréal, Montréal, Québec

Olivette Genest, Faculté de théologie, University of Montréal, Montréal, Québec

Marc Girard, Département de sciences religieuses, University of Québec at Chicoutimi, Chicoutimi, Québec

Michel Gourgues, O.P., Collège dominicain de philosophie et de théologie, Ottawa, Ontario

Élisabeth J. Lacelle, Départment de sciences religieuses, University of Ottawa, Ottawa, Ontario

Jean-Jacques Lavoie, Départment de sciences religieuses, University of Québec at Montréal, Montréal, Québec

André Myre, Faculté de théologie, University of Montréal, Montréal, Québec

Jean-François Racine, St. Michael's College, University of Toronto, Toronto, Ontario